With Forks and Hope

AN AFRICAN NOTEBOOK

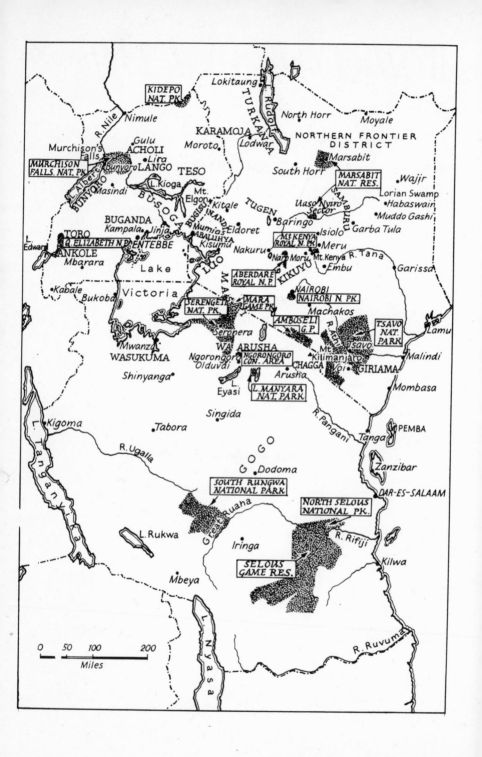

With Forks and Hope

AN AFRICAN NOTEBOOK

By

Elspeth Huxley

Illustrated by Jonathan Kingdon

1964

WILLIAM MORROW & COMPANY   NEW YORK

CONTENTS

CONTENTS

CONTENTS

AUTHOR'S NOTE

This notebook is based on a visit to parts of Tanganyika, Kenya and Uganda between February and May, 1963. Much has happened since. Kenya's independence came on December 12, 1963, following that of her sister state, Uganda, on October 9, 1962, and Tanganyika on December 9, 1961. Federation before the end of the year was at first promised by the three Prime Ministers, but later postponed.

Writing about modern Africa is like trying to sketch a galloping horse that is out of sight before you have sharpened your pencil, and I can only ask indulgence if events have outstripped the writer, publisher and printer of these impressions. Perhaps it is foolish even to try; but it is just because so much *is* happening—because the scene sparkles with new hopes and plans, because nothing is static and nothing seems impossible—that I was tempted, hoping that what so fascinated an observer would have at least some points of interest for the general reader. And, behind the dance of politics, the features of the ancient landscape, the birds and beasts—so splendidly captured here by Jonathan Kingdon—and the dilemmas of the people remain; "for in truth," as Winston Churchill wrote in 1907, "the problems of East Africa are the problems of the world."

"Lamuria" has previously appeared in *Blackwoods'*, and "The Two Faces of Nationalism" in *Encounter*. I make grateful acknowledgment to the editors of these magazines. The essays have been slightly edited for the present book.

With Forks and Hope

AN AFRICAN NOTEBOOK

ROUND IN CIRCLES

Camp Followers

We drove in Land-Rovers south from Seronera on a fine
morning, across a great treeless plain, open as the sea: in fact,
the Serengeti is a kind of land-ocean, coloured the tawny buff
of ripening wheat and stirred by a wind that creates rippling
waves among the panicles of red oat grass, and gives you a
tremendous feeling of freedom.

Here horizons have the simplicity of the primeval. Above
them hang billowing cumulus clouds that cast dark stains
over sunlit grass in an ever-changing pattern. These great
clouds, at once fluffy as whipped cream and substantial as
ice floes, move imperceptibly across the blue and yet never
seem to obscure the sun. I have often puzzled over this
mystery, and never solved it.

We saw few beasts at first, but many birds, mostly raptors:
a big tawny eagle, the handsome grey-and-white Montagu's
harrier, augur buzzards, the black-shouldered kite. And abun-
dant rollers, most brilliant and exciting of birds. (Both
species are common here, the lilac-breasted and the even finer
European roller with his dazzling azure breast.) Plovers
wheeled and called, a black-shouldered heron brooded majestically, mottled sand grouse squatted until almost run over.

There are no hills, but sudden piles of rocks erupt as if

tossed there by some giant at play. A few jackals, the silver-backed and the larger Asian variety; a bristled warthog with his coarse tusks and look of mock ferocity; small bands of Thomson's and Robert's gazelle playing last-man-over-the-track with sudden spurts of flat-out speed.

Soon after we had left the road and headed across the open plain for Lake Lagarja, on the Serengeti National Park's southeastern extremity, we came to the first signs of the great migration: not the wildebeest themselves but camp followers, scroungers and sutlers. These were hyenas; the spotted variety. They stood or sat about in small groups, with long necks sprouting from the grass like sea serpents surmounted by cats' heads.

Try as one may to be fair to hyenas—they do a useful, needed job, just as dustmen do, or undertakers; why should we despise or shun them?—try as one may, one cannot like hyenas. They are ugly, mangy-looking, cringing, debased. A copulating couple scarcely glanced up as we jolted by.

I suppose this aversion to hyenas arose because they eat corpses. But then so do lobsters, I believe, and we devour *them* with relish, as we do *Tilapia,* who thrive on manure. In African tales and folklore the hyena displays two main characteristics: greed and stupidity. There is no doubt about the greed, but there seems no evidence to suggest stupidity. They will themselves kill only the small, defenceless, weak or injured; otherwise they tag on to lions and sneak in to finish up the scraps of someone else's kill. This would appear crafty rather than stupid.

Certainly it's an ignoble role, but, like scavenging, necessary. Hyenas help to keep down the wildebeest population by waiting on the migration's fringes to feast on newborn calves, which must struggle to their feet and trot after their mothers before they are dry. If they get left behind, they are doomed.

A warden told me he had timed the process and the calf was on its feet in two minutes; an impala, on the other hand, had taken fifty.

No wonder the hyenas looked satisfied—and jackals, too, scavengers just as much as the hyenas, but so much more attractive, lithe and graceful in their movements. Clusters of heavy, bald-headed vultures squatted on the ground like lethargic old men.

Moving Armies

We came soon to the first of the wildebeest, a few outliers; then to the start of the herds, which spread out into long, close-packed lines of these ungainly antelope reminding one of bison. Their coats are silvery grey and shaggy over the shoulders, they have sloping quarters and long, melancholy, clownish faces fringed by yellowish-grey beards. As they move they make queer, abrupt, grunting noises to which the closest parallel is the croak of a bullfrog. These are the white-bearded gnu, *Connochaetes taurinus albojubatus*.

The country became more rolling and the slopes looked as if thickly strewn with slow-moving black boulders. Bullfrog grunting filled the air. One stream we passed through, a file stretching far out of sight, was estimated by Mr. John Owen, director of the Tanganyika National Parks, to contain perhaps thirty to forty thousand animals. But it was anyone's guess, and hard to say where one file ended and the next began.

The wildebeest paused now and then to crop grass, not pressing or hurrying. In October and November, when the eastward movement starts towards fresh grass evoked by rain, they gallop as if chased by furies. At this time of year, in April, they proceed at a more sedate pace.

Between two glistening, croaking streams we came on a
party of lions out in the open: a mother and four half-grown
cubs. One of the cubs was caressing its dam, paws round her
neck, licking her face. Its own face looked wise and solemn,
its paws were big and flat like plates. All the lions moved
with a wonderful flowing motion as their muscles rippled
under supple skins, fluid as the wind that rolled the panicles
of grasses. Farther on a family of cheetahs vanished into a
fold of the plain. We saw many birds: flights of red-legged

larks, and a green-and-yellow flush of stubby-tailed little para-keets, the Fischer's (or Tanganyika) lovebird.

The Serengeti Park has an awkward shape with a narrow-ing wedge thrust westwards towards Lake Victoria. The boundary runs to within one and a half miles of the lake, but does not touch it. This is where rainfall is highest and where the wildebeest and zebra spend the dry season, not in big herds but dispersed in small groups. Some stay within the Park, but a great many move outside it, and then poachers and hunters, and cultivators whose little plots of maize, beans and cotton ring the boundaries, get busy.

Once an animal sets hoof outside its sanctuary, its life is cheap. Everywhere the fecund humans are pressing in on areas whose dedication to wildlife preservation most of them resent. Animals, when all is said and done, are, from a human point of view, there to be eaten. If Christians believe that God created them for man to have dominion over, the hu-manists, who place man on the top rung of the evolutionary ladder, authorize him to look down on them. Animals must know their place and stay there. We all need something to look down on, even if it's only a snail or a chimp. If we can eat it into the bargain, so much the better.

But why this little niggle of guilt about our predatory in-stincts? Sometimes it becomes much stronger than a niggle, as when people deflect staghounds with false scent and would gladly tar and feather fox hunters. Is this due to progress, *Angst* or decadence? Impossible to say. It seems a new emo-tion. Romans never had it, few Latins do now, the British were little bothered by such qualms in the days of cockfight-ing and bearbaiting.

At any rate, this little worm of guilt is here and it is why we have national parks. Parks are now seen to be an economic asset, the raw material of tourism, so they have become respectable. But this was not the real cause of their birth. They were started by people who did not wish the animals to be exterminated because they are beautiful, fascinating and, above all, free. While men create works of art, animals constitute them. Trying to preserve them is a tribute to freedom, to which the sound, hardheaded business arguments have been tacked on with a sigh of relief.

But it has been a battle and it still is, nowhere more than on the Serengeti; a battle that may yet be lost. Humans are encroaching and are much more of a threat than the hyenas. While hyenas have immensely powerful jaws, humans have miles and miles of steel wire for snares, picks to dig trenches and a great many muskets and rifles; also a deep delight in killing and a lot of ingenuity. Against them the bearded, clownish wildebeest are defenceless.

During October, if all is normal, rains fall in the dry eastern sector of the Park. Hundreds of miles to the west zebra and wildebeest start to draw together into big herds and to move eastwards at a quickening pace.

What starts them off? How is the message communicated? These are great mysteries, of the same nature as the mystery of how and why birds and insects are driven by instincts none can locate or account for to cross oceans and continents. Migration is one of the great unexplained urges of the animal kingdom. It is also the mechanism whereby a balance is maintained between the creatures and their food, the eater and the eaten.

Man wounds and can destroy his habitat—he has demolished forests, dried up rivers, eroded soil, created deserts, fouled seas and lakes; he has spread like a mushroom cloud over fertile ground and left it sterile. Animals, if they are left to their own devices, do none of these things. They work out for themselves a natural rotation which rests pastures when they need rest in dry seasons and maintains a just balance between forest and plain, tree and grass, soil and vegetation, which allows rivers to flow strong and clear, springs to rise, grass to seed itself, trees to give shelter and conserve rainfall.

So off go the zebra and wildebeest in their long files, smelling perhaps the distant short grass and sweet water, or remembering it, corporately, in some secret channel of the mind. Often two or three zebra lead the way. It is the zebra who have the initiative and force of character: sometimes a long file of wildebeest will wait near a water hole until half a dozen zebra have finished their drinking.

Files converge into "armies" of tens of thousands. Numbers fluctuate: at the time of my visit the estimate was between 350,000 and 400,000 wildebeest and zebra combined. The Serengeti also holds perhaps half a million of the smaller antelope such as Thomson's and Robert's gazelle, topi, waterbuck and others; in all, probably a million quadrupeds.

This is by far the greatest collection of plains-dwelling animals left in the world today. It is a microcosm of what most of East and Central Africa was like little more than half a century ago, a surviving pocket, a remembrance of one of the greatest sights the world has ever known. This is all we have left. There are about five thousand square miles of it, which sounds a lot but is little on an African scale—less than 1.4 per cent of Tanganyika's area. If you stocked this type of land even with the little, thrifty zebu cattle, you would need fifty acres to support a single beast; and there is very little permanent water.

Wildebeest and Masai

Next morning I flew over the migrations with John Owen, who has taken up piloting in order to quarter his domains, and also to get quickly to and from his Ministry; for his job is at least half political.

Tall, blue-eyed, vigorous and determined, he is a fitting son to one of Kenya's best-known and most controversial earlier figures, the Reverend Walter Owen, Archdeacon of Nyanza from 1918 to 1944, who belonged to the old school of fighting missionaries—fighting for the right as he saw it, a Christian who pulled no punches and was known to those whom he had punched as the Archdemon.

I was interested to learn that although Swahili is Tanganyika's official language, John Owen has refused to learn it. "I am the hired consultant, the technician," he explained. "When I cease to be of use to Tanganyika, I shall go. Meanwhile, as a foreign expert, it's not my place to learn the language. All the people I deal with speak English and prefer it so."

As we flew east, soon after sunrise, every tree beneath us stood out like a peg, casting a sharp pencil of shadow over tawny grass. A herd of buffalo, fat as black pigs, clustered beside a seasonal stream marked by a fold in the ground and a line of flat-topped thorn trees.

Everything was peaceful, gentle, serene and smiling—no sign of man, the destroyer. "Here the world is young and fragile" reads a message carved on a board at the Seronera airstrip, where most visitors enter the Park. The word "fragile" immediately arrests you—does it fitly apply to a slice of raw Africa? In the sweetness of this golden early light, you see that it does.

We came to the wildebeest armies soon after we had flown over a long, straight furrow marking the Serengeti's eastern boundary. The migrating armies had crossed this boundary and were outside their sanctuary and in the Ngorongoro Conservation Area. In 1959 over three thousand square miles were excised from the Park to fulfil promises made to the Masai, who claimed this area as part of their traditional grazing grounds.

This excision was made in accordance with the principle that when the interests of men and those of wildlife conflict those of men shall prevail. But no one inquired too closely into *which* human interests were to have precedence: those of a few nomadic herdsmen—and less than one hundred Masai were reckoned to live permanently in the Ngorongoro Crater, although many more used it seasonally—or those of the very much larger number of visitors who come, and will come in ever-growing numbers, to the Serengeti.

By excising this area, which includes the superb Ngorongoro Crater and its highlands—a magnet for tourists—the Serengeti ceased to be the ecological unit that its creators had intended it to be. The wildebeest and zebra migrations no longer take place within its borders. In fact, the animals now spend at least half the year outside the Park. As a rule, they are safe enough within the Conservation Area, where hunting is forbidden, but elsewhere Tanganyika's citizens have the right to hunt and do so. There are, for instance, at least 120,000 old-fashioned muskets in African possession. If each musket accounts, at a very conservative estimate, for five animals a year, some measure of the slaughter can be estimated—at least six hundred thousand head; and that is quite apart from the heavy toll taken by snare lines at water holes, by pits and trenches and by arrows tipped with poison easily made by boiling down leaves and bark of the common *Acocanthera* tree.

That morning we flew over two separate wildebeest and zebra armies, seething below us like streams of ants, their coats and beards silvery grey in the sunshine. They were on the so-called short-grass area, where rainfall is low and the

9

normal vegetation a sparse herbage only three or four inches high. These plains animals love it, but only after rain does it offer sustenance. When it is severely grazed a low, bushy shrub called *Indigofera basiflora,* with a pretty little reddish flower, covers much of the steppe. There are practically no trees. These short-grass areas lie outside the present boundaries of the Serengeti Park.

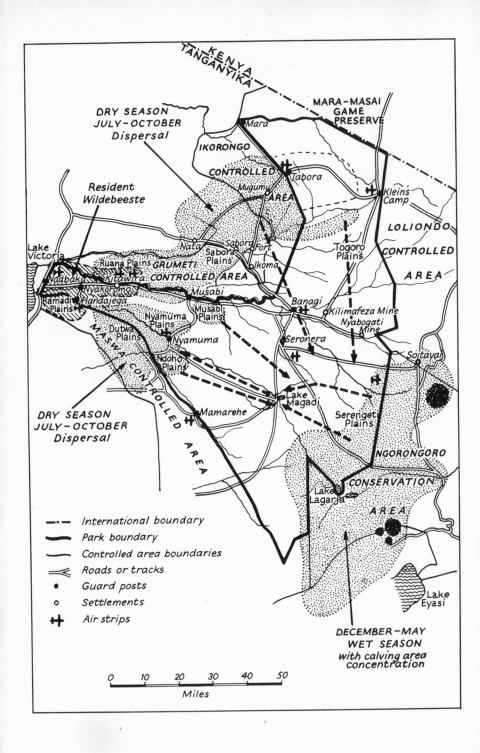

KENYA
TANGANYIKA

DRY SEASON
JULY-OCTOBER
Dispersal

MARA-MASAI
GAME
PRESERVE

Mara

IKORONGO

CONTROLLED   Tabora

Resident
Wildebeeste   Mugumu   Klein's
                                                          Camp
                              AREA

                                                                    LOLIONDO
                        Nata   Sabora Fort
Lake   Sabora   Togoro   CONTROLLED
Victoria   Ruana Plains GRUMETI Plains   Plains
            Kitawira CONTROLLED AREA Ikoma   AREA
Ndabaka
     Nyakoromo   CONTROLLED AREA
Ramadi Handajega   Musabi   Banagi
Plains   Kilimafeza Mine
         Dutwa   Musabi   Nyabogati
         Plains Nyamuma Plains   Mine
MASWA   Plains Nyamuma   Seronera
    CONTROLLED   Ndoho   Soitayai
         Nyamuma   Plains
    AREA   Lake
DRY SEASON   Magadi
JULY-OCTOBER   Mamarehe   Serengeti
Dispersal   Plains
                                                          NGORONGORO

                                                          CONSERVATION

                                Lake   AREA
                                Lagarja

- · - · -   International boundary
～～～   Park boundary
———   Controlled area boundaries
≫≫   Roads or tracks
•   Guard posts   Lake
○   Settlements   Eyasi
✚   Air strips
                                              DECEMBER-MAY
                                              WET SEASON
                                              with calving area
                                              concentration

0   10   20   30   40   50
            Miles

Is it to reach this short-grass grazing, sweet with young growth after rain, that every year the animals trek for hundreds of miles? Does a need for certain minerals underlie their craving? No one knows. Cattle like this grass too, but during the wildebeest calving season the Masai drive their herds off the plains and into hilly country towards Ngorongoro and the mountain Lemagrut. They do this because they believe the afterbirth of the wildebeest to carry a disease lethal to cattle, called malignant catarrh.

Wildebeest calves are born with fluffy gingery-brown hair on their chests which stays for about four months and then moults. The Masai, observing this, believe the calves to remain infective until all the gingery fluff has dropped off.

Blood samples taken from wildebeest calves and examined at the research laboratories at Muguga, outside Nairobi, have told the story. The virus of malignant catarrh is not carried in the afterbirth, nor is it connected with the fluffy hairs, but it *is* carried by wildebeest calves. They themselves are not affected by it, they merely pass it on. So the Masai were correct in their observations, but wrong in their deductions—like so many countrymen who, to the despair of meteorologists, connect the vagaries of the weather with every unrelated phenomenon, from phases of the moon and the behaviour of oaks and ashes to flights of midges and nuclear explosions. By keeping their herds away from the plains when the wildebeest calve there, the Masai successfully keep at bay the virus of malignant catarrh.

They are observant people. Dr. Philip Glover, a wise ecologist, assured me that they have a name for every plant in his own large collection. A complete muster of Serengeti plants made recently by Dr. P. J. Greenway, a noted botanist, has distinguished over two thousand species—as many as in the entire British Isles.

Frontiers of Knowledge

Towards the end of May the wildebeest armies join up again, re-enter the Park and head west towards the narrow corridor reaching almost to Lake Victoria. They may cover, in the process, up to a thousand miles. In the corridor they disperse, and spill once more across the Park boundaries into so-called controlled areas to the north and south, where hunting is theoretically limited by licence but staff is lacking, public opinion antagonistic and poaching rife.

It is here that "cropping" the animals to an agreed scientific plan might be tried, as a way of satisfying the needs for meat and profit of the cultivators who surround the Park. If the animals could be used, and be seen to be used, to satisfy a human appetite, local opinion might veer away from poaching and support control, combined with a planned and humane culling of the herds. It is a long way from doing so at present.

And there is much more to be found out before cropping can be safely and efficiently embarked upon. What biological reasons lie behind these great seasonal movements of plains animals? What routes do they follow and why? Does each beast follow the same route each year? Do some never migrate at all? What is the herd structure; does it vary from year to year, even from day to day?

In 1959, Michael Grzimek, son of the director of the Frankfurt Zoo, was killed in a flying accident while counting animals on the Serengeti. A simple stone memorial on the rim of the Ngorongoro Crater, commanding a magnificent view across its great floor, preserves the memory of a young man of enterprise and courage in the words: "He gave all he possessed for the wild animals of Africa, including his life." Money subscribed by his many friends to a memorial fund was spent on a small research laboratory at Banagi, near Seronera, on the Serengeti. Six biologists are at work there under the direction of a distinguished Belgian, Dr. Jacques Verschuren, until recently chief biologist to the Parc National Albert, in the Congo.

His first task has been to assess the Park's carrying capacity in relation to its animal population: in other words, to answer the question, is the Park overstocked? After a careful aerial count a preliminary assessment suggested that while overstocking had not yet become a serious problem, if existing tendencies developed it might well do so.

What are the remedies? Cropping, perhaps; also to spread the animals more evenly over the Park. Range management, in fact (the American term), applied to wild animals.

All such animals have strong food preferences, which may even vary according to the season. Are these connected with the mineral content of the herbage? What minerals do they seek—could these be supplied artificially, so as to enlarge the use of pasturage and thus increase the Park's carrying capacity?

Or, again, there is the question of those short-grass areas so much favoured by plains-dwelling species: could areas with longer grasses, some of which are undergrazed, be converted to short-grass pastures? If this could be done, more wildebeest and zebra might stay for longer periods within the Park, instead of seeking the favoured foods they like outside.

Only in the last few years has the discovery of the technique of "darting" made such studies feasible. This consists of anaesthetizing animals by firing into them darts, or plastic syringes, loaded with some such drug as succinyl choline chloride, which temporarily paralyzes the neuromuscular system. The biologist can then brand or otherwise mark the drugged animal and subsequently pick it out and map its movements.

The darting technique is now well developed. Practitioners know the right dose for most species, from a rhino to a gazelle. Doses vary enormously: a tough zebra, for instance, needs ten times as much as a wildebeest. Age also counts. Mr. David Orr, a warden previously engaged on darting in the Ngorongoro Crater, told me that he concentrated on animals between six and eighteen months old, the most resilient group, and he did not lose any.

A German scientist at Banagi, Dr. Klingel, has carried things a stage further by discovering that just as no two human fingerprints are identical, so are no two zebra alike in their markings. Now he has worked out a technique by which he can identify an individual zebra from its stripes on photographs, one taken from each side.

A British member of the team, Mr. Murray Watson, studying wildebeest migrations, is following up a clue provided by an analysis of river water on the Serengeti. The fluorine content is exceptionally high: fifteen parts per million, as against a normal content of two parts. Too much fluorine can damage teeth and even rot the bones. Wildebeest prefer rain water, if they can get it, to rivers. This suggests the possibility that a root cause of the migrations may be not only a search for short grass, but for sweet water.

Nowadays the Serengeti's birds attract as much attention from the visitors as its mammals. This part of Africa is fantastically rich in bird life. Over sixteen hundred species have been recorded, more than twice as many as in the whole of the United States. At Seronera the skins of some three hundred and fifty species, many of a gemlike brilliance, repose in trays waiting to be set up in a museum, which in turn awaits the money to build it with.

That is the crying need—money. Tanganyika is a poor, sprawling country, newly come to independence, with un-developed natural resources and all to do at once for a back-ward population—schools, hospitals, clinics, roads, housing, agricultural development, projects of every kind. It cannot also develop its parks without help from other countries, whose citizens come in increasing numbers to enjoy them—help, as its Ministers so often say, from "the Outside." What better cause for "the Outside" to support than the parks?

Seronera

John Owen told me that he has a three-pronged objective: to get across to Tanganyikans the beauty, value and interest of their own parks; to promote and find money for research, on whose findings he may base his policies; and to develop the parks for the benefit of visitors from home and overseas.

When the Ngorongoro Area was lopped off the Park, the sole safari lodge went with it and a new start had to be made. Now there is an airstrip at Seronera, several wardens' houses and a new safari lodge, far from completed. It all costs money, and money is tight. Ambitious plans are afoot: seven new lodges, no less, on the Serengeti alone.

I must admit to a quailing of the heart: roads full of speed-ing cars, aircraft buzzing overhead, diesel fumes, litter baskets, packed luncheons, comfort stations, caravan parks, and even-tually, no doubt, Coca-Cola bars, dance halls, drive-in movies. . . . Why not, if people enjoy them? It's bound to come and, if done with intelligence, perhaps may lead to more happi-ness, rather than less. Or perhaps not?

Seronera Lodge has made a good start with a bar well de-signed by a young Nairobi architect, Mr. Robert Marshall, shaped like a crescent moon and roofed in palm thatch, built in undressed stone and enclosing in its arms an open-air patio with slabs of stone to sit on round a campfire. This gives out a pungent smell of thorn-log smoke loaded with suggestions of long-past, half-remembered camps under the stars with all infinity around you, all time blurred.

The sounds are unchanging: crickets ceaselessly shrilling, the weird whooping call of a hyena and, quite close, a resonantly grunting lion. A half-moon behind a tracery of acacia branches and leaves. Wood smoke sweet as incense, a clean-tasting drink; distant, hunched-up shapes and shadows, a wink of light, a sausage fly hurling itself against something hard, knocking itself out and falling with a plop to the ground—is all this a bit stagy, larger than life? Perhaps that is what people come for, to be enlarged, feel the tug of a greater dimension. Everyone becomes an individualist here.

Wardens, of course, have to be. They are on their own: no voices on the ends of telephones to issue instructions, no buildup from secretaries, files and committees, no group solidarity. They command tough, simple, unsophisticated men, the game scouts, drawn mainly from fighting tribes who obey orders but will serve only men they respect. And the respect has to be earned. Wardens have great distances to cope with, hard travel, quick decisions which can be matters of life and death. It is tempting to romanticize them, turn them into Hemingway figures because their lives seem so far removed from those of chemists' assistants, clockers-in at factories, stockbrokers' clerks.

No day goes by when poachers are not at work in some section of the Park. Modern poaching is no matter of a rebel against property owners bagging the odd hare or tickling a salmon. Here poaching is, in the main, big business, with miles of steel-wire snares and trucks carting away meat worth three shillings (forty-two cents) a pound.

Anti-poaching patrols are out all the time: on foot, in Land-Rovers and airborne. The Park now has three light aircraft presented by generous donors, and several of the wardens, besides the director, have learned to fly. Patrols keep in touch with headquarters by radio link. While I was there news came in of a series of trenches, found two hundred miles to the north, in one of which were several trapped buffalo.

All poaching is cruel, often hideously so. In dry weather the animals, desperate for a drink, walk into steel snares as they approach the pools and die slowly, smelling the water they crave but cannot reach. "Poachers have only to wait," a warden said—like hyenas, who gnaw alive the captured creatures, while vultures peck at eyes and anus. The toll is enormous. In the last few years this single warden has taken twelve thousand snares and secured the conviction of over seven hundred poachers. Far more snares escaped detection, far more poachers got safely away.

Here is an extract from one of his reports.

> I came on a big bull buffalo lying in a mud hole. As he lurched to his feet, I noticed five feet of steel-wire snare hanging from his neck. Through the glass I could see a ring of blood and flies round his neck, and at fifty yards' range the smell was frightful. I destroyed this buffalo. The back of the neck had a gap of five inches of exposed flesh black with flies while below the jaws the blood was still running freely. I never did see the noose itself, it had disappeared deep into the suppurating mass of flesh. The snare must have been on at least a month and the buffalo was dying by inches.

It is not surprising that wardens carry on their anti-poaching war with fervour as well as with courage.

Men and Beasts

Such adventures form natural conversation-fodder round a thorn-log campfire, under the Serengeti stars, the grunt of lions never far away. My companions went on to speak about the ethics of killing animals when you want to preserve them —not mercy killings, like the buffalo, but for a living.

This arose from the topic that today, like lions at Seronera, is always within earshot—Africanization. The white wardens know that they must go. When, none can say; there is no indecent hurry; Africanization rolls on like a locomotive whose wheels have started turning and must gather force and speed as it advances down the track. Everyone knows its advance to be just and inevitable. In two, three, five years at the most no expatriates will be left in the government service.

"There's nothing else we're fitted for," said this warden. "Only hunting." Before he joined the parks he had earned his living as a white hunter, and supposed that he must go back to it. He is Kenya-born, a rancher's son, and has a wife and children.

"You'll never go back to it," the director suggested.

"A man must eat."

"To go back to butchery—licensed butchery for millionaires . . ."

The warden shrugged his shoulders. He's in his forties now, slightly deaf as a result of wartime service in tanks and armoured cars.

Of course there is a love-hate relationship between men and beasts. We pet them and eat them, preserve them and hunt them, pity them and torture them, pamper them and slaughter them, win their confidence and then have them destroyed. When they do as they are told we sentimentalize them and make fools of them and of ourselves, when they defy us they are wiped out without any nonsense. We fear them and laugh at them, worship them sometimes, at others keep them as toys. A farmer will minister for a year to a single beast as if it were an emperor, grooming and cosseting and making much of it, leading it out on a halter, letting it feed from the hand, and then send it off without a qualm to Smithfield to be judged and slaughtered—content, if it wins a prize, to boast about the price of the carcass.

I once asked a Wiltshire neighbour then employed in a slaughterhouse—a mild and gentle villager, fond of cricket, a model father with a shy, apologetic manner—if he didn't find the work uncongenial. He was astonished. "Lovely work," he said, and added unexpectedly: "I never feel so good as when I've got my arms in blood up to the elbows." Another villager, a passionate gardener, had castrating for his hobby. "No tom-cat's safe from Frank," his friends respectfully said.

To move from killing creatures to preserving them is a natural progression. By learning how best you may destroy them you learn so much about their habits, minds and ways. You get to respect and love them, then to regret the need to blot them out. You give your killer's impulse a twist and it becomes an even stronger urge to preserve, and to deflect others from a course you yourself followed so enjoyably.

But can you subsequently move the other way? Revert from protecting to your first position, that of killer? Or, in the warden's case, of midwife to others who often kill only to boost an emasculated ego, and then to brag about a courage they seldom possess? Perhaps you can do anything to make a living. We left the question unresolved.

In his house, sited beneath a *kopje* full of rock hyraxes—the Biblical coney—who come out every evening to be fed, the warden has a most unusual book collection—unusual because it spans so wide a field. There's a bit of everything: history, biography, philosophy, travel, fiction, mythology, ancient religions, modern science. Every book looks read.

Like, perhaps, the animals he protects, this warden is a survivor—he prefers to almost every other pleasure that of *buying* books. He knows, he said, of no better moment than the arrival of a parcel which he wrenches open (a vicious struggle, these days, with clinging cellotape; not like the clean snip of tidy string) to pluck out the fresh, brightly jacketed volumes. Then he starts at once to devour them with that obsessive and now rare reader's greed, grudging evenings when he can't sit back with one in his hands.

There is no trash on his bookshelves. I don't mean he has only learned tomes; there are Waugh and Wodehouse and Hemingway, Firbank and Scott Fitzgerald, as well as works of, or about, explorers like Hilary, Costeau and Burton, and people who sail round the world in small boats. There are books about the notable from Tamerlane to Hitler, and the significant from the Gautama Buddha to Teilhard du Chardin. Boswell stands next to Buchan, the *Seven Pillars* prop up *The Anatomy of Melancholy*. A favourite is *Death in the Afternoon*. "Just now I'm fascinated by the conquest of Latin America," he said.

Birds came and shared our veranda breakfast, coneys sunned themselves among the rocks, a small herd of topi and some tommies grazed just beyond the lawn. The night's predation was ended, peace and serenity returned. There's a Garden of Eden quality about these wind-swept, smiling plains where men have drawn their own fangs.

One more quotation from the warden's report.

> The dusky fly-catchers are very tame around my house and join us at meal times on the veranda. One day Hoppity came as usual but did not look his normal self and even declined a succulent moth. He adopted a constipated attitude and after some

effort succeeded in doing a "job" and then vomited a seed from the fruit of the *Commiphora* tree nearby. Fly-catchers pick up and swallow the whole fruit lying on the ground, and after digesting the fleshy portion, regurgitate the stones. Having done so, Hoppity renewed his desire for moths and joined us on the breakfast table.

IN A CRATER

Tourists' Heaven

An early colonial atmosphere lingers in crevices of the log cabin on the rim of Ngorongoro's crater, where tourists eat. There's a big stone fireplace at one end, where a cedar fire smoulders; on the tables are chianti bottles with candles stuck into their necks; the tongues of half a dozen nations mingle in the smoky air. Soon this will go; some visitors have objected to the logs because of insects, or even snakes, they fear may lurk in the crevices, ready to emerge and savage them; so the cabin has been condemned.

The visitors who shared our table had no such fears. They looked like portraits by Grant Wood of middle-aged, honest, upright, God-fearing Middle Westerners, and did, in fact, come from Iowa; newly retired, they were going at their leisure round the world. Their comments were shrewd, kindly, sensible and not at all dogmatic. The fertility of Africa impressed them, and also the improvidence with which it seemed to them to be squandered. And why no hogs? They shook their heads over this, it worried them. In Iowa everyone raised hogs.

Here everyone talks nineteen to the dozen; Germans, Italians, Israelis, Americans, Australians, Greeks, Lebanese—even an English trio deep in a discussion (believe it or not) of equine performances during Badminton's three-day event. A microcosm of the world sitting on a bit of its roof. No Tanganyikans, though—few could afford it and those who could perhaps prefer city life.

The early morning view is fabulous. Poised on the rim, surrounded by tall junipers which scent the crisp air with a fresh, cedary mountain aroma, down you look into the crater, a good two thousand feet below, its floor half hidden by wisps of cloud laid gently across like strips of fine muslin later to be drawn aside by the sun.

Before sunrise the sky and hills beyond the far wall are the grey-blue of a dove's breast, as clear as the bottlebird's bubbling call. The sky flushes apricot and saffron, and is streaked just above the horizon by long pink and mauve clouds. The distant mountains, creased by dark clefts of forest, are the blue of a ripening plum; below them lies the crater's floor with its lake like quicksilver. The sun emerges to flush with gold the crater's western slopes and illuminate as if by floodlight all the trees and rocks and gulleys. The whole sky turns gold and then the clear, pure blue of a blackbird's egg.

The Rivals

With Mr. Henry Fosbrooke, Conservator of the Ngorongoro Conservation Area, we bumped down a steep Land-Rover track into the crater, passing a detachment of the Tanganyika Rifles who were helping to install a pump. Mr. Fosbrooke leaped out to harangue them on the problems of the Area and the need to safeguard and develop simultaneously forests, grass and game. He and his staff let slip no opportunity to instil into the minds of Tanganyikans of every age and kind the doctrine that this is their country, these are their resources and their whole future depends upon the use they make of them.

On top of the crater we had passed a pleasant little hostel built to accommodate groups of students and schoolboys who come in batches for two or three days to be shown how the task of conservation is tackled, and to be taught something of Ngorongoro's ecology: its trees and grasses, its animals domestic and wild, how they interact upon each other, and how the Masai's need to graze their cattle can be reconciled with the preservation of the wild animals and forests.

This Conservation Area includes that part of the Serengeti which was excised from the National Park in 1959. There were, at the time, only five permanent Masai *manyattas* (encampments shared by livestock and people), holding less than one hundred souls, in the crater itself; but the Conservation Area as a whole, all three thousand square miles of it (about the size of Kent and Sussex), held probably ten thousand tribesmen.

The Masai pressed their claims to the crater and its surrounding highlands largely because they had been so badly handled in the past by successive colonial governments. When the National Park was scheduled in 1947, they were not even consulted. Although so few live or regularly graze their cattle in the crater, they look on it as a dry season reserve, and in times of drought throng from all sides to the walls, where a higher rainfall keeps vegetation going for longer than on the surrounding plain. The wild animals need grazing no less urgently in times of drought. Although the Masai do not, by tradition, kill these animals, when short of keep they drive them away from water holes, which comes to the same thing.

And they are growing increasingly to resent the presence of the game. Once there was plenty of room for all; now, as Masai herds increase and multiply, there is mounting pres-

sure. "The Masai grievance," Mr. Fosbrooke said, "is that they had to give up their rights to their traditional grazing within the Serengeti Park when the boundaries were redrawn, but since then no effort has been made to keep the game on its own side of the boundary. Probably this isn't a practical proposition. But it rankles with the Masai all the same."

Wild animals are not the only rivals to the Masai herds. The crater highlands, rising to nine or ten thousand feet, are thickly forested, and here the rivers rise. The Masai are no respecters of forests. Trees, to them, are enemies which rob them of potential grazing, rather than allies which anchor soil and make of it a sponge to absorb rainfall and return it in the form of springs. The Masai drive their herds up into the glades and start fires which destroy the vegetation.

Across the Rift, on the southwestern slopes of the Mau Escarpment, you can count at least a dozen fires every time you fly over the mountains. You can see blackened patches and clearings hoed for crops (a lot of these Masai have Kikuyu wives who cultivate) and the gloomy spectacle of human predators colonizing and spoiling the forests. Already springs are dwindling, and soon rivers that have always flowed the year through will be turned into seasonal streams that come down in spate in wet seasons and dry up altogether in between. Then what will the Masai do for water? When their streams turn into dry, sandy riverbeds, they will shrug their shoulders and say *shauri ya Mungu:* the affair of God. Perhaps it is, for tolerating so much human stupidity.

So this is no simple issue of the interests of human beings versus those of wild animals. Rather it is one of the short-term, immediate interests of those Masai who want the grazing and the long-term interests of the whole community.

Ngorongoro is unique. One of the world's largest craters, it supports as rich, varied and magnificent a collection of ani-

mals, birds, plants and trees as you can find on earth. It excites
wonder and delight. People come to see it from all over the
world. Scientists become nearly awe-struck at its interest and
variety. Surely there is a case for saying that its beauties belong to the world? Have the Masai a right to destroy them,
any more than a small, local group of Europeans would be
justified in demolishing Chartres Cathedral or St. Peter's,
blowing up the remains of the Parthenon or the Crusader
castles, or throwing the contents of the Louvre into the Seine?

These are questions perhaps lying beyond the scope of civil
servants and committees who decided on the crater's future.
At any rate, they were brushed aside. Ngorongoro and its
highlands were taken out of the National Park—but, with the
usual British compromise, they were not simply handed over
to the Masai. They were called a Conservation Area, and
placed under the control of a local committee consisting of
five Masai elders and four junior officials, chairmanned by a
District Officer. This was a low-level committee exercising
low-level powers, and split between the Masai elders, hostile
from the start to all forms of interference, and young technical
officers obliged to refer every decision of importance to their
seniors.

Doomed to failure from the start, the scheme duly failed.
The Masai invaded the forests, drove game away from water
and started to spear the rhino, a thing they had never done
before—probably as a way of showing their resentment against
what they considered to be perpetual interference with their
rights. Other troubles arose. The mixed committee was abolished and Mr. Henry Fosbrooke appointed as Conservator
directly under the Ministry of Lands, Forests and Wildlife.

By this time the Minister had become a Tanganyikan, Mr.
T. S. Tewa: a cosignatory, with President Julius Nyerere and
Chief Fundikira, of the Arusha Manifesto of September, 1961,

an important turning point in Tanganyika's policy. After describing wildlife as "an integral part of our natural resources and of our future livelihood and well-being," the signatories pledged themselves "to do everything in our power to make sure that our children's grandchildren will be able to enjoy this rich and precious inheritance."

Meanwhile a grant of £182,000 ($509,600) had been made from the Commonwealth Development and Welfare Fund—it runs out in 1964—to get the Conservation Area going, and experts had drawn up a Management Plan. The aim of this is:

> to conserve and develop the natural resources of the whole Area (including water, soil, flora and fauna) so as to provide a stable environment for the human occupants and the animal occupants, domestic and wild, thereby maintaining the existing residents' rights and promoting the national interest by conserving the Area's unique tourist attraction, aesthetic value and scientific interest.

An unimpeachable aim—more briefly, to have your cake and eat it. The plan runs to 160 pages and is full of sound projects and useful information, not all of it reassuring. The success of any plan depends on the staff who will carry it out, and Ngorongoro staffing has never been adequate either in numbers or in quality. Good work has been done, bold projects launched, but in fits and starts. In other words, all has not been plain sailing. Nor has the conflict between the Masai on the one hand and wildlife, forests, rivers and the outside world on the other been resolved.

Dwindling Rhinos

Down on the crater's floor lies a lake soured by soda but still drinkable, and shared between Masai cattle and herds of zebra, wildebeest, topi, eland, gazelle and other wild creatures. We came upon two rhinos, a mother and her half-grown child, standing monumentally out in the open, without a bush in sight.

Rhinos like shelter normally, and are bush dwellers. Here, perhaps, they felt safer in the open, where, despite poor eyesight, they could not be approached without warning. Three or four years ago hundreds of their kind inhabited the crater and its surrounding hills; now there are thirty-seven, and some think this is an overestimate. They have taken a terrible beating from the Masai, and from people living outside the crater, such as the Wa-Arusha and Mbulu. Everywhere rhinos are dwindling so fast that the survival of their species is threatened.

The Olduvai gorge, about thirty miles west of the crater, used to be full of rhinos which cohabited the bush peaceably with archaeologists digging up bones at the Leakeys' camp, and with the Masai whose cattle grazed the surrounding plain. And then, in 1961, in the space of six months, the Leakeys counted over fifty rotting carcasses in the gorge, all speared by Masai. Whether or not their motive was political, they had taken the profit; every horn had been removed.

Since then the Leakeys have not seen a single rhino at Olduvai. This is typical of what is going on all over East Africa. The rhino cannot hold out much longer. There have been rhinos on these plains, of one sort or another, for at least two million years, according to the archaeological evidence. They shared the terrain with the human species until the last few years, when the desire for sexual excitement of the Asian male and greed for money combined to end the truce.

Our pair had, at any rate, learned to be suspicious. Mother and child stood together gazing towards us—in our Land-Rover we could not be smelled, and were, I suppose, nothing but a blurred and faintly menacing shape—with their heads up, horns curved back over their heavy, encrusted heads, their feet planted squarely on the short grass, looking like massive fat pigs, grey as boulders. If it weren't for those phallic-shaped horns, no one would bother them. Because of those, because of the legend of the horns' aphrodisiac properties and because of the greed and gullibility of man, they have perished in their tens, their hundreds of thousands. A meticulous analysis carried out in a Swiss laboratory failed to reveal the slightest trace of any aphrodisiac agent.

Whenever I see a rhino, I feel guilty of what has been done to them by my own species and for the reasons, so shoddy and cruel. Not only is the superstition false, but how can there be a *need* to stimulate the sexual potency of Asian males? With a birthrate like India's, Pakistan's and Southeast Asia's? Had the rhinos been slaughtered in the hope of damping down their ardour, there might have been more excuse.

"An all-out drive by the C.I.D., using modern methods, combined with much stiffer penalties," I was told, *"could* smash the smugglers, but . . ."* The usual "but"—no money, no skilled staff, no real flexing of the will. So the rhinos dwindle towards a point of no return.

A Cigar-Shaped Hovel

A tall, glossy-skinned young Masai leaned gracefully against the Land-Rover to scrutinize with supercilious curiosity everything within, to laugh and to say to Mrs. Fosbrooke: "Mama, will you drink milk?"—the traditional offer of hospitality. Nearby was his *manyatta,* as scruffy a cluster of low, cigar-shaped, dirty mud hovels as you could hope to find, devoid of dignity or interest. A few vultures brooded on the only nearby tree, in itself a sorry specimen; pied crows perched on a broken-down stake fence, waiting for offal. Here, to all outward appearances, has not stirred the least puff from the wind of change.

This tall young man was dressed in the traditional manner, his hair gathered in a queue like an eighteenth-century sailor's, but matted with grease and with red ochre, which also dyed his short calico cloak and reddened his limbs. He had the almond eyes of an ancient Egyptian, with a disturbing glitter; an air of arrogance; shining bangles and bracelets and dangling earrings; a strong musky smell; and above all, that strange effeminate, half-drooping attitude proper to the Masai warrior.

I do not know why these well-built young men, with their reputation for endurance and bravery and swagger, should look so like girls, or at least stand and move like them, but they do. Their bodies are quite hairless. Beside them a hairy-chested European has an apelike appearance. They are smooth as statues and fluid in their movements. I suppose they are one of the most publicized, photographed, anthropologized and sentimentalized people on earth.

All the same, they *are* photogenic, and I clicked away as all tourists do. "His usual fee is thirty shillings [$4.20]," Mr. Fosbrooke warned me. Because I was with the Fosbrookes, I was permitted to click for nothing. Not long ago one of our party had picked up a Masai with his spear, dressed in the same fashion, as a guide. He proved to be an ex-sergeant major, a trained driver and carpenter who had served in Burma and Malaya, and after the war, returned to his *man-yatta* to herd cattle, content with his cigar-shaped mud hovel and resolved never to take a job, drive a vehicle or use a lathe again.

The young man who offered Mrs. Fosbrooke milk owned a part share in a truck. A number of warriors had clubbed together to buy it for £2,000 ($5,600), and used it mainly to get about in, not to market anything—they have nothing to market but their cattle, which, as a general rule, they are reluctant to sell. They enjoy travelling, and go sometimes to Arusha. On the way from this busy little town we had passed several trucks halted by the roadside, while pig-tailed Masai exchanged milk in old gin or whisky bottles for maize meal with the Wa-Arusha. It is no longer true that Masai will eat only their rancid cheesecake made from sour milk, cattle's blood and a dash of urine. So, after all, there have been changes.

As for the part ownership of trucks, it's mostly a matter of *heshima:* that quality which impregnates African life as intimately as the sap impregnates a plant's tissues. Pride, face, dignity, prestige: the motive force, the mainspring, the sustaining factor.

Above all, this quality of *heshima* is linked with cattle. A man without cattle is a man without *heshima:* conversely, the more cattle, the more *heshima.* So, to some extent, wealth and *heshima* are one, but there are subtle differences. Prowess and courage can win *heshima* for young men, wisdom and contact with ancestral spirits for the old.

This, in a nutshell, is the problem with the Masai: to persuade them to treat their cattle less as the measure of their wealth and *heshima* than as an economic asset to be exploited and managed. It is no longer a problem of "we," the Westerners, teaching "them," the Masai. White men are now in Tanganyika only as experts and advisers, when called in by Ministers in Dar es Salaam. Nevertheless, there is still a "we," although its face has turned black. An African "we" wishes to change an African "they." Nothing, really, has altered, except a few complexions. And there are still plenty of white ones about.

This is a terrible dilemma, the root of African uncertainty, insecurity and contradictory behaviour. Africans are torn in two ways. They do not want to go on merely being "them," to be changed and remodelled by a "we" which remains basically Western, and therefore white, in origin and philosophy. They want to be themselves, to find their own way and to have their own personality. At the same time they don't want to forgo and renounce either the ideas or the technical skills of the Western "we." They don't want to remain any longer as raw material for anthropologists, as primitives, as interesting survivals, like the rhinos. They want to join in and catch up with and ultimately perhaps to lead the twentieth century. They want to read and write and look at television, to wear suits and shoes and dark glasses, to drink beer and eat steaks and have electric light and plumbing, to use cars and airlines and, eventually, nuclear power, H-bombs and astronauts in orbit. All these things are part of *heshima*.

As for the Masai, they don't want to give up vaccines. All would be well if they did, because the numbers of their cattle would be controlled as nature in the past controlled them, by disease. It is the vet's needle that has changed everything. Vaccines now keep alive nearly all the animals that used to die. Flocks and herds increase and multiply, overgraze the pastures and destroy their own habitat.

Tons of paper, rivers of ink, loads of typewriter ribbons, have been used up in seeking ways to control the numbers of Masai livestock; people have had nervous breakdowns and been sacked and even speared over it; and the answer remains elusive. In 1961 a drought, the worst for half a century, killed thousands of cattle and forced the Masai to sell thousands more, halving the number in the crater. Then came two good seasons. And again numbers are rising fast and the "offtake"—the number sold, eaten or lost through natural causes—lags well behind the natural increase, despite official persuasion to put the cattle through markets run especially for this purpose, and despite the country's shortage of meat. A change of government hasn't meant a change of heart.

Learning to Want

There is a plan, if they can be persuaded to follow it, for the Masai to become "home-based"—no longer nomads, but to keep two herds, one static and consisting of improved cattle regularly dipped against disease, the other a ranching herd that would not be dipped but, as at present, acquire immunity to East Coast fever by losing up to two thirds of its calves. The owners would have to sell their surplus beasts, like it or not, and to "learn wants."

It is ironic that people must be taught or bullied into acquiring wants, when most of us struggle so hard to satisfy the wants we seem unable to suppress. Shouldn't we do better to shed *our* wants and simplify our lives, rather than lure the Masai after us into this acquisitive mantrap? Are "we" caged by greed, egged on by jealousy of "their" freedom from wants?

In this case our motives appear sound: "we" are trying to stop "them" from ruining their country and know no other way to go about it. "The challenge is the growing degradation of the grassland and forests and their proper management," says the Plan. So men must learn to want, learn to be discontented, learn to be greedy and envious and covetous and unhappy. Eat of the fruit of the tree of knowledge and learn merely that they are naked, surely the least satisfying of rewards for defiance of a divine command. Learn that they are ignorant of knowledge which can bring only unhappiness.

What are they to learn to want? "Television sets on donkeys' backs," someone suggested. If that is taking matters too far, they could perhaps learn to pay for the water they do in fact already want, in piped supplies for their cattle, and for the vaccines they get at subsidized rates; they could learn to want cattle dips, dispensaries—few children are without eye infections, and venereal disease is rife—and even schools.

For a long time the Masai resisted schools. Years ago I visited one of the first they had reluctantly agreed should be started, after a lot of bullying; it needed a site of five thousand acres because no father would sanction the attendance of a son unless two or three cows went with him to supply milk and blood, and a woman to look after him and do the milking. Now there are a number of schools and the Masai are demanding more, because they know that they are being left behind in the race and do not want to be governed by men of other tribes. From among the few already educated Masai the Government has selected one as Area Commissioner (District Commissioner that was) at Loliondo, headquarters of the Tanganyika part of Masailand.

One of the wants that a few of the bolder Masai are acquiring is for better housing. Certainly nothing could be worse, at any rate by "our" standards, than their traditional dwellings, in which no one can stand upright, there are no windows and thick smoke saturates the air, chokes the lungs and injures the eyes; flies abound; roofs leak in heavy rain on to mud floors and sometimes turn the place into a quagmire, and goats and sheep share a hut full of fleas. It is surprising that these handsome, clean-limbed young men emerge, like dragonflies hatching out in dirty ponds, from such squalor.

A "better" house is always roofed in corrugated iron. The crater is to be developed for tourism as a relic of the old, wild, unsullied Africa *au naturel*, the wilderness that was, the wildlife sanctuary. Will visitors appreciate a wilderness aglint with sheets of corrugated iron winking like heliographs in the sun? Can you in fact combine progress with preservation? Here is another clash of interests, as yet unresolved.

Lions and Flies

There are lions in the crater, but nothing like so many as there used to be. Some have been speared by Masai, but many more died two years ago as a result of an ecological accident. Mr. Fosbrooke showed me deep scratches on the bark of a thorn tree made by lions who had climbed into the branches to escape biting flies called stomoxys. Normally these flies do no more damage than gadflies or "stouts" in an English meadow, which pester cattle but do not destroy them. Stomoxys breed in the swampy margins of the crater lake. This lake shrivels every year in the dry season; the margins dry up, and the flies cease to breed.

In 1961 there was first a devastating drought, then a prolonged period of heavy rain which fell all through what should have been the next dry season. The lake, far from shriveling, advanced, and in its swampy margins no less than nine consecutive generations of stomoxys bred. The population built up to fantastic numbers and attacked everything in sight. An eland which stumbled became black with flies within a few seconds and was dead within the hour. Cattle showing the least sign of weakness were set upon and bitten to death. The unfortunate lions clambered into trees—in vain; one was seen with its side half scratched away and caked with blood. Before the plague roughly sixty lions inhabited the crater; after it, fifteen.

Beside the scratched tree stands a rock from whose flat surface had been scooped a double line of shallow depressions, made for the game played all over Africa, played for many centuries and known by many different names. The Swahili word is *bao,* which simply means board, in which the shallow holes are often made; though they can be just as well marked in the dust under a shady tree. Into these depressions you drop beans or pebbles to a fixed number, and your object is to capture your opponent's counters. The rules are far too complicated for me, at any rate, to grasp. Men will spend hour after hour at *bao,* like chess players, and indeed it is a kind of African chess.

These depressions in the rock must have been made long before the coming of the Masai, who, according to the latest reckoning, did not enter the crater until about 1850. The earlier inhabitants, peoples called Iraqw and Tatog, have disappeared.

Nearby, a clump of bushes on the crater's floor conceals the tent of a young American who is experimenting with a plastic collar he has invented to catch wildebeest and zebra for the purpose of marking them. We passed a redheaded youth in a Land-Rover, a member of the Voluntary Service Overseas Corps, spending his holidays searching with binoculars for marked animals among the herds and, if he detects any, putting dots on maps.

Westerners are still busy asking why. The Masai, driving docile herds of tiny humped cattle to water, aren't worrying. Either they asked all the questions long ago and have forgotten the answers or they have dismissed the questions as irrelevant. Content with their rancid cheesecake, their warm fire, their children and their fertile cattle safely penned, they want little more. Nothing, at any rate, worth the trouble of asking a lot of pointless questions on a hot day.

The flats all round the crater's lake, swampy now from recent rain, are full of birds. Two flamingo species, greater and lesser, share the alkaline shallows round the lake's margins. Sacred ibis are there in force, very handsome with their snowy breasts and backs and coal-black rumps, and a queer streak of blood-red on the undersides of their wings. The glossy or *hadada* ibis, with its queer bronzy-purplish lustre, is much less spectacular but has a subtle beauty of its own. The brown Hammerkop stork provides a note of the grotesque with a long crestlike excrescence on his head. Gaily plumaged Egyptian geese; storks of several varieties; the showy black-and-white blacksmith plover; ducks and egrets, bustards and herons, spoonbills and grebes: birds of every shape, size, habit and colour, a dazzling variety.

And what a setting! A rim of grape-blue hills against a sky turning gold with evening and long, long lights resting on their gently sloping shoulders, above them, a frieze of rose-red cloud. The air is soft and drenched with a diffuse golden essence that at once soothes and amazes; even the toylike zebra calves look gingery, with golden-tinted manes. Silver-backed jackals do not trouble to turn their pointed faces and pricked ears in our direction as they trot by.

Peace suffuses the air, peace and gentleness and harmony. There is a pause at this time of day. The heat has abated, the harsher business of the night not yet begun. "Here the world is young and fragile," and a short truce reigns between hunter and hunted, predator and prey. The sun withdraws behind the mountains, and the light changes; there's magic still, but a hint of darkness, of the breaking of the spell. A flight of ducks wheels above the silvery lake, and one's thoughts turn to the shelter of walls.

Not the least of the pleasures of the safari lodge, with its good food and welcome drinks and sweet-smelling wood fire, is that the log cabin has no radio.

The good food is cooked by a true Tanganyikan: half German and half African, she has one daughter married to a grandson of the first German settler in the crater, another to an African teacher. Sometimes her grandchildren pay her visits and mix as children do, without any racial restraint. A microcosm of the future Africa, or an aberration? One of the questions that can be asked, but not answered.

The Leakeys' Camp

A stone slab marks the grave of a hominid—not a man, but one of his precursors—who died about one and three quarter million years ago, in an age called the Lower Middle Pleistocene. It is a large, solid concrete block and shows where, in 1959, the two Leakeys dug up his skull, which was resting on a floor covered with pebble tools—probably his, although this cannot be stated for certain.

"He had a flat skull and a very long face," Mrs. Leakey said. They called him *Zinjanthropus;* the Leakeys believe he was one of several different types of hominid then coinhabiting the earth. He dates from a considerably earlier period than Professor Dart's *Australopithecus,* discovered nearly forty years ago in the Transvaal, another hominid precursor of man whose bones have contributed to the current theory that the African continent gave birth to *Homo sapiens.*

Olduvai is an extraordinary crack in the eastern Serengeti plains which cuts through layers of rock and lava, revealing, about three hundred feet below, deposits mostly laid down on the bed of a very ancient lake. Until you are right on top of the gorge, you have no idea it is there. A German scientist called Professor Kattwinkel stumbled upon it in 1911—it is said when pursuing a butterfly—and saw at once that it was

45

rich in prehistoric material. Many fossil bones were dug up there in 1913 by Dr. Hans Reck. It was to investigate these finds that Dr. Louis Leakey visited the gorge in 1931, at once started to collect hand axes and recognized in this miniature Grand Canyon one of the richest deposits of prehistoric fossils and enigmas in the world.

Olduvai has, since then, been Leakey territory, a source of pregnant finds and ideas which have led to the revision of much archaeological dogma in the last thirty years. And it is like an ocean from which only a few trawls have been taken; shoals and shoals of undiscovered fish remain.

It is also like a fiery furnace. Heat is trapped there in the grey volcanic ash in whose brittle, dusty surface specks of quartz and lumps of feldspar catch the light and hurl it back at you. Dark glasses are essential, the light is so blinding and aggressive. Although heavy rain had fallen on the Serengeti, everything looked and felt as dry as one of the excavated bones. Every drop of water has to be brought in Land-Rovers thirty miles from the top of the Ngorongoro Crater. As the track is appalling, wear and tear on vehicles is heavy and water more precious than gasoline. You must need a bath very often in this camp and seldom get one.

The Leakeys' living quarters are an open-sided thatched shed with a table, a few chairs, a large refrigerator, a radio link on which they talk daily to Nairobi, and for the rest a jumble of bones and skulls and teeth and lumps of quartz and lava, bottles of glue and chemicals, choppers and head axes and tins of unidentifiable objects—the kind of disorder from which order emerges in neat little labels, beautifully reconstructed skulls and erudite papers in scientific journals. A haunch of meat hangs from a rafter, a long shelf is jammed with paperbacks, in one corner a bespectacled African glues together fragments of vertebrae with meticulous care. Three large Dalmatians bound about.

The camp is dusty, exceedingly hot and full of insects, but all this Mrs. Leakey finds less distracting than coachloads of tourists who stop here en route from the crater to Seronera for a little sight-seeing.

"I'm glad they're interested, but every time a coachload comes I have to stop and show them the digs, and it's very time-consuming. After they've bumped all this way on these roads, you can't just shoo them off." A guide? There's no one else who can explain; while the Leakeys have excellent home-trained African assistants, they have no one who is archaeologically qualified.

At the time of my visit Louis Leakey was away, lecturing in America, and his wife was on her own, save for her African helpers, the Dalmatians and a great many Masai who inhabit a nearby *manyatta* and gather at her camp every morning demanding medical treatment. To keep time clear for their true function is the greatest of the Leakeys' difficulties. The more remote a place appears to be, the more you are at the mercy of the increasing number of interested and no doubt well-meaning people who nevertheless have few scruples, whether they are Masai or European, in asking for that most precious of all commodities, the time of the talented.

Time in Layers

Of this time we took our ration, and bumped past the monument to *Zinjanthropus* into the gorge. Four strata have been laid down, over the millennia. Bed I, between one and a half and two million years old, of volcanic ash, is the product of cataclysmic eruptions which then convulsed this part of Africa. Here the Leakeys have unearthed bones of

47

archaic forms of hippopotamus, elephant and crocodile, and also very crude tools made from waterworn pebbles. Their makers, early hominids—not necessarily our ancestors, but precursors of the human branch—may have been the earliest tool users in the world.

Here also the Leakeys found the skulls first of *Zinjanthropus* and then of a child of about eleven, who may be even older, but whose genus was probably inhabiting the region at the same time. Both genera, the Leakeys think, probably used pebble tools.

In Bed II appear simple hand axes, more skilfully made. Above this lies Bed III, a brick-red layer of slags and sands laid down during a prolonged dry period when the lakes vanished and the whole fauna must have changed. No wonder there are few fossil animals; but hominids were there, gradually improving their tools. Here, too, have been found bolus stones, which those early hunters looped together with thongs and hurled at the legs of wild beasts to bring them down. Some of the animals present after this later Pleistocene drought, whose bones were found in Bed IV, were modified by natural selection or else arrived from Asia. A higher proportion now differed little from their modern descendants, but there were still many giants.

Bed IV consists of a top layer of river sands laid down after the long drought ended, perhaps two hundred thousand years ago. By this time the first true men were on the earth. Underneath it all lies the basement complex of sedimentary and metamorphosed rock dating back over two thousand million years—the oldest rocks in the world.

I suppose no one will ever know the exact spot, if indeed there is one, where man or his precursor made the greatest of all discoveries, greater even than that of fire, and long before it: how to shape a natural object, such as a pebble, into a tool, and then to use that tool to better his material condition. It could have been at Olduvai.

Until he did this, Dr. Leakey has pointed out, man or his precursor was a scavenger, in the same class as the hyena and vulture. No doubt he could catch and tear apart small beasts with his hands, but he could eat the larger ones only if they had been killed by some other predator and their skins had rotted; otherwise he could not have penetrated their tough hides. So, at some point, he discovered how to sharpen a pebble in order to split a hide. "Progress," Dr. Leakey has said, "came with man's urge to extend his food supply." He

has himself made these pebble tools in twenty-five seconds. After our mutual ancestor had made his discovery, he left the scavenger class and joined the hunters. "His skill was related to more efficient killing," as it still is.

The Birth of Tools

Was *Zinjanthropus* the earliest of all tool users? Impossible to say, or even to be certain that he was the user of the pebble tools on which his skull lay. And since his disinterment a momentous series of observations made by a young biologist, Jane Goodall, has suggested that the first users of tools were not hominids at all.

For more than three years Miss Goodall has shared the lives of chimpanzees inhabiting a sanctuary on the shores of Lake Tanganyika. After a while the chimpanzees grew so accustomed to this solitary fellow creature that they would stroll in and out of her camp and take away her clothes and blankets, and accept bananas from her hand—regarding her, she believed, as another kind of chimp, if an eccentric one.

In the sanctuary are mounds covering the nests and galleries of termites. These are ventilated by channels, or pipes, which show on the surface as small holes. Jane Goodall has frequently watched a chimpanzee break a twig from a tree, strip off its leaves and thrust it down one of the ventilation channels. Then it withdraws the twig and proceeds to lick off the termites clinging to the sides and tip.

This, in her estimation, and that of Dr. Leakey, constitutes the use of a tool, of which his definition is "a natural object, or part of a natural object, deliberately altered by hand for a specific purpose." The chimpanzees will strip leaves and shoots off a twig, thus altering a natural object, and adapt it to "fish" for termites, thus using it for a specific purpose. For how long this has been going on, no one can ever know. That some primate other than the ancestor of man may have been a tool user is a possibility that will put a big cat among the archaeological pigeons. "Jane Goodall," Dr. Leakey has commented, "has carried out what is probably the most wonderful piece of primate research ever done."

At Olduvai, Mary Leakey showed us some heaps of black lava rock arranged in a rough circle she believed to be manmade. If so, the only purpose the Leakeys can deduce is that the rocks were so arranged to support wooden uprights. These could then have been packed with brushwood, or even hung with skins, to make a rough shelter against wind and weather. These would be the earliest shelters ever known.

All speculation, of course; but the Turkana, in northern Kenya, make temporary shelters much on these lines today. Were we looking at the birth of the idea of a house? If so, was the shelter used by *Zinjanthropus*, or by some earlier being? No one can say.

Giants and Dwarfs

At the dig half a dozen Africans, crouching in a hot, shallow trench cut into the side of a wall of the gorge, were prodding cautiously with dental picks and gently sieving crumbs of gravel. The jawbone of a giant pig was just emerging from the rock.

These fossils, dating back before the Middle Pleistocene interpluvial period which changed the fauna, reveal that there really were giants in those days. Mary Leakey showed us in her workroom the reconstructed skull of a Middle Pleistocene rhino, alongside a contemporary skull. It looked, to an untutored eye, very much the same shape but just about twice as large, and it needed two men to lift it. The skulls of giant sheep and buffalo have also been disinterred. Why have their descendants become so much smaller? Another unsolved mystery.

Strangely enough, the newest finds the Leakeys are investigating have revealed many examples of pygmy creatures, as much smaller than their modern counterparts as those at Olduvai are larger. A farmer at Fort Ternan, about thirty miles from Lake Victoria, wrote to say that he had found a few broken fossils. Here, in a very difficult terrain—long grass, bush, heavy rock deposits and a sixty-inch rainfall—the Leakeys found a rich deposit of bones dating far back into the Upper Miocene, perhaps thirteen or fourteen million years ago. This is the most important find, the Leakeys think, for years: bones of rhinos, giraffes, hippos and other animals—and all dwarfs. With them are bones of early primates, possibly ancestral to man.

Why dwarfs? And why so many bones concentrated in so small an area, and in such good shape—some are even still articulated—after thirteen million years? To the first question it is impossible even to hazard an answer; to the second, Dr. Leakey thinks this could have been the site of a tectonic spring which now and then emitted poisonous fumes. These would not only have killed the animals who came to drink at the spring, but prevented the scavengers from dispersing their bones.

PLANTS AND MEN

A Mating Display

The plains of Olbalbal were looking their best because rain had fallen and fresh green growth, tender as young beech leaves, had begun to thrust up under the brown. Their colour was an umbered green or lime-green bronze, like ripening wheat just on the turn or the old gold of oak leaves when the tightly clenched buds begin to unfold.

"I love this country," one of my companions said. "There's always something new round the corner, something unexpected. A water hole you didn't know about, a plant or bird you hadn't seen before, something fresh. . . ."

And just then we saw a sight fresh to me, though fairly common at this time of year: a greater bustard cockbird practicing his mating display. He stood alone on a slight mound in the tawny grass, rigid, his big pale grey neck puffed out to three or four times its normal size, taut as a frying sausage, and his head thrown back: his inflated neck looked like some big, fat white snake. Then he flung up and spread his black-barred tail in a big fan, bent it over to lie almost flat against his back and began to strut and side-step, apparently in no particular direction. Nor could we see any sign of the hen.

This was the kori bustard, a bird larger than a turkey that can weigh a good thirty pounds. His method of puffing out his neck so fantastically remains mysterious; apparently a thick, slimy mucus inflates the tissues and can be pumped in or withdrawn at will.

This was in April, the time for such displays. Cock whydah birds in their full, glossy black mating plumage go through the same antics; you can see them bobbing up and down in the grass like bouncing balls, their absurdly disproportionate tails thrown up and waving high above their heads. These black, flowing tails are perhaps eighteen inches or two feet long and quite weigh down the whydah, itself no larger than a thrush—it is a kind of weaver—and when in flight the bird positively staggers through the air in an upright position, fluttering desperately and paddling with its feet, as if drunk in charge of a tail.

What is the object? Surely birds would mate quite happily without all this fuss? One cannot believe a hen bustard or whydah would turn her back on males with ordinary plumage any more than sparrows do, or wildebeest, cattle or cuckoos, frogs or dogs, or any other species; or that other cocks take it all too seriously. From the point of view of survival, mating plumage displays must make the cockbird more vulnerable to enemies. Why do some species go through all this buffoonery and not others? No one seems to know. Always something new round the corner—something unexplained.

Such as the barkans: the most peculiar sand dunes I have ever seen. Wind-built into the shape of a perfect crescent, they jut without rhyme or reason from this short-grass plain. The one we inspected measured about fifty yards between the tips of the horns and was twenty feet high in the middle. The concave side was vertical, the back (as it were) tapered in a long slope to merge into the plain.

Year by year these queer dunes inch their way forward, rolled imperceptibly along by prevailing winds. No one seems to know how, when or why they were formed, the pace at which they move or what will become of them. Even their name seems inexplicable. Eventually, it is thought, they get anchored and grassed over. At present only three mobile ones are to be seen, one of them a baby.

Africa abounds in such mysteries and is short of solution seekers. A scientist is like a hound chasing a pack of hares; a dozen fresh ones start up from every field into which he chases his quarry.

Deserts Could Happen Here

One of the scientists took us to see a fence intended to exclude wildebeest and zebra from a neck of land cupped between two rocky ridges, in order to find out what happens to the natural grasses of these plains when no animals graze them. To put up fences stout enough to keep out zebra is expensive, and the game biologist, Mr. David Orr, had hoped the two steep and rocky ridges that enclose this neck of land would act as barriers, with a fence thrown across at each end. This worked with wildebeest but not with zebra, who found a way over the ridges; and the wildebeest followed.

This experiment forms part of a general inquiry into the complex plant life of the Ngorongoro Area and the Serengeti Plains. The object is to study the interrelationship, responses and behaviour of the vegetation under different conditions. And this in turn forms part of a wider inquiry into the changes in the vegetation brought about by man, by his domestic livestock and by the wild animals, all of whom interact upon one another and upon the habitat. The ultimate aim, of course, is to learn how to control the various factors so as to improve the habitat instead of, as at present, harming it: in short, to gain the data on which to base a sound plan of range management. At present things are going downhill.

Fires and overstocking are the ugliest villains. In the Conservation Area at the moment—the number fluctuates—there are reckoned to be rather more than 150,000 cattle. Last year the Masai put fewer than 4,500 through the markets, a sale of only about three per cent. No one knows exactly what the figure should be, and the Masai ate more beasts than they sold, but probably to keep the herds stable they should have marketed three times as many as they did. The herds are building up again after the drought of 1961, and pressure is once more mounting on pastures which, on these light volcanic soils and in these regions of low rainfall, can stand very little pressure before poor grasses drive out good ones, grasses yield to weeds and finally (and much more quickly than most people expect) a desert forms.

This is no panic threat or bogey. It has happened already in many places and it is happening today. Parts of Kenya Masailand are already little better than deserts, scoured with deep gullies, bare as a vulture's head; seen from the air, like a carcass stripped of flesh with tired grey bones showing. It has happened in Somaliland. One of my companions on the Serengeti, Dr. Philip Glover, a scientist of wide outlook and many parts—zoologist, botanist, but ecologist above all—who has collected plants in that part of the Republic of Somalia formerly a British protectorate, has seen the trees and grasses vanish and a grey, heat-baked, sterile desert take over within twenty years.

Until the coming of the white man the nomadic Somali clans, their numbers kept down by constant raids and warfare, remained in balance both with their camels and their cattle, sheep and goats, and with their habitat, a balance always precarious in this land of marginal rainfall. Grasses adapted to

the harsh conditions protected the soil from wind and sun; trees stabilized and sheltered it, wild animals abounded— elephants, rhinos, hartebeest and zebra, cheetahs and gazelle and herds of wild asses.

It was the old story: good intentions paving the way to a new hell. The vet's syringe and imposed peace between them, both presumed to be benefits, when conferred upon Somaliland ruined it, probably for good. Camels and the cattle multiplied and trampled and destroyed the pastures, men cut down trees, wind and storms swept away an ashy soil and finished off the rivers. Now even the drought-resistant *Euphorbia candelabra* tree is threatened, and another species of *Euphorbia*, whose poisonous sap protected it from man and beast alike, has succumbed because the topsoil deteriorated into dust and left it no anchorage.

In order to avoid being eaten, certain species of plant (of the genera *Sloanea* and *Lithocaulon*) learned to imitate rocks or pebbles so closely that they escaped detection, even by goats. But so desperate did the hungry quadrupeds become that even this ruse proved ineffectual; the plants were hunted down and all but exterminated. The search for sustenance became so intense that the Somalis loaded their beasts on to trucks and rushed them to any area where rain had fallen and a little fresh growth begun to sprout. "Against such ruthless treatment," Dr. Glover commented, "nature has no answer but unconditional surrender."

Some years ago the last elephant died in Somaliland—from starvation. The wild ass has dwindled to a few small, scattered and probably doomed herds. And much of Somaliland has become a desert.

It is a sad, familiar story, and it could—quite easily—happen here, in the drier regions of East Africa.

How Plants Survive

Every year the Masai start fires which sweep across these plains and destroy or damage the trees and often eat into the forests. Dr. Glover told me he had seen a tree whose rings showed it to have lived through thirty-seven rainy seasons; it was about a foot high. Every time it had tried to put on growth, another fire blackened and disheartened it. Yet it was still alive. Because some species are more fire-resistant than others, and some scarcely resistant at all, these fires largely determine the structure of the vegetation.

What makes a plant fire-resistant, or the reverse? Many things: type of seed, habit of growth, root structure. There is, for instance, one among the many species of acacia that is especially fireproof: *Acacia lahai*. Not only has it developed a thick, corky bark to protect its trunk, but just under the surface of the soil it has a thickened callus from which its roots emerge. Fire may consume the tree but spares the callus, which sprouts new roots after rain.

Dr. Glover also pointed out a ring of darker vegetation surrounding each of the umbrella thorns, *Acacia tortalis*. Heavy storms break their force on this tree's mat of outspread branches, and the rain, instead of cascading down to sweep away the light soil, descends gently and beneficially, penetrates the soil and stimulates the vegetation. Each umbrella thorn creates around its base a small oasis.

Plants, like men, can be remarkably ingenious in the devices they adopt in order to survive. Among the grasses is one, frowned upon by man because his cattle dislike its coarse, thick tussocks, called *Eleusine jaegeri*. To resist fire, it has developed a root system of extraordinary density and a method of forming new shoots under the protection of the old, deep in the ground. And it fends off the tongues and teeth of livestock by its sharp-edged distastefulness. So the more severe the burning and trampling by cattle, the more this tough but unpalatable grass will thrive.

Experts on pasture research were asked, several years ago, to suggest ways and means of driving out this grass to make way for species acceptable to cattle. But (as so often happens) further inquiry showed that it plays an important local part in the eternal cycle of growth, decay and then regeneration round which all life revolves. Its mat of thick fibrous roots anchors soil exposed by the overgrazing and trampling of tenderer species; and its tussocks act as "nurseries" to the seedlings of other plants. Dr. Glover has counted thirty-three young plants sheltering in a single tussock.

When the pressure lifts, out spread these seedlings from their "nursery" to recolonize the trampled earth. After a while, if rainfall is sufficient and cattle keep away, these more appetizing grasses take over. In an area where nothing has been seen but *Eleusine jaegeri,* livestock were kept out for several years and a thick sward of Kikuyu grass and *Cynodon,* eighteen inches deep in places, replaced the tussocks. Only little hillocks standing out above the general level of the sward revealed the former presence of clumps of *Eleusine.*

So balanced is this natural cycle, so delicate and yet so strong, so intricate and so incredibly well designed, that to destroy it is the most perilous act mankind can embark upon. Yet it is embarked upon, frequently, through ignorance or plain indifference. One day, perhaps, out of the spent and unconsidered earth the cities will not rise again—or, rather, there will not rise the vegetation which feeds the beasts which feed the men who build the cities, and who are going hungry even now in many parts of the world.

Out of the Crater

Fires damage not only the better grasses but, even more irrevocably, the forests which cover—or used to cover—the hills and mountains that both surround the plains and protrude from them, such as Lemagrut, Ol Moti and the Elanaiobi highlands, all of which rise to over ten thousand feet and are the birthplace of rivers. If the forests go, so do the streams. It is as simple as that. Apparently, however, the Masai do not grasp it, for every year they start fires without taking any precautions to ensure that these do not spread into the forests. Looking up at Lemagrut, we could see that it was practically bare.

Official efforts to protect the forests of the crater highlands round Ngorongoro have been more successful, although it is a constant struggle. These are thick, dark, tangled forests full of birds and beasts and many kinds of trees: above about nine thousand feet the light green feathery bamboo, below that such native species as *Juniperus*—these are the sweet-scented cedars with their lichen "beards"; *Hagenia* and *Dombeya*, with its attractive white flowers. Above the forest line are stretches of moorland populated by plants like the giant *Lobelia*, *Senecio*—cabbages on stalks—and *Helichrysum*, and by various tufty grasses; below it comes what is called "montane acacia woodland" with varieties of the ubiquitous thorn such as *lahai* and *abyssinica*. Below that again, other acacias of the parkland kind such as *tortalis; Euphorbia* trees, *Croton*, and then *Commiphora* bushland and thicket. Ngorongoro is a paradise for ecologists: its vegetation runs through every gamut, from alpine down almost to desert.

But it is changing, or being changed by man. Such changes could be beneficial. The root problem is that virtually all the changes going on are deleterious, first to the vegetation and ultimately, of course, to man. To stop people cutting their own throats is the task in a nutshell. And it has to be done by persuasion, not by giving orders.

Along the southern and southeastern borders of the crater highlands press cultivating tribes such as the Wa-Arusha and the Mbulu, who would also like to detsroy the forests, in their case to grow crops rather than to graze cattle. The road leading from the crater's rim down to the plains, and so on to Arusha, runs through part of the Mbulu's territory, and we saw some wonderfully fertile-looking soil, efficiently farmed. The land was clean, the crops looked healthy and prolific and the Mbulu were getting away from hand hoe and peasant plots; tractors were at work on the hillsides, there was contour ploughing and there were small plantations of coffee.

The Mbulu scoop their houses out of a hillside and camouflage the flat mud roofs so skilfully that in days of tribal raids their attackers sometimes ran right over the rooftops without realizing that houses lay underneath. Masai raiders used to fire burning arrows into the thatch of their victims' huts. The Mbulu successfully countered this—there was nothing to fire burning arrows into; and women, children and livestock could shelter inside their caverns, secure from anything short of a total defeat of the warriors in battle.

Old Mbulu houses are still lived in; more recent ones have come out into the open and stand on level ground, but you still have to bend double to get into one. A skinny, toothless grandmother welcomed me in. The men and younger women were out at work, and the homestead was populated by innumerable children, and by goats wandering in and out.

The house was square and dark, lacking windows. Inside, a forest of fire-blackened beams supported the flat roof. A mud-and-wattle partition parallel with all four sides of the house formed a passageway, subpartitioned into chambers where the life of the household took place. Beds roughly constructed from poles tied by leather thongs occupied two or three of the compartments; others were used for storing bags and jars of grain, maize cobs, onions, hides and waterpots and everything else that needed storage; one compartment, extending along the whole length of the wall, was a pen for sheep and goats. Another was the kitchen, with its usual three stones and smouldering fire, whose smoke filled the air and choked the lungs. Outside was a pile of rich compost, composed of refuse from the house, whose earth floor was swept out every morning and looked clean and shiny from the tread of many feet.

A red tractor stood nearby, and one of the sons of the house drove it away. An interesting contrast: the old defensive house—an African counterpart of the medieval baron's castle —and the modern tractor; goats and gourds and cooking stones and beaded women in the house, and modern cultivation tied to world markets outside it. When Mbulu farmers make money—and I was told that many of them now enjoy incomes few Europeans would despise—they evidently do not rush to spend it on improving standards of living. They go on living in the same houses, sleeping on their pole platforms, carrying on without wooden floors and glazed windows, let alone bedroom suites and dinner sets and refrigerators and electric light.

What do they spend it on? First, cattle to get another wife; next, trucks, cars and tractors. Mortality among all forms of vehicle is high. Few Africans have any firsthand mechanical knowledge, garages or service stations exist only in the larger towns; conditions are hard, and cars and trucks are expected to go on going, just as women and cattle are expected to go on breeding. The connection between oil and mechanical survival is not always grasped. So life for vehicles is hard and short.

Arusha

"We used to call them provinces, but we thought that sounded too imperialist, so now we call them regions instead," the Regional Commissioner explained. Districts have become areas for the same reason.

Arusha, a pleasant small town still predominantly Asian in flavour, is the capital of Tanganyika's Northern Region. The chief incumbent of its handsome and substantial headquarters, built by the colonialists just before they left, is now, of course, a Tanganyikan, and the flagpole erected to support a Union Jack displays the native banner. Otherwise there do not seem to be any obvious changes.

There are changes, however, in the concept of a Regional Commissioner's duties. Under the colonial system he was a civil servant to the marrow; now he is a politician. Soon after independence all the British Provincial Commissioners were replaced, somewhat abruptly, by officials of the Tanganyika African National Union. (The Commissioner who received me in so warm and friendly a fashion in Arusha was a member of the National Assembly—an M.P.) The intention was to make all branches of local administration part and parcel of the country's government—that is, part of TANU. Only in this way could policy devised at the centre be carried through with consistency in the outer regions of this huge country—as large as Britain, France and West Germany combined—and the grip of TANU be maintained.

No one could have been more approachable and jovial than the large, expansive, extroverted Regional Commissioner, Mr. Walwa, beaming from behind his desk in a spacious office flanked by Tanganyika flags and portraits of the President. Here was a man who clearly relished his life, his job, his prospects and his achievements. If he had his worries he was not allowing them to harass him; he seemed right on top of his job.

"We must be photographed," he insisted. "But there is a difficulty—my regional photographer is out for the day. . . ." It was solved by the summoning of a private practitioner; but the official photographer had not, in fact, left Arusha, and soon there were two, and the Commissioner and I were kept busy posing in the office and then on the sunlit steps outside.

While photography proceeded we touched on the Region's affairs, which seemed in good shape. It was true that stock thefts were troublesome, leading sometimes to spearing affrays; among the remedies was the introduction of stiffer penalties. "That will be done," said the Commissioner. "We can't allow people to defy law and order." Soon afterwards the National Assembly passed a law to reintroduce flogging as a penalty for theft—on the instalment system, half the lashes to be delivered at the start and half at the end of the prison sentence.

There was still a sprinkling of expatriates in Arusha, as in other regional headquarters. Such is the backward state of women's education that it will be some time before competent secretaries are forthcoming in the needed numbers. The Commissioner's private secretary was British, and I think every Minister and senior official I subsequently saw in Dar es Salaam was similarly served. The Commissioner's Permanent Secretary—his head civil servant—was also an ex-member of the British administration who was staying on until an adequate Tanganyikan could be found to succeed him. One by one these senior officials are going, but enough still remain to provide the experience and continuity which keep the wheels turning—creaking a bit here and there, perhaps, but not seizing up.

All the District Commissioners have become Area Commissioners and all are Tanganyikans. But quite a lot of expatriate technicians—the mercenaries of peace—remain: vets and foresters, agricultural and livestock officers, surveyors and engineers. As with private secretaries, it will be some years before there are enough trained Tanganyikans to go round. Tanganyika's problem is not to get rid of expatriates but to hold on to them. It is not that most expatriates object to working for an African government—on the contrary, those I spoke to preferred it to the old regime.

"They hire you, pay you and leave you to get on with the job," one of them said, summing it up for most of the others. "The attitude is: 'You're the expert, it's up to you, and don't keep bothering me with your problems.' So there's far less interference, and I've had all the backing I could want. It suits me."

Of course there are snags. Letters aren't always answered, paperwork is weak and punctuality goes against the grain of custom in all sun-soaked, heat-laden lands, where casual talk, exchange of courtesies, hospitality and the enjoyment of living are put higher in the scale of things than hours and minutes. (No one in Africa has ever invented any form of timekeeper, not even an hourglass.)

This casual view of time results in a disregard of appointments, and can handicap the conduct of affairs in a modern society. It certainly frustrates expatriates trained in a different school. Some find a way round. One officer, finding his work brought to a standstill by a prolonged silence from his regional headquarters despite his frequent letters, wrote out a set of instructions to himself, drove to his Commissioner's office, waylaid the Commissioner and secured his signature without the least demur, drove back with his instructions in his pocket and carried them out. "A great improvement," he remarked, "on arguing the toss with everyone who thought he knew better, getting it all turned upside down by the Provincial Commissioner and then referred to Dar es Salaam."

Every expatriate knows that his place will be filled by an African just as soon as a passable one can be found. There is no ill-feeling or dispute about this. It is the whole point of independence. No expatriate can look forward to finishing out his time. The tide is coming in; however pleasant the beach, no family man can run the risk much longer of getting cut off by rising waters at too advanced an age to start again.

So expatriates are going, for the most part sadly, for they love the beach; and seldom with anything but regrets and goodwill on both sides. A visitor's impressions must be superficial, but no where did I, at any rate, encounter anything but warmth and friendliness between human and human. It is when people commit themselves to doctrines that they start to scowl.

STUDENTS AND WITCHES

Haven of War

Dar es Salaam lies like a dormant bush baby curled round a blue bay fringed with coconuts and flamboyants. Brightly painted yachts are moored upon a silky ocean, tamarisks and lush greenery half conceal white-fronted houses, a red sun sinks behind darkly silhouetted palm fronds, a moon comes up as yellow as a Cheshire cheese and many twinkling lights leap and waver on a sleepy sea.

The haven of peace, its Arab name: soft, dreamy, humid, squashy as an overripe plum. Life's natural tempo is easy, the people's natural mood easygoing. In Arab days men in long white *kanzus* strolled the dusty streets between sprawling palm-thatched houses, women swathed in black were so closely veiled as to reveal only the dark eyes. Dhows came and went in the harbour with spicy cargoes, ivory and slaves and mangrove poles; imams drew people to white mosques, and the slaves came down their ancient route of purgatory, yoked and defenceless, to be sold in markets whose very sites have been forgotten.

The Germans left their mark in houses well adapted to the climate: double-storeyed, so that life could take place well above the street and any breeze that blew would lap through the spacious doorless rooms, linked by archways in the Arab fashion. Verandas ran all the way round, and big fans revolved in the centre of each ceiling.

A few of these attractive houses survive, but most have gone and all are doomed, to make way for tall piles of cement-block boxes exactly like buildings everywhere else. Air conditioning makes them tolerable to work in, but they are much stuffier, pokier, and less well adapted to the climate than the old houses. They *look* modern, that is all, especially when fitted out externally with sawed-off drainpipes to shadow-pattern their surfaces. But they will be overcome by shoddiness before many years have passed.

The oddest thing about Dar es Salaam is that to this sleepy languor, this sticky heat, this focus of goodwill and easy race relationships, should have gravitated so many firebrands and nationalists from those remaining parts of Africa not yet independent, to establish centres of what one side calls subversion and military plotting likely to endanger the peace of the world, the other side freedom fighters and resistance heroes: centres to co-ordinate forces being marshalled to set free the rest of Africa.

Whichever way you view them, here they are: nationalists on the run from South Africa, Rhodesia, Angola and Mozambique, plotting and conferring and drawing up manifestos and bargaining for arms, dispatching secret parties of recruits to learn the arts of sabotage and guerilla fighting in Ghana, Algeria, East Germany and other Iron Curtain countries, and possibly in China as well. Tanganyika, its rulers have declared, intends to raise and train an army of half a million Africans to march south and free their brothers.

Dar es Salaam will certainly be one of the launching centres for the military action the independent African countries mean to mount against Portugal and South Africa. It has always been a centre of the pan-African movement, whose main

headquarters have, since the conference there of May, 1963, been moved to Addis Ababa. So appearances are deceptive: in the torpid blood of this tropical paradise angry viruses proliferate.

One of the Ministers I saw in his air-conditioned office, behind a wide desk, said with an air half defensive, half aggressive: "We are seriously considering the purchase of nuclear weapons." Remembering Tanganyika's slender and precarious budget, its financial dependence on Western nations, its staggering dearth of every form of expertise and trained personnel, its thousand pressing and multiplying social needs, I thought at the time that he was trying to fool me. But now I believe that he meant what he said. Young men will always spring from the dinner table when the trumpet sounds; Tanganyika is governed by young men and the trumpet has sounded, the pan-African trumpet, which is to herald an assault upon the last redoubts of white rule.

Students

When that day comes, and unless the trumpet brings the walls down without a struggle, the young men from the University College of Dar es Salaam will no doubt be, if not in the forefront of the battle, at least in its operations room.

There are not many students yet—a total, at the moment, of 77; the full complement will be 550. The first degrees are to be awarded in 1964. Only one Faculty is in full working order, that of Law. Here lawyers for the whole of East Africa are to be trained. There is need of them. Tanganyika entered independence without a single native judge, and with exactly one African magistrate. Dar es Salaam is the youngest of the three colleges which joined together in June, 1963, to form the University of East Africa, with Dr. Julius Nyerere as the first Chancellor.

In a world where every other university is besieged by would-be students and turns away thousands of deserving applicants, the University of East Africa has hundreds of empty places, and its enrolment dwindles rather than grows. The ratio of teachers to students must be the highest on earth. The Faculty of Veterinary Science, for instance, attached to Nairobi's Royal College, at present has a teaching staff of eleven to instruct four future veterinarians. In the Faculty of Science one course in mathematics has enrolled two students, and a course in geology just one. To instruct fewer than five hundred students, the Royal College employs more lecturers and professors than Cape Town University, which has between five and six thousand undergraduates.

There are two principal reasons for this extraordinary state of affairs. The secondary schools are failing to turn out a sufficient number of potential undergraduates; and a majority of those they do turn out, instead of taking up places so expensively provided for them in their own countries, are going overseas. In round figures there were, last year, just under fourteen hundred university students in East Africa and about eighteen hundred officially known to be in North America and the United Kingdom. If you were to count up all the East Africans studying in all foreign centres of higher learning, including those in India, Russia, China and Eastern Europe, and students who have gone privately without official cognizance, you would find at least twice as many overseas as on their home ground.

This is not because of any local inferiority. On the contrary: Makerere, the Royal College and Dar es Salaam have attracted first-rate teaching talent. Dons of promise and renown face lecture halls three quarters empty. The reason is rather that most of the world's major nations, anxious to scramble aboard the African bandwagon, are tempting students with bursaries, scholarships and grants to their own already overcrowded universities, sometimes regardless of the students' capacity to benefit from their studies.

In one of the few surviving black-and-white German buildings, the headquarters of the Ministry of Education, I found one of the few surviving expatriates wrestling with a kind of shopping list of students submitted by various nations. He had just sent sixty off to Russia, in two batches—emphasis on engineering, agriculture and medicine—but had been asked for five hundred, all expenses paid. Most of them, he thought, would stay there six or seven years.

He showed me a list of the numbers already sent this year under official auspices: to the United Kingdom, about three hundred; just over two hundred to the United States; then the Russian contingent; forty to West Germany, twenty to India, fifteen to Pakistan and smaller numbers to Italy (mainly priests), Ethiopia, Switzerland, Yugoslavia, Bulgaria, Liberia, Australia, Canada, Ghana, Ireland and Israel. At least as many more had gone, he believed, through unofficial channels.

This lively and ever-mounting thirst for Tanganyikan students is sucking up not only some excellent material but some that is, in my informant's words, pretty ropy. "There just aren't enough to go round." I heard this echoed in Kampala and Nairobi. "The bottom of the barrel . . ."

Teachers

Are the secondary schools to blame? It's a question of logistics and teachers. The shortage of graduate teachers is chronic, acute and frustrating. In the whole of Tanganyika, with its population of about ten million, there are exactly eleven African graduate teachers—or were, at the time of my visit; there may well be less by now. Any African graduate can take his pick of jobs and very likely become a Minister, if he chooses, with a £3,500 ($9,800) basic salary, a house, a car and innumerable perquisites; or director general of a public corporation, or an ambassador; it's a wonder there's a single African graduate left in teaching, and soon, probably, there won't be. The great majority of graduate teachers are expatriates, and their numbers dwindle as they take their "lumpers"—compensation—and go.

"The whole secondary school system of the country," I was told, "would have broken down if it hadn't been for the T.E.A. scheme." This—Teachers for East Africa—is run jointly by Columbia University in New York, with money from the U. S. Government's A.I.D. programme, and by Britain's Department of Technical Co-operation. Its aim is to plug the gap between the departure of expatriate teachers in the secondary schools and the arrival—which seems likely to be long delayed—of enough trained Africans to replace them.

It is a bold, imaginative and generous scheme, and it now supplies about half the total graduate teaching staff in East Africa. But it has its drawbacks, like every other emergency measure. The main one is that the teachers stay for only two years, too short a time to gain an understanding of East African conditions and then to act upon such understanding; just as the teachers begin to find out what it's all about, they go. And no pupil can ever be carried through his four-year secondary course from start to finish by one set of teachers. Over half the volunteers, being American, are trained in teaching methods wholly different from those, modelled on the British, in common use in East Africa. The Anglo-American mixture sometimes turns out to be lumpy rather than smooth, and gives the pupils indigestion.

Pupils

While the top rungs of Tanganyika's educational ladder are shaky, the bottom rungs are too narrow. If there is one activity where the constant cry of "higher production" is being answered, and answered with gusto, it is in the production of babies. They pour from the fecund wombs of African mothers in an ever-mounting stream. Any educational system in the world would be hard pressed to keep its head above these rising waters.

Everywhere small bush schools, often built under self-help schemes sponsored by local branches of TANU, are springing up to meet a demand that grows more and more insistent. Most are basic not only in their equipment but in a staff relying heavily on untrained teachers with a minimum of schooling themselves. By these expedients the primary system may be just keeping up with the fast-rising child population, but the ideal of primary education for every Tanganyikan child still recedes as the mountain peak does before the climber. And four out of every five children who enter primary schools drop out before they reach their fifth year.

The full primary course lasts for eight years. Then comes the eye of the needle: entry into a secondary school. And at present only two out of every hundred children who complete the primary course—in itself a very small proportion of the whole school-age population—continue into a secondary school.

This tale is like that of the ten little pigmented boys, or the ten green bottles hanging on a wall. The number of young Tanganyikans who surmount all these educational hazards to reach the university level is minuscule. Of all the school-age children in the country—I don't know how many, but there must be well over two million—less than three thousand sat this year for the Cambridge Overseas School Certificate, which is roughly the equivalent of the British O-level. And of these only six out of ten, that is about eighteen hundred in all, were African. The rest were Asian, with a sprinkling of Europeans.

This is only O-level—a key which, while it unlocks an enormous range of African doors, is not supposed to let people into universities. For this a Higher Certificate, the equivalent of A-level, is needed.

Very few secondary schools as yet even have the fifth and sixth forms, in which pupils are prepared for this test. In 1962 the output of all Tanganyika's sixth forms was less than two hundred pupils—African, Asian and European combined. Of these only 102 qualified for university places at the British standard, which is maintained in East Africa through an association between London University and the local examining boards.

This tiny handful was 1962's total harvest, from the wide fields of Tanganyika's youth, of grain considered fit and ripe for the mills of higher education. Numbers will, of course, increase year by year, but only slowly; in 1965 there are not expected to be more than seven hundred and fifty Higher Certificate passes, of whom probably only about half will measure up to university standard. Considering that the entire government, civil service, industry, commerce and professional services are to be wholly and speedily turned over to African direction, the situation would be ludicrous were it not tragic.

What can be done? The first thing is to recruit more graduate teachers, who can come only from overseas. "We must have help," said the Minister, "from the Outside." This Minister, Mr. Solomon Eliufoo, a Makerere graduate with a mild, patient air of sapience, soft-voiced and friendly, was himself a teacher, and is reckoned to be among the ablest of the Cabinet Ministers. But even with financial help it won't be possible to secure all the needed teachers; cloth that has not been woven cannot be cut into a coat of any kind.

Britain and the United States have helped a lot already, and now other nations are moving in; for instance, the Scandinavians, who are building near Dar es Salaam a Nordic Centre

77

to combine primary and secondary schools with a health centre and an experimental farm, and perhaps something on the
Danish Folk High School lines. And Israel is offering short
crash courses to students willing to become teachers even
though they lack the full qualifications. As for the university,
unless it lowers its standards of admission, many of its places
must remain unfilled.

Lion Men

White sand too hot for bare feet; all-devouring sunshine; a
tepid, cradling sea creaming against a distant reef; a thatched
beach shelter, lilos, books, the waves' whisper, peace and silence. . . . The citizens of Dar es Salaam are luckier than they
know to enjoy for nothing what others spend fortunes to
reach. All day the beach was empty save for a small group of
Asian children gravely paddling and two gogglers with frog-
man feet and snorkel masks setting forth towards the reef.

Why, amid such languid innocence, conversation should
have strayed into the dark and tortuous thickets of witchcraft
I do not know: perhaps because lawyers were present and the
trial for murder of three young witches was, at the time, filling
the local newspapers. This trio was, it seemed, composed of
apprentices learning their trade. They had gathered with
others in a hut outside the capital to hack off the head of a
young woman (she was newly married) and cut out bits of her
body to eat and preserve for use in medicines needed for the
practice of sorcery.

Such cases are not uncommon, but this drew attention because of its brutality, its proximity to the capital and because
one of those periodic waves of witchcraft which sometimes
run through a district or a country appeared to be in spate.
Hundreds of miles to the west of Dar es Salaam, near Lake

Victoria, over seventy witchcraft murders had taken place in the past few months, obliging the Government to impose a ban on poisoned arrows, the main weapon being used, and to raid the people's huts to confiscate their armouries.

One of my companions had been stationed for some years at Singida, a small government post on the bush-clad steppe of central Tanganyika, which would never have been heard of but for its extraordinary cult of lion men. No one has ever sorted out fact from fiction, reality from illusion, in regard to the happenings at Singida, though many have tried, and men have been hanged for their part in them.

How old the cult is no one knows; certainly it was there long before the coming of the European. In 1920 over two hundred lion-men killings in the district, among the Turu tribe, were attributed to a clique of wizards who had hired out assassins and established a reign of terror. One man avowed that he had been kidnapped as a child, clad in skins, kept in a pit and trained to kill with lions' claws. Fifteen men were tried and executed after this outbreak.

All was peace and quiet around Singida until murders started again in 1946. Every victim was clawed as if by lions. The confusing part was that some of the victims had un-doubtedly been killed by man-eaters. Genuine lions are plentiful in the district, or were then, and now and again, in any lion district, one of them—generally an aging female with worn teeth, no longer spry enough to catch an antelope or zebra—will take to man-eating. Probably lion men do not operate unless there are genuine man-eaters about.

During the outbreak of lion-man killings between 1946 and 1948, over a hundred violent deaths were investigated. Some were found to be the work of genuine lions, but most were attributed to men equipped with lions' claws and pads. In the High Court, in 1947, fifty-seven lion men were accused

79

of murder and twenty-seven convicted. Some got off on appeal, but six were executed. The outbreak then subsided; and a chief, asked why this was so, replied: "Too many eyes are watching now." During these two years about fifty people were killed by genuine lions.

It is a widely held belief among the people of Singida that lion men capture small children and bring them up in caves where they never see the light, are wrapped in lion skins and grow to believe that they *are* lions, in fact to *be* lions in everything save anatomy. Then they are sent out to kill, with gauntlets like lions' pads on hands and feet so that they leave claw marks on their victims, and imprints on the ground, indistinguishable from those of the genuine article.

"I saw a lion myself," said the eyewitness from Singida, "with all its feet cut off, presumably by lion men—but that, again, is a presumption. No lion man has ever been seen or captured by a European." But many Africans claim to have seen them.

Do people really see lion men, or imagine that they do? Can they be hypnotized into these beliefs? My informant gave this example.

Immediately after the discovery of a fresh murder, the people of the village to which the victim belonged reported that a lion man had taken refuge in a certain hut. The forces of the law surrounded this hut and closed in with the utmost caution. A cat slipped through the door and made off. When the police broke in, they found no lion man; everyone in the village believed that he had escaped in the guise of the cat.

Another theory is that by the use of some power Europeans do not understand—indeed, they haven't really tried to do so —the men of this cult can call up genuine lions to do their bidding. It sounds farfetched, but there are men, we know, who can communicate with animals by imitating their "language"; Sir Arthur Grimble witnessed the summoning of porpoises in the South Seas; and did not Conrad Lorenz bring down a cockatoo from the sky by calling to it from the platform of Altenberg Station?

Even my friend from Singida, a rationalist with legal training, was not prepared to dismiss the calling up of animals as hocus-pocus. He remembered an experience of his own.

"We were trying to get an irrigation scheme going. Most of the people were willing, if not keen, but there was one man who obstructed everything. His shamba was right in the middle of the scheme, and so he managed to block almost everything we wanted to do. He was very unpopular. Discussing it on one occasion, the local chief said: 'One day he'll be sorry' (or words to that effect). 'The elephants will fix him.'

"And one day they did. The odd thing was that this herd walked straight through all the other shambas and completely ignored them, didn't touch a single banana tree; they made for this man's shamba and bashed it to bits and then walked out again. No one was in the least surprised. One of the man's enemies, they believed—and they knew which—had called up the elephants. Coincidence, perhaps; but it makes you wonder. . . . No one's ever really investigated these things."

The Waxing of Witches

That witches are on the wane is a comfortable belief held by most expatriates, as well as by educated Africans; one cannot suppose, in 1964, Cabinet Ministers to dance naked upside down at midnight and ride through the darkness on the back of a hyena, as witches are commonly supposed to do. Yet there is no evidence to show that witchcraft *is* dying out, and some to point to the reverse. An anthropologist working among a tribe called the Mbugwe, who live near Lake Man-yara, about sixty miles west of Arusha, reached the startling conclusion that as recently as 1956 at least half the population—a conservative estimate—were witches.[1]

To know that every other person you meet every day, the members of your own family, perhaps your own wife or husband, your son or daughter, practices these sinister arts, and may at this very moment be weaving some spell to injure you, must destroy all peace of mind in home and village. The only people you can trust are those of your mother's lineage; everyone else, including your father's blood relations—even your own son—is suspect.

Even in the hottest weather, Mr. Gray records, meals are taken indoors, and no guest is ever invited, lest the food should be bewitched.

> When a group of men are away from home and cannot retire into their houses for meals, the precautions are not in the least relaxed. Unless the men should all be lineage-mates, they disperse at mealtimes, and each man eats in seclusion behind a tree. If it is a large group and cover is sparse, each man goes off a little distance and covers himself completely with his cloth while he eats. . . .

Meals must lack the conviviality found in less witch-haunted societies.

If all precautions fail and your food does get bewitched, your illness will depend less upon the medicine administered than upon the kind of food that has been tampered with. Sweet potatoes, when bewitched, cause the stomach to swell; meat so treated affects throat or rectum; water drives you off your head, and the worst of all is butter, which causes leprosy. The only hope then is to consult a diviner, find out who has put on the spell and get him to lift it.

1 "Structural Aspects of Mbugwe Witchcraft," paper by Robert Gray, in *Witchcraft and Sorcery in East Africa*, ed. Middleton and Winter. Routledge and Kegan Paul, 1963.

Every Mbugwe witch owns one or more hyenas which are
branded invisibly with his mark, visit his house at night, keep
their cubs there and are milked by their owners, who call
them "night cattle" and ride about on them all over the
countryside. "The riding of hyenas," Mr. Gray observes, "is
regarded as a difficult art, requiring a long course of training
for the novice witch." At regular intervals rallies are held in

the bush, where all these mounted witches gather to boast of their achievements, swop professional secrets and indulge in obscene orgies proper to witches all the world over—rather like pony clubs, apart from the obscenity.

That such beliefs should thrive in Africa today, unshaken alike by the scientific outlook of the age and by TANU's rallies, one man, one vote, self-help schemes and the whole educational system, is hard to credit. Mr. Gray evidently felt the same doubts, and records in his paper that he "made extensive inquiries in a critical and sceptical manner."

> I expected to find that the more worldly elders, and the boys who had been through school, while perhaps believing in the fundamental reality of witchcraft, would at least be incredulous about the milking and riding of hyenas. My findings did not confirm this assumption. On the contrary. Some of the youths who had attended the local mission school at first denied, as they had been taught to do, that witches existed, or at least that they had power to harm people. But when the discussion turned to hyenas, they all gave eye-witness evidence of hyena riding. They had often seen the eerie light of a witch's torch as it flickered in the distance; one reported that he had been almost knocked over as a mounted hyena rushed past him in the darkness; and it was a common experience to have smelled the acrid odour of burning hyena butter where a witch had recently passed. When these fragmentary experiences are put together, the evidence of the senses seems to reveal an authentic picture of a witch riding naked at full gallop through the night, mounted on a hyena and carrying a flaming torch which he refuels from time to time from a gourd of hyena butter slung over his shoulder.

No wonder hyenas are feared and shunned by the Mbugwe and wherever possible destroyed, although to do so is dangerous and you must cut off and bury the ears, tail and one of the front legs, which carry the owner's invisible brand.

Although witchcraft practices and beliefs vary from tribe

to tribe and region to region, almost everywhere two obscene acts seem to be required of novices before they can qualify as full practitioners. They must commit incest, and they must eat human flesh. These are, presumably, the deadliest sins that any human being can commit, the most outrageous offences against common decency, and to perform these acts has the same effect as did the worst Mau Mau oaths: it puts the perpetrators beyond the pale and fills them with the desperation of the damned. And so long as witchcraft continues, victims must be sacrificed to supply the organs for initiates to eat—as one had been sacrificed, only a few months before, near Dar es Salaam.

A TALK WITH THE PRESIDENT

The Nyerere Enigma

"It's sad to see the old place these days," an ex-colonialist lamented. "All those guard dogs and barbed wire . . . Nothing like that in my time." He was talking about State House, formerly Government House, a handsome, white, colonnaded mansion, full of light and air and archways, standing in shady gardens by the sea.

In the ex-colonialist's time there wasn't even a fence around it, and about all the sentry did was to click to attention when the last Governor-General, Sir Richard Turnbull, sped by on his bicycle at sunrise to pedal vigorously along the seafront and into the back quarters of the town, waving jovially at the children as he went by. Now the garden's full of Alsatians and helmeted policemen with automatic weapons, and floodlights illuminate the place all night.

Would-be assassins have had several goes at President Nkrumah and succeeded in the case of Togo's Olympio, and Dr. Julius Nyerere is a great deal less expendable than the very best colonial Governor. His image overshadows everything. Is he, or isn't he, the stuff of which dictators are made? If so, is he benevolent, or just biding his time?

Can dictators stay benevolent? Is he TANU's master, or does TANU—which he created and leads—master him? Why is he resolved to introduce by legislation the single-party state and no parliamentary opposition when that's the *de facto* position anyway? Can he avoid the occupational disease of all absolute rulers: power corruption, paranoia, self-deification? Does he really mean to lead a *jihad* against South Africa? Such questions cluster round the head of President Nyerere like bees around a hive.

Slight, dapper, energetic, fluent, approachable, very much on the ball, he could charm coneys out of rocks. As head of state he's polite, considerate, decisive, quick, persuasive and well informed; off duty, blithe, ebullient and the best of company. Aged about forty-three, he looks younger, eats sparingly, rarely touches alcohol, never smokes. He nearly always wears an open-necked green shirt—green is TANU's colour—and sandals, spurns formality, has a boyish, debonair sort of gaiety and can enjoy the sweets of life.

A graduate of Makerere and Edinburgh, he started as a teacher; he's a practicing Roman Catholic, married, with a nursery score of seven so far, mostly at the tot stage. He must work like a demon, for everything goes through his hands and many things originate in State House. He doesn't just sit there making decisions. He generates policies, initiates action, sparks off ideas. His has been the vision and the driving force behind the move to federate East Africa. Today's Tanganyika *is* Nyerere, in so far as any country so vast and sprawling and loosely connected, at once lethargic and excitable, can have a single motivator. And just lately, in his spare time, he's translated *Julius Caesar* into Swahili.

Three major themes, at the moment, occupy his mind. The search for (as he put it) "a superior system of government, easy to practice, that guarantees democracy and is understood by all our people"—not on the Westminster model, by any means; to develop, reform and revolutionize his country's social system and its economy; to unify East Africa and, that accomplished, create as a major world force a great United States of Africa. Even for so able, dynamic and revered a leader all this adds up to no mean task.

The single-party state is his first aim. In the circumstances of the time and place, he immutably believes (as African nationalists do everywhere) a parliamentary opposition, offering an alternative set of rulers, to be a luxury no African country can afford. Nor does he believe it to be an essential element in democracy. Knowing its dangers, Western liberals are disturbed by this creed; but nothing they can do or say will, I am sure, make the least dent in the nationalists' armour of certainty.

An Interview

After President Nyerere had been kind enough to talk to me, I sent him my notes, and they came back revised and approved: in parts they were unchanged, in parts toned down or formalized. Here is the gist of his replies to some of the questions.

Q. Do you intend to prohibit any party other than TANU from being formed?

A. Yes.

Q. If you suppress opposition, won't it then take unconstitutional forms?

A. Every citizen can be a member of TANU, that is his constitutional right. In the Party he is quite free to express his ideas. That is the place for him to speak his mind. Of course, if he chooses to go underground, no one can stop him. But why should he? He can use TANU, for TANU is his.

Q. How can you maintain discipline? For instance, what happens if a majority of TANU votes against the Government in the Assembly?

A. I find the question of discipline very hard to answer, the hardest of all. Every government needs a majority to govern with. Perhaps we shall have to change the present system, where every time a vote is taken in the Assembly it is regarded as a vote of confidence. We might say: "On this important issue the vote will be a vote of confidence, but on those smaller issues it will not." Our problems and our situations are not the same as those of the British, and our difficulties arise when we follow the system of the British, which ties the government to the legislature. In America this doesn't happen in the same way. President and Congress sometimes go in different directions. Perhaps we can reach a blend of the two systems; I don't know. We are feeling our way. The answers will appear in actual practice. We are making our system as we go along, out of our experience. What we are trying to avoid is dogma.

Q. TANU has achieved its object: it's the ruling power. If it is to have no rivals, isn't there a danger of apathy? Won't people lose interest in it?

A. Yes—psychologically, this danger is real. An "enemy" is always useful in keeping a party united and avoiding apathy. Nations sometimes create fictitious enemies, and find them very useful in maintaining national unity and purpose. But this is dangerous. Instead we must find an *internal* reason for our unity and dynamism. Fortunately, a young nation like ours should do this without difficulty. We're all engaged in an exciting task—building a new nation. Our enemies are there all right—poverty, ignorance and disease.

Q. What would happen if TANU disagreed with the policy of the Government?

A. Then TANU would prevail. The final voice of the people

is TANU, acting through the National Executive. I, as President, am also Chairman of the National Executive, but the Executive is the stronger of the two. I appoint the Cabinet; if I don't agree with what the Cabinet wants to do, then I can say: "You go." They'd go, I'd stay. But I don't appoint the National Executive of TANU. They are elected by the people. If they disagree with my policy, then I go, they stay. That's why TANU must always be a people's movement. The will of the people must be expressed through TANU. And if the Government tries to depart from TANU's will, then TANU must act. That is not dictatorship.

Q. How has Tanganyika managed to avoid the tribal tensions that are so strong elsewhere?

A. I think it was because nobody believed that we were going to succeed. So we got in first. People laughed at us to start with, no one took us seriously. In 1954 a visiting mission from the United Nations said we might perhaps be ready for independence in twenty-five years' time. Twenty-five years! [1] We were the first in East Africa to launch a movement for independence, and it all seemed so remote that it didn't arouse jealousy. The people who could have got into power through tribalism, or used tribalism to wreck our tender national unity—they didn't see their opportunity. So those of us who understood that we could achieve independence *only* through national unity, we got our way. The tribalists, the backward-looking people, lost their chance. By 1958 we had got such a hold on the country that no one could oppose us and hope to succeed. And by that time we had overcome tribalism, we had made it discredited, and religious bigotry, too. These things we would never allow in TANU—tribalism, religious bigotry and racialism. Even in 1957, when the Afri-

---

[1] Dr. Nyerere, giving evidence before the Trusteeship Council in 1957, suggested independence in ten to twelve years. It came in four.

can National Congress tried to tempt people away from us with the bait of racialism, they failed. We were against race, tribes, class, sects, all distinctions, from the word "go"; and our policy succeeded. If we'd failed, then these racial and tribal divisions in our country would have been exploited. But by the time they tried it, the divisionists had lost the fight. It was because we saw from the very start that unity was our only road to independence, and because to put down tribalism was a key part of our policy—it was because of this that we succeeded.

Q. What about Kenya, where they missed that bus?

A. There is Jomo.

Q. Isn't Jomo a tribalist?

A. Jomo is *not* a tribalist. When I finished my studies at Makerere in 1945, I was invited to join the staff of St. Mary's School, Tabora. My purpose in deciding to take up teaching was to help my people, and by "my people" I meant my own tribe, my small tribe of forty thousand Zanaki. I had previously entered for a competition in authorship run by the East African Literature Bureau, and the subject I chose was "my people," and I wrote a history of my tribe. So, if you like, I was a tribalist then. Jomo's book, *Facing Mount Kenya,* is a study of his tribe—the work of a sociologist. But Jomo was already talking about *African* independence even when he was in London. Kenya's not another Tanganyika, but they will succeed in becoming united.

Q. Within an East African Federation—which in turn will be a step towards something bigger?

A. A step towards the final goal—the United States of Africa. From the Atlantic to the Pacific is no farther than from the Atlantic to the Indian Ocean. It will come.

Q. In your lifetime?

A. Does that matter? I hope so, but I don't know how long

I shall live! If it comes later, that's all right—there must be time for these great ideas to take root and spread. But it will come, we shall achieve it.

Q. Does the economic future worry you?

A. Our first problem is to create the machinery to carry out the main task we're committed to—raising the living standards of our people. For this we shall need quite a different structure of administration from that which we inherited from the British. The British administration was fundamentally designed to maintain law and order. It was simple, and it served its purpose. But now our primary purpose is to tackle these enormous problems of poverty, ignorance and disease. Without the machinery to plan and execute development projects, we can't make use of overseas aid. Without this machinery, we can't direct the vigorous self-help spirit of our people into productive channels. And without sufficient trained and skilled experts, we can't *create* this machinery. We shall proceed step by step, as briskly as we dare, but it's going to take a long time, years in fact, to train enough men and women and create the complex machinery that will carry forward our development. We've made a start. Our people know this—that's why they're not talking, and we're not talking; we and the people are one and the same. We know that Tanganyika has the latent resources, and that it's up to us to develop them. We have our first development plan, and now we are at work on a big one that will carry us forward for the next ten years.

Q. You have spoken about the growing gap between rich and poor. This is one of your worries?

A. Yes, it's very difficult. The gap is so big. The peasant in his shamba with his hoe, his little hut, his children perhaps without a school: the Minister with his big house and good food and car. But even so, the Minister hasn't got enough. We tried to keep down the pay of the Ministers, but it didn't work. The Minister is like the chief—he feeds everyone, all the people come to him and he can't turn them away. His house is like a hotel. Every Minister is running a big hotel, that's his trouble; he's helping everyone; people write every day, or they come to his house. He gets a big salary, but it's never enough. And still less has the man on the shamba got enough. We've got to create more wealth for all to share. That's our economic problem. We're trying to solve it through our development plan. We shall succeed because the will of the people is behind it. But we shall need time.

A Liberal Dilemma

One, at least, of President Nyerere's convictions sticks uncomfortably in liberal throats. This is his sincere belief that in establishing the single-party state he is entrenching, not destroying, democracy. "It all depends on what you mean by democracy. . . ." In his view, the democratic principle can take many shapes. There isn't just the "Westminster model."

Here Western liberals face an awkward dilemma. It's quite true, they agree, that there isn't just the one model. But certain principles must underlie all democracy's expressions, and one of these is that the people must be able, constitutionally and smoothly, to dismiss one set of rulers and install another. No one has been able to design a better way of doing this than by means of periodic elections based on votes; and through an opposition party whose leaders spend their time arguing in parliament, and not languishing in jail.

The single-party state doesn't tolerate an opposition; a change of rulers, if it comes about at all, must be effected elsewhere than in parliament, and by other means than through elections and votes. (In Tanganyika's case, according to its President, in the conclaves of TANU, culminating in the National Executive.) In the view of most Western democrats, this is a dubious expedient. In these matters of principle there can't be one law for Western nations and another for Africa: that would be to admit a fundamental difference cutting across the belief in fundamental equality—a form of philosophical apartheid.

That so brilliant and respected an African leader as Julius Nyerere should propagate such heresies is deeply disturbing: as if the Pope were suddenly to question the divinity of Christ. The more realistic observers understand the reasons for his insistence on a single party—the dangerous fissures in society which make the need for unity overriding—and sympathize. They know that if the African leaders fail to weld their countries together those countries will fall apart and all the work will be undone. Practically, the African leaders are beyond doubt right; in countries torn by tribalism, the single-party state is a necessity. So pragmatists are not unduly worried; but for the true believer the dilemma remains.

The Mystique of TANU

In the President's philosophy, everything can be put right by TANU. In this nationwide party he holds an almost mystical belief. For him, TANU *is* the people; their voice is TANU's; to him it speaks in special tones of intimacy. Again and again this feeling for TANU comes through, a dedicated feeling akin to that of a priest towards his church. Partly, perhaps, this is an expression of the love of the creator for the thing he creates; born of his spirit, now in turn it is inspiring him.

The President's connection with TANU is his taproot, thrusting down into the soul of Tanganyika and drawing from it the sustenance of understanding and support. Anything that threatens TANU must therefore be a dangerous enemy, not merely to Nyerere personally, but to the life of the whole country, the Tanganyika tree. Once this is understood, it is easy to see how the President has come to believe that the single-party state is not only a practical necessity, but that fundamentally it is more democratic than a two-party system could ever be. It expresses the will of the people, which is the whole purpose of democracy.

The two- or multiparty system (in his view) destroys the will of the people by dividing and weakening it; ultimately it may destroy the country altogether, and let in the virus of neo-colonialism. In the African context it is Nyerere and his TANU who are the democrats, supporters of an opposition who are anti-democratic and who would, if they had their way, finish off true African democracy. All this, of course, stands on its head the idea of democracy as it is practiced in the West—where it was, after all, invented as a political system, if not necessarily as an underlying idea.

We are, I think, apt to forget that Africans never *asked* for Western democracy; it was imposed on them from outside, by the will of the Parliament in Westminster. The British came first as missionaries, to convert East Africans to Christianity; next as consuls, to impose British law; and finally as missionaries again, to preach a democratic form of government. The whole colonial civil service, with its (by and large) upright, energetic and dedicated men, could be regarded as a corps of missionaries sent by a secular church to spread the gospel of democracy and introduce its dogmas: elections, parties, local government, taxation, estimates and budgets, welfare services and trade unions, Cabinets, committees and votes.

Now the missionaries have gone home and must expect changes in dogma to result from changes in their church. It is sometimes hard to realize that when people rule themselves they will alter the rules. They will rule themselves as they wish, perhaps badly, and not as Westerners think they should.

If this can be hard for Westerners to digest, Africans do not always face the dangers implicit in the single-party state. It is not, after all, exactly an innovation. No doubt recent experiences with single parties and their leaders have soured Western opinion and tarnished its belief in the ability of single parties to remain moderate, just and humane, and of their leaders to resist the temptations inherent in the unrestrained exercise of power. Acton's famous warning echoes in the ears of Westerners. And Voltaire: "I disapprove of what you say, but I will defend to the death your right to say it." This, to most Africans, seems a very stupid idea.

The single-party state, they say, carries on the African tradition of government. Just what that tradition is it's hard to say. Indigenous forms of government were so many and so various that I doubt whether anyone could extract a satisfactory common denominator. Absolute military dictatorship such as Chaka's; tightly organized confederacies based on military conquest as in Ashanti; petty tyrannies such as those of Buganda and Bunyoro; shepherd kings as in Ankole, priest kings as among the Nuer and other people of the Sudan; a loose control by witch doctors as among Masai and Nandi; fragmented rule by councils of elders drawn from ridge or village, as among the Kikuyu or Ibo; government by a central tribal council like the *gkotla* of Bechuanaland; the straightforward rule of chiefs, for the most part hereditary, such as many of Tanganyika's tribes acknowledge and which is, I suppose, the commonest form; it is impossible to speak, in view of this variety, of "an African tradition of government."

If there is a feature common to nearly all African systems— and this is disputable—it is that while the individual may be free to speak his mind in an appropriate council to which, as a rule, he is admitted on a basis of seniority, once the majority decision has been taken he must loyally accept it and cease to criticize or cavil. In the general African view, criticism is not a helpful and constructive effort to remedy wrongs; rather it is a selfish, subversive and dangerous attempt to undermine authority. The critic pulls down walls, he does not build them; he threatens stability; he coats his arrowheads with the poison of doubt. He goes against the grain of an orderly society. He is a menace—the shadow of a lion man, of a witch.

Meanwhile, despite a few high-handed incidents, Tanganyika has a long way to go before it becomes a police state. There may have been some pointers. Non-Africans deported summarily without reasons given; trade union leaders accused of fomenting trouble rusticated; threats against the freedom of the press; powers taken to hold without trial anyone suspected of plotting against the Government; a hotel shut down by a Commissioner because its guests failed to stand up when M. Sekou Touré of Guinea, whom they didn't even know by sight, walked in; tales of the beating up by Youth Wing thugs of citizens who failed to obey the branch secretary of TANU with alacrity; the pattern is far from unfamiliar. It also appears to be far from general. There is plenty of lively speaking out in the Assembly and even more at TANU rallies, and Ministers are kept on their toes.

The ultimate leadership isn't questioned. If Julius Nyerere has a mystical feeling for TANU, his people reciprocate with a mystical feeling for him. Over this huge and sprawling and still, in any Western sense, poor and backward country, scarcely as yet uniting over one hundred and twenty separate tribes, there spreads the shadow of his wings—not the sinister outline of a predator but that, perhaps, of the raven, who brought bread and meat to Elijah, and is the wisest of birds.

DAR ES SALAAM

Expatriates Come, Expatriates Go

The first fruit of independence seems to be the arrival of a great many foreign missions, anxious to make friends and influence the newest member state of the United Nations to roll off the assembly line. The first action of each mission is to acquire an embassy and living space for all its members, from ambassadors to cypher clerks. As accommodation suitable for such purposes is limited, houses of any size became immensely valuable; property in Dar es Salaam is said to have doubled or trebled in value.

The Chinese Embassy is reported to be the largest and to have the longest, sleekest cars; its members go to parties wreathed in smiles but impeded by the language barrier, and so far their main activities seem to have concerned cultural exchanges—tribal dancers for jugglers—and expressions of goodwill about trade. It is still early days, however. So far twenty-eight new missions have set up shop in Dar es Salaam, and others are to come.

So, on the whole, more expatriates are coming than going, but those who are going are perhaps more useful than the newcomers. Most of them are senior civil servants who are staying on until they can be Africanized. "The jam in the sandwich," they have been called, spreading their expertise

between a political Minister above and a mass of juniors below whose abilities may be promising but whose experience
is nil.

To start with, expatriates were shot out like bullets from
guns; the Commissioner of Police, for instance, arriving one
morning at his office, found a note on his desk—"in long-
hand," I was told, "not even typed"; that seemed to make the
insult worse—instructing him to wind up everything by
twelve o'clock and not to come back after lunch. But all that
is over; in fact, the Government wants most of the remaining
expatriates to stay until they can be replaced by trained and
qualified men rather than by TANU branch secretaries of
tender years.

Nevertheless, they are going and, inevitably, leaving gaps.
Although the Tanganyikans who fill these make up in enthusiasm what they lack in technique, a certain clogging of
the wheels can't be avoided when about twenty years' experience is just missed out. One result is that Tanganyika, as
the President hinted, is finding itself unable to make full use
of the aid which so many "outside" nations are so anxious to
provide—basically because there is no one able to fill in the
forms.

This—the form filling—is not so easy as it sounds. The
Americans in particular, hurt and alarmed by the way some
of their foreign aid money has been squandered overseas,
have tightened up their system of distributing largesse to such
an extent that Washington must know in advance how every
cent of every dollar is to be employed. The necessary estimates, as a result, are so complicated that many men must toil
for many months to put them into the right shape, having
first found out just how much it is going to cost to provide
the community centre at Ujiji with an epidiascope, and sanitary buckets for a nursery school built for the families of

labourers employed at the rural institute at Mpapwa. A man in Nairobi told me that the application to the U. S. Agency for International Development for a single project connected with the city's water supply weighed twenty-four pounds—about the same as an eighteen-month-old child.

"Nairobi is the only city in East Africa with a staff to cope with this," he added. "Everywhere else aid is grinding to a halt for lack of people who know how to ask for it." Rather like Aladdin stranded outside his cave, unable to remember the word "sesame."

The Americans are themselves helping to alleviate matters by sending forth experts in different managerial skills. The Massachusetts Institute of Technology, for instance, supplies planners, and not only that, but young men who know how to plan the organization of planners. This has become a skilled technique, brought to a high pitch of refinement by the French.

The Ten-Year Plan

When I was in Dar es Salaam, a high-powered French economist had just arrived to direct the framing of a ten-year development plan and a new Ministry, under Mr. Nsilo Swai, been created to put it into effect. The impetus behind this ambitious, all-embracing project came, like almost everything else, from the President, who watched with a mixture of admiration and caginess (beware neo-colonialism) the way the French have both guided and expanded the economies of their former dependencies and revitalized their own economy.

"They've got something, the French," he remarked, shaking his head in the manner of a man at once fascinated, cautious and a little incredulous; whatever it is, Tanganyika needs it, and so a Frenchman trained in the school of M. Jean Monnet has been summoned. Now he broods invisibly and, at the moment—since he has no English, let alone Swahili, and few here can speak French—incommunicado, in the Treasury in Dar es Salaam.

Neo-colonial traps are sprung behind every bush, in TANU opinion; nonalignment is the way to avoid them. In practice, nonalignment boils down to the old adage that there's safety in numbers. To let loose an unchaperoned Frenchman to plan Tanganyika's development would be to walk straight into one of those traps. So the President has invited not one planner but six. Each is of a different nationality so that they will, neo-colonially speaking, cancel each other out; economically, everyone hopes that six sets of ideas will be better than one.

There have arrived in Dar es Salaam, to reinforce the French director M. Jacques Faudon, a German, an Englishman, an American, a Swede and a Yugoslav. The arrival of the Englishman, a banker, was heralded by a telegram asking whether Dar es Salaam had a good club he could join.

French logic is at work already, clothing itself in a series of circles, arrows, boxes and other diagrammatic devices, which emerge in a steady flow from the invisible M. Faudon and appear on the desks of somewhat puzzled civil servants and presidential aides. One on whom I called was studying a very complex diagram, clearly a work of art, with the same expression as that to be seen on the face of someone who, confronted with an action painting, is wondering which way up it should be, and about to say: "But I don't *understand* modern art. . . ." After inspecting the diagram with the same blend of awe, confusion and ignorance, I borrowed from one of the M.I.T. Fellows-for-Africa a paper in which the relationship between General Equilibrium (Horizontal) to Vertical Commissions on Global Optimization was set forth in terms that any simpleton could understand.

A Theory of Social Change

The young man from the M.I.T. presumably understood it, but he was deeply immersed in a theory of social change recently advanced by an American sociologist. This, he said, explained how a shift could take place from the uncreative to the creative personality, by breaking the vicious circle of traditional respect for the *status quo*.

In each personality, it seems, there is maintained a balance between the creative impulse, which welcomes opportunities for action offered by the world, and the uncreative impulse, based on anxieties arising from a fear of failure. Hitherto the African personality has been dominated by anxiety. Tribal Africans have felt the outside world to be beyond their capacity to cope with or to change. The way to break this vicious circle is to undermine respect for the traditional authority: the father, the elders and the chief. Here the theory delivers a backhanded good word for the colonialist who made a dent on this status respect by treating the big shots of African society, the chiefs and elders and magicians, as inferiors.

The reaction of the first generation to this behavior was simply stupefaction; that of the next, and present one, rage and anger; but the generation after that, partially liberated from status respect, should get over this and begin to change from uncreative to creative personalities. In this they will be aided by a fundamental change in the relationship of the sexes. The dominant and lordly male, seen by his spouse to be angry, bewildered and perhaps humiliated, no longer appears infallible; she turns for emotional satisfaction to her children, and begins to regard them not merely as creatures to be protected and not respected as individuals, but as individuals in their own right. And so the child finds the world to be responsive, and learns that he can influence the attitudes of others, his surroundings and events. The child's response changes from one of anxiety to one of pleasure, and so the creative personality is born.

"It will take five generations," said the Fellow-for-Africa. "Then we may see a really creative African personality. The pace will be uneven. Everything will depend on how quickly and generally the average mother's attitude towards her children changes, and on how thoroughly the mould of status respect can be smashed."

The M.I.T. young man told me he was supposed to be training a successor to fill his place as a link between the planners and those who carry out the plans. "But I'm not training anyone at present," he added, "because there's no one to train."

Villagization

It seems a far cry from this cerebral dynamo in the Treasury, converting the most sophisticated techniques evolved in Europe's most sophisticated nation into plans for Tanganyika's progress, to the round mud hut in the bush, the woman hoeing her patch of mealies with her baby on her back and her husband, most likely, drinking home-brewed beer under a tree when, if he were only toiling on his shamba and doing what the experts repeatedly advise, he could treble his cotton crop, and hence his income, without planting an extra rod, pole or perch of land.

Can the dynamo somehow be connected with, and galvanize, this easygoing peasant? "Our plants," I was told by one of the President's aides, "will come up from the villages; we don't mean to impose them from the top. In each village there's to be a committee to put up ideas for development; at a higher level there'll be district committees, then regional committees, and they'll send in their plans to the Ministry. Plans must come up from the grass roots; we must carry the people along. . . ."

One difficulty seems to be that, while there is in Dar es Salaam a brand-new Ministry, out in the country there are not yet the villages whose inhabitants will form the committees whose members will think of the plans.

Tanganyika is still a land of scattered homesteads in the bush. Sometimes these are called villages for lack of a better name, but the description is inaccurate because each group of huts normally belongs to a single family. An African family —an "extended family," as anthropologists say—is, of course, a great deal larger than a European one, embracing as it does not merely father, mother and their offspring plus a grandparent or two, but also their sisters and their cousins and their aunts, and a great many other relatives of varying degrees of consanguinity and age.

Such communities often look like small villages, but in reality are single units, cells in the tribal structure, rather than (as in Europe) communities of people bound by economic ties, providing for one another mutual services and skills (the butcher, the baker, the shoemaker and the smith) and forming miniature units of government. African homesteads are generally too small to support schools, clinics and the various amenities often gathered up under the umbrella phrase "community development." Even such amenities as water, sewerage and electric light cannot be laid on to so many scattered little globules of humanity.

So, in TANU's new philosophy, homesteads equal backwardness. They imprison people in an old and rigid mould of peasantry and tribalism, a mould in which the whole archaic social system is contained: the son who must seek permission from the elders to cultivate a piece of land, and hand it back if they so decide; the daughter who will know no other destiny than to hoe and reap and breed; the equation of authority with age; the council of elders, the fat and well-wived chief, the father's autocracy, the bride-price bargaining, the permanent subjection of youth to age.

This mould must be broken and replaced by a flexible pattern that will allow Tanganyika's people to take a great leap forward into the nuclear power, mass production, jet aircraft age. Though they be liberated from colonialism, ahead lies a struggle for the greatest liberation of all: from the past, from backwardness, from poverty and from an archaic tribal mould.

So "villagization" is the newest TANU aim. This is to be combined with self-help schemes among the peasantry to create, by the use of voluntary labour—which in colonialist days might well have been decried as "forced"—new schools and roads, bridges and dams and wells, rest houses for Commissioners, accommodations for teachers, community centres: the minimal equipment for communal living that Tanganyika so desperately needs.

"There is no other way," the President said when I asked him about the scheme. "When people are scattered in the bush, they will go on the same way without change. They must come together in villages. And they want this. There is no opposition. On the contrary, the demand is coming from the people, from the bottom, because they know it to be necessary. It is coming from TANU; the TANU people come to me and say: 'We need villages. We are starting ten experimental ones as part of our development plan.'"

A Ministry of Youth

The villagization programme, potentially the boldest and biggest of all Tanganyika's hopeful projects, is to be administered by a new Ministry of National Culture and Youth. This is presided over, appropriately enough, by a young man, Mr. L. N. Sijaona, who is not yet thirty, or barely so.

The mobilization of Tanganyika's youth—girls included—in the service of their country is the first aim: two years' national service for all. Although training is to start with drill and discipline, the idea is not to turn the conscripts into soldiers, but to draft them out into the countryside to carry out good works—make roads, dams, plantations, terraces; above all, help to build the new villages.

Ghana's Builders' Brigade forms an obvious model. The first batches of future group leaders, Mr. Sijaona told me, have gone to Israel and Yugoslavia to be trained. An adviser from Israel is at work in the embryonic Ministry. TANU's Youth Wing, which has at times got out of hand and beaten up people who, in their estimation, have not put their backs into various "self-help" schemes, is to be absorbed into the scheme—a move which will win the unreserved approval of almost every citizen of riper years.

Among the ironies of life is a tendency among the governments of newly independent African states to introduce, with all the zeal of freedom-loving reformers, measures which when originally propounded by the colonialists had been resisted by the people as glaring examples of imperialist oppression. Villagization is an example.

The only part of Africa, so far as I know, where it has been successfully introduced by official action is in the Kikuyu, Embu and Meru districts of Kenya, where it was a by-product of Mau Mau. When forest terrorists were at their most ferocious, the Kikuyu were gathered from their scattered home-steads into villages, partly for their own protection, partly (on Malayan lines) to deny the terrorist gangs supplies of food.

Emergency regulations gave the Government power to force these drastic measures through. Villages were created and, while some have since crumbled, the village habit came to stay. Independent Kenya does not wish to undo them. Whether villages can be created in Tanganyika on a really big scale without the exercise of similarly drastic powers remains to be seen. Certainly the President's vision, his lieutenants' enthusiasm and TANU's organization make a combination tough enough to put most things through.

National Culture

The other half of Mr. Sijaona's task is cultural. "We're going to build an institute in Dar es Salaam," he said, "to foster our Tanganyika culture—drama, folklore, dances, a writers' workshop where our writers will be given facilities to produce creative work. There will be a national theatre. Later we shall have cultural centres in each of our regions. . . . But at present there are no funds. We must get help from outside."

What *is* Tanganyika's national culture? "Music—dancing—there are carvers—basketwork—on the coast we have the Arab ruins, Swahili poetry. . . ."

Tanganyika is a new country, and most of its culture is still to be made; like (one may hope) Greece in Mycenaean times, it stands on the brink of a golden age. The foundations on which its artists must build are slender.

Centuries ago—how many no one can be certain, but possibly as far back as the Paleolithic era—the inhabitants of the great central plateau painted their caves and shelters with images of the animals around them, of hunts and fights, elephants and warriors. Some of these, in a succession of styles, are still to be seen round Kondoa Irangi. (And there can be no more urgent task for Mr. Sijaona's Ministry than to arrest the deterioration being caused in these caves by both weather and tourists getting in.) Then came a gap of a great many centuries, and then the Arabs and their wholly alien culture, which now survives mainly in some splendid ruins of old palaces and mosques, in a few traditions and in the Swahili tongue.

In between, very little. The mainly Bantu-speaking peoples of Tanganyika created nothing to match the achievements of West Africans in sculpture and carving, song and dance. Even such objects as masks were few and crude. A visit to the excellent little museum leaves an impression of innumerable weapons, drums decorated with cowrie shells, painted shields, boldly executed bead designs on stools and aprons and a little carving, crude but strong. Now that the West has flooded in with an alien inspiration and sophisticated techniques, the task will be to fuse the two worlds, to join the two streams and give a wholly new shape to the arts.

Boundless confidence, soaring hope, friendly manners; a refusal to be daunted, a conviction that help will come, and go on coming, in quantities to which no limit can be seen, from "the Outside"—these are the main impressions Dar es Salaam leaves on the mind. The sun shines, rain falls, birds sing, trees give cool shade, the sea sleeps; everything will be better tomorrow, even if it's not quite right today.

> *They sought it with thimbles, they sought it with care,*
> *They pursued it with forks and hope;*
> *They threatened its life with a railway share;*
> *They charmed it with smiles and soap.*

What are they seeking? Hard to say; something splendid, something great. The plan that works, and aid as of right from "the Outside"; freedom without chaos, power without abuse; nonalignment, pan-African unity, African socialism; peace without conquest, democracy without opposition, nationhood without discontent, prosperity without sacrifice; freedom from hunger, freedom from neo-colonialism, freedom from interference; knowledge without guilt, life without tears; the end of an old shame, the dawn of a new dignity; the truth about the African personality—the face in the glass.

Every man has his Snark. We must hope that few will find, as the Baker discovered when he softly and suddenly vanished away, that the Snark was a Boojum after all.

THE INHERITORS I

Happy Valley

We corkscrewed by Land-Rover up a rough, steep track to the forest boundary, halted at well over nine thousand feet and looked down over an enormous panorama below. Tumbling valleys flattened out and merged into a wide plateau, which stretched to the invisible scarp of the Rift. Around us, in the tall bush, magnificent wild delphiniums, peacock-blue and purple, reached to my shoulder. *Hypericum* was in vivid yellow bloom.

We were on the slopes of Kipipiri, one of the three peaks of Kenya's Aberdare Range. Above us cedar forest lay in dark folds over the mountain's crumpled shoulder as far as the bamboo line; above that moorlands took over, but they were masked in cloud. The crisp air was chilly; so were the streams that rise in these forests. In former days they had been stocked with trout.

"No fish there now," said my companion, a young English District Officer soon to leave with his "lumpers," as we looked down the long, steep valley. "The settlers have had them all." One of the minor changes that has come to Kenya in the last year or so is that the word "settler," like the civil service, has been Africanized.

The great sheet of land below us shimmered with little pinpoints of light, like daytime stars winking. Each pinpoint reflected sunlight from the corrugated-iron roof of the house of a new settler. The iron sheets are issued to the settlers to enable them to catch rainwater off their roofs, and thus save their womenfolk a long daily trek to the nearest river. But I saw no guttering on the roofs or storage tanks beside the shacks.

"The idea hasn't caught on. In fact, the settlers have hammered out the guttering to make ridging for the roofs," my companion explained. "The Settlement Board offered them a lot of old oil drums for next to nothing to store the water, but they weren't interested." So wives, daughters and grandmothers still plod to and from the nearest stream, humping heavy drums, as they have done for centuries—except that old oil drums have replaced gourds. The Kikuyu don't believe in idle hands among their womenfolk.

Below the forest boundary all the trees are coming down: every one. Their charred stumps poke up like blackened teeth from clods of rich chocolate-brown earth turned up by the hoes of the settlers, who are cultivating on slopes that are all but precipices. Rainfall here is high—fifty or sixty inches annually. It seems inevitable, despite contour ditches, that heavy storms will wash much of this fat, good earth downhill and scour the hillsides.

Everywhere hoes peck away, wielded by girls in faded, tattered cotton garments and bright head scarves; by shaven-headed wives with bodies coarsened by repeated childbearing, their newest babies slung on their backs; by skinny grandmothers, with wise and wizened faces and long, dangling ear lobes hung with coils of wire on strips of leather adorned by multicoloured beads. Even tots, five or six years old, have their little hoes.

The industry of these Kikuyu women is phenomenal.

When they are on their own land, working for their own families, they never pause. In their different sphere the men, no doubt, are just as busy, but it is a sphere more of tongue and wit and less of muscle: buying and selling, bargaining, seeking out new opportunities in old trucks.

The last of the forest is going up in smoke from dozens of small fires, scenting the air so sweetly that we drew in deep breaths for the sheer pleasure of it. Perhaps I was sentimental to regret the trees. But our guide said: "In a few years' time what will have happened to the streams? They're bound to dwindle; in a drought they'll dry up altogether. This is a catchment area. It's sheer lunacy to let the forest go." But whose forest is it? Not Britain's, anyway.

We were looking down over the Wanjohi, the once notorious Happy Valley, haunted perhaps by the raffish ghosts of people like Lady Idina, six times husbanded; and Joss Erroll, one of the husbands, destined to be the victim, in middle age, of a *crime passionel;* and Boy Long, whose handsome looks and gaudy shirts and broad-brimmed hats dazzled eyes and broke numerous hearts. And many others. All this took place a long time ago, in the twenties; the great depression of the early thirties obscured and eventually dispersed those Happy Valley dwellers who had survived *delirium tremens,* Muthaiga Club parties, needle pricks, and being shot at by jealous lovers on railway stations.

Gin-soaked as they were, they enhanced rather than damaged the natural charms of their valley by leaving the native trees alone and creating gardens of outstanding beauty, by paddocking green pastures for butter-yellow Guernseys, stocking streams and building attractive, rambling, creeper-festooned bungalows of local timbers with shingle roofs.

After they faded out, a different lot of settlers—white still— replaced them; they changed the valley, still without abusing it. They planted pyrethrum, an attractive crop with sheets of white flowers and sage-grey foliage; they bred good sheep, some of the finest in Kenya, from imported rams and ewes; and sold butterfat off pastures they improved by modern methods of grassland management. The Wanjohi became a productive valley: still happy, on the whole, but on more bourgeois lines than in the days of its notoriety.

Now it has passed to a third lot of settlers. The plan is to settle fifteen hundred Kikuyu families here and on the slopes of Kipipiri, between forest and plateau. Many of the small holdings extend to only seven acres—not much at an altitude too high for maize, the Kikuyu staple, and best suited to live-stock, for which most of the plots are too small. On poorer land, plots are larger; but poorer land produces less.

The Million-Acre Scheme

All this forms part of the so-called million-acre scheme, an outcome of the momentous Lancaster House Conference of January, 1960, when the decision was taken to end Kenya's sixty-year-old experiment of white settlement, abandon the outmoded hope of multiracialism and hand over the reins as quickly as possible to a wholly African government, with no privileges or protection for white or brown minorities.

Deep in every African heart burns a hunger for land. Ever since the colonial government leased land to white settlers in Kenya's highlands, this hunger has been growing, and so has the resolve to satisfy it by reclaiming from the Europeans land which the Africans of Kenya, and especially the Kikuyu, regard as rightfully theirs.

Two factors have intensified this pressure. The first is the steep, dangerous and spiralling rise in the population. No one knows how many Africans occupied the area that became

Kenya when the British first took it over; the estimate was about two million. Today the population stands at nearly nine million and is rising at the rate of three per cent a year, which means that nearly three hundred thousand souls are being added annually and that numbers will double in little over twenty years. This is part of the "population explosion."

When people multiply like that, there cannot possibly be room for everyone to possess a plot of land. But almost everyone still wants to. And there are nothing like enough industries to absorb the surplus people. Eventually, of course, a lot of people will have to overcome their land hunger, but meanwhile the pressure is too great for any government, let alone an outgoing colonial one, to withstand.

The other factor is political. The nationalist demand for independence has been linked with a demand for land. One became a symbol of the other, the very proof and essence. No independent African government could tolerate a situation where so much of its most productive land belonged to ex-colonialists. So the million-acre scheme was launched—very quickly, more or less as an emergency measure to let steam out of the political boiler.

The total area of the white highlands was about seven and a half million acres. Most of this lies in regions of low fertility and rainfall—thirty inches or less—suited only to ranching; about three million acres consists of mixed farming land that can be cultivated. The Government is therefore buying one third of the mixed farming land formerly leased to Europeans. This is an expensive exercise. The land alone, with all its improvements, is costing twelve million pounds ($33,600,-000); the whole scheme, nearly thirty million pounds (eighty-four million dollars), spread over five years. That, at any rate, is the estimate, and it will be surprising if in the end it doesn't cost a good deal more. The aim is to settle about fifty thousand families—equal to roughly one year's natural increase in the population. Only one third of the cost is to be given away; the rest is on loan and is supposed to be repaid by the settlers, with interest, over thirty years. Whether they really will repay this loan money is a moot point.

It would have been much cheaper, of course, merely to have opened the weir and let loose a land-hungry black flood over the once-white highlands. But the white farmers were producing four fifths of the country's exports and most of its taxable revenue. Less than five per cent of the total land area of Kenya was theirs and only about one fifth of that area was classified by agriculturalists as "land of high potential," but on this they had built up an economy which sustained the whole country. If all this were to be submerged beneath a tide of peasants without capital or expertise, consuming what they grew and herding only goats and scrub cattle, the economy would simply collapse.

So there had to be orderly settlement; phased, planned, controlled, supervised and paid for.

One of the first decisions was to buy mostly from those Europeans farming on the perimeters of land already owned by Africans. So the small holders are being settled tribally: Kikuyu here, Kamba there; Nandi on this scheme and Kipsigis on that; not jumbled together. This follows their own wishes. Kikuyu Kamaus don't want to mix with Luo Ohangas.

Settlers

There are two types of schemes: high- and low-density. On the first, plot holders provide scarcely any cash of their own; their names are drawn from a drum, and each one gets anything from seven to about twenty acres of good or fair arable land, on which it is reckoned he can support a family and make a small cash income. The British taxpayer is finding the money for these high-density schemes.

Low-density projects offer plots ranging from twenty acres up to several hundred. Settlers are hand-picked and need, by local standards, quite a lot of capital—from £350 each ($630), in cash, up to about £1,000 ($2,800). So a different type of settler is entering the low-density schemes: men of substance, often successful traders, artisans or farmers in their own right. These projects are not designed to help the landless, but to get more salable produce off the land.

Can any family support itself—and nearly always there's an awful lot of family to support—in modern times off the produce of seven acres? Another moot point. Much of the land lies at high altitudes which oblige the owners to concentrate on pyrethrum and potatoes. Pyrethrum prices have slumped to a level where the crop barely pays; potatoes succumb to a disease called bacterial wilt, and easily glut a restricted market.

This minimum of seven acres marks a compromise between those who were anxious to settle families on even smaller plots, in order to relieve unemployment and give the landless somewhere to go, and those who believe that in the long run more human distress will be caused, not less, by creating agricultural slums. Behind the scenes a running battle has taken place between the two schools of thought, and the agriculturalists have been gradually gaining ground. The cash income "target," at first a mere £25 ($70) a year, has been changed to £40 ($112) a year and then to £70 ($196). Now the agriculturalists want to get it up to £100 ($280). This may seem low enough, but it is high by peasant standards anywhere, and especially in Africa, where many families wring a living from a single eroded acre or even less, and have nothing at all left over for sale.

Back to Hoes

When the first white settlers came, they took over forest, bush and plain almost empty of humans, whatever African politicians may subsequently have claimed. Most of the country belonged to the wild animals, then in a marvellous abundance never to be seen again. White men inherited from elephant and buffalo, zebra and eland; they slew or drove away most of the beasts and took the land. Skin-clad little Dorobo hunters had set traps here and there, and taken honey; on the plains, Masai had intermittently driven flocks and herds across illimitable pastures. A Scots settler, not yet seventy, once described to me how antelope had walked right up to him, innocently approaching to within a few yards, to see what he was. No man had ever taught them fear. That was put right; he shot the inquisitive beasts. "The porters had to eat."

So most of the first settlers made their farms from uninhabited and untouched bush and forest. They felled trees, uprooted stumps, fenced paddocks; they made dams, dug wells, sank boreholes; experimented with crops that failed, imported animals that died, died themselves sometimes of mysterious diseases until the newcomers found out what would, or wouldn't, thrive, and how to live and make a living in this strange land where snow lay on the equator. By and large they succeeded. All that is an old story.

Now the new settlers take over going concerns. They inherit fences, boreholes, paddocks, houses; knowledge of how to get high yields from crops and grass leys; machinery, plantations, orchards, dips, driers, cow sheds, pigsties, barns; pedigree and productive flocks and herds: a store of fifty years' experience.

But in order to enjoy their inheritance they must first carve

it up. A good deal of it anyway: the going concerns. These are
being split into small units. Fences are coming down, plantations being razed, grass leys broken up, pedigree herds dispersed, machinery dispatched to auction sale-yards: all very
strange in this day and age, when every other country in the
world is moving towards the bigger unit—towards mechaniza-
tion, mass production, centralized marketing; an age, like it
or not, of assembly lines and computers, nuclear power and
automation, the collective and *kibbutz*.

Only in Kenya can you actually see a combine-harvester
chugging off one end of a five-hundred-acre wheat field and
barefoot peasants coming in at the other to hoe the stubble
and press in with naked toes seeds of maize which at this
altitude take eleven months to ripen and are almost certain
to be killed by frost. It's like *Through the Looking-Glass,* or
watching the hands of a clock being put back. Everyone's out
of step but my Johnnie—or my Kamau.

I asked the manager of one of these schemes what he himself would have done. "Divide the farms into economic units,
a hundred acres at the least, and lease them to Africans with
capital; syndicates probably, men with business ability—
capitalists if you like. Let the homeless and landless work for
them as paid hands. That mayn't be socialist idealism but it
would work, and it would keep up production. Whereas
this . . ."

These farms we were discussing, he added, would barely,
under the new dispensation, support more families than they
had before. The white farmers had employed a lot of black
labour. Every man with four years' residence or more was
entitled to a plot. More recent arrivals had departed, to be
replaced by those who had drawn the title to a plot out of
the drum; the net result had been a gain, in terms of human
numbers, of about ten per cent. An official estimate is that

only twenty to thirty per cent more people will ultimately find places on the farms bought for resettlement.

For none of these limitations to the scheme's effectiveness are the men in charge, the agricultural technicians, to blame. They have planned it with immense care, they are enthusiastic and hard-working and they have saved it from what would have been disaster had the plans been badly framed or not framed at all. They have excellent projects for training the settlers in many branches of husbandry, for establishing co-operatives, for stepping up production, improving quality, organizing markets.

The shortcomings of the scheme arise basically from one cause: that it was begotten not of technical or economic need, but of political expediency. It is an attempt to lessen (not satisfy) land hunger and take the sting out of racial discontent. Judged by this standard—perhaps the only fair standard, that of what it set out to do—the scheme has met with a considerable degree of success.

On the Kinangop

It had rained heavily in the night, and the Kinangop was covered in dense cloud, the road streamed with runnels. The Settlement Officer, an ex-naval commander and fisheries expert, brought a Land-Rover to meet us, and we traversed muddy tracks and lurched over tufty grasses and rolling slopes in a truly nautical fashion, tacking and pitching. Here was another scheme: eighty old white settlers bought out and a target of eight hundred and fifty new black ones to be moved in.

One bought-out farmer had come here from New Zealand after World War I, acquired virgin land just below the forest line at over eight thousand feet above sea level, developed a farm, built a house, raised a family and, an old man now, gone back to New Zealand, taking his money but (I would suppose) leaving his heart on this mountainside with its distant view over plains and hills as purple-blue in this light as the wild delphiniums. Certainly he left behind a good house: walls of local stone, a roof of plum-red Italian tiles, made on the farm by prisoners during World War II. In the garden fuchsias were tumbling over stone walls, creepers rampaging, lilies shining among deep herbacious borders, but all was tangled, overgrown and gone to seed. The house stood empty. "We hope it will become a school."

Behind the house was a mature apple orchard which last year produced over £2,000 ($5,600) worth of fruit. Must that also be obliterated? "We're looking for a settler who'll take it over as it stands. No luck so far—they're not trained to it, not interested. I'm afraid it'll have to go."

The Settlement Officer was explaining how the departed New Zealander had farmed his land. "Pyrethrum yields of up to two thousand pounds an acre . . . fifty-inch rainfall . . . seed potatoes and butterfat—maize is hopeless . . . these enormous families . . ."

Kariuki, one of the new settlers, had come to him and said: "It's no use to give me seven acres." "Why not?" "Because I should need most of it for a village for my family." "A village?" "I've three wives and twenty-seven children." And more on the way. He beamed with pride, and got thirty-five acres.

We called at Kariuki's and found, indeed, a village: a sort of barrack, and a swarm of children darting in and out. Others clustered over a broken-down cart embedded in the mud outside. I tried to count them, but they dodged about like chickens; I made the number fifteen or sixteen. The rest were out hoeing or at school, the babies with their mothers in the fields,

Kariuki himself had gone off in his pickup van. He owned an old sedan as well and ran a taxi business on the side, and did a bit of trading. Formerly he had driven a tractor for a European.

"He's got his head screwed on," the Settlement Officer said. "He's bought a hammer mill and a secondhand tractor with a power take-off, and he's going to grist the other settlers' maize. He got two cows with his loan money and then another five off his own bat—plenty of capital. And a small flock of ewes. He'll come out all right."

So he should, with three wives and probably a dozen children working for nothing. He has only two paid hands and they are paid very little.

"The Agricultural Workers' Union? They've no hope up here." On tea and coffee estates, where labour can be organized and is employed by Europeans, wages are treble what Kariuki pays, and strikes almost as frequent as in the British motor industry; but few African employers have any time for trade unions, a colonialist idea. The Tanganyika Government has already passed a law forbidding strikes.

While Kariuki holds the procreative record on this settlement scheme, others do not lag far behind. Most are of the same complacent mind about their fecundity, but I did encounter one disturbed by doubts.

"I need another cow," he said sadly. "One isn't enough. My children drink all the milk and leave me none for sale, so how am I to pay their school fees and buy their clothes? Pay, pay, pay—that's all I do for my eleven children! I sell cabbages, potatoes, a little milk when there is any, but I never have enough. . . ."

Europeans, I suggested, have smaller families not by accident but by design. His eyes shone, he waved his hands.

"Yes, yes, I have given my wife birth control! But I found

it too late! What good is it now we have eleven children? If I had only known before! Four or five would have been enough, all at school, well clothed. Everyone should have birth control! That is the only way to raise our people!"

He glowed with the ardour of the converted, but he was the only one I encountered of this mind.

Off to Sea

There is a Settlement Officer in charge of, roughly, every ten thousand acres. All are practical farmers. Some are men bought out by the Settlement Board, or their sons, signed on in its employment for two years—all are on two-year contracts —to split up their own farms, among others, and settle small holders on what was formerly their own land, or their fathers'. The job gives them a breathing space while they decide what to do, and must provide them with a strange experience. As one remarked: "You learn to be numb to a lot of things."

The ex-naval commander's farm had been bought but not yet taken over, and he was engaged in an exercise he described as "running it down." His was a small farm, only sixty acres. He started with a fishing plot bought from a Nairobi businessman; by wheedling his neighbours he doubled his acreage, put up a homemade piggery, bought a few pedigree sows and started to breed and fatten baconers for the local factory. Soon he was sending away three hundred a year, all in the top grade. His pigs' manure fertilized his potatoes, which gave generous yields twice a year; he irrigated cauliflowers, worked up a record output of pyrethrum and went in for sidelines like milling and blending stock feed.

Everything was shipshape, well planned, orderly, a perfectionist's dream. The upshot of it all was that off his sixty acres he was selling annually £8,000 ($22,400) worth of produce, a record for these chilly, mist-wrapped uplands. Now his farm is to be split into four holdings, each of fifteen acres, and leased to four Kikuyu families. The "target" for these plots allows a cash income of £40 ($112) a year. If every settler scores a bull's-eye totally they will sell in a year, off this farm, produce to the value of £200 ($560)—one fortieth of its former output.

"The only chance of keeping up production would be to get a co-operative to take it over as a going concern, and keep on the piggeries, the irrigation and so forth. That doesn't seem possible. The settlers have no co-operative experience, and anyway, they aren't keen. It isn't what they *want*. What they want is each man with his own individual plot of land."

The Kikuyu are passionate individualists—that is, taking the family as a unit. To co-operate and share outside that circle goes against the grain.

All these farms, when they were bought from Europeans, were on a "ring" water main. Water was piped from a spring on the mountain, taken round the perimeter of the block of farms and sold to each farmer for three shillings (forty-two cents) a thousand gallons. When the Kikuyu settlers moved in, they cut the pipeline to avoid the meters, left the water flowing and wasted so much that the Settlement Officer had to disconnect the supply. Now the settlers' women plod a couple of miles to a stream to fill their drums.

When I looked round the solid, double-storey stone house above the river with its full bookshelves, the silver cups and old brasses, the pictures and Indian rugs and all the possessions of a lifetime, I found it hard to realize that soon all would stand silent and empty: windowpanes cracked, chimney cold, garden run to seed. Or perhaps the new settlers' wives would squat over three stones while cooking fires blackened the floorboards and tethered goats bleated from the veranda.

"They might use the place for a school or a community centre, but they've got more houses than they need for that sort of thing."

And its former owner? He has built himself a boat from timber cut on the farm, about all of his property that he'll be able to take away, and in it he and his wife intend to sail round the world.

"We shall take our time, there's no hurry. I've always wanted to see the Great Barrier Reef. . . ." After that, no plans.

LAMURIA

A clean, cedary smell is what I principally remember: the split-log shack was lined with strips of cedar cut from the surrounding forest, cedar logs spat and crackled in an open fireplace. I think the shack had two rooms separated by a weatherboard partition, and a narrow veranda facing the plain. We had slept in tents pitched in a clearing amid rough-barked junipers whose sharp-scented foliage was hung with drooping grey-green lichen beards. Among them grew tall *Podocarpus* and the knotted olives, and shrubs like *Lamuria,* whose clusters of creamy pink flowers drenched the air with the scent of jasmine. The dew-soaked sunny morning quivered with the song of birds.

That was about forty years ago. I was a child then; we had ridden our tough little Somali ponies across the plains to look at land high up on Mount Kenya's moorlands, over nine thousand feet—good for sheep, people said. We stayed the night with Berkeley Cole. He had built this shack beside a mountain stream which rippled down so limpidly that you could see every pebble on its bed, except where the water was rock-curdled into foam. It came from the glaciers and was ice-cold. Thick bush choked the banks, and there were no trout in those days: it was stocked later. Anyway, an angler would probably have hooked a rhino or flicked the muddied hide of a dozing buffalo.

Berkeley Cole was one of the old, colonial Kenya's legends, impossible now to pin down; a man whose brilliant colours faded, when he died, like those of a tropical fish or a blue-and-orange lizard. He had fine looks, supple conversation, grey eyes and a gay Irish wit. He never made money, entered politics, took life seriously or married. It was he, I think, who started the fashion for cobalt-blue or tomato-red Somali shawls, woven from very soft yarn, flung over the shoulders, and for tall, proud, fierce Somali attendants, or squires.

People bracketed him with the even more legendary Denys Finch-Hatton, a man never forgotten or explained by his friends, who left nothing behind him but affection, a memory of gaiety and grace, a kind of melody or aroma, like a trace of the *Lamuria* scent on the air. He, too, had wit. I can recall only one illustration: of how once, when he was on safari in the farthest, wildest regions, many days' march from contact with mails and telegraphs, a cable from London, forwarded from Nairobi by relays of runners with cleft sticks, caught up with him in the bush. Its content was brief. "Do you know George Robinson's address?" Back went the reply as it had come, by relays of runners travelling for weeks with cleft sticks. It was even briefer. "Yes."

He crashed when piloting his own small aircraft some time between the wars. Karen Blixen wrote of him in *Out of Africa* and described how, in the Ngong Hills, lions haunted his grave.

At Lamuria, in the early morning, I followed a narrow path down to the river and met a bushbuck standing stock-still, his dewy coat dark chestnut, with creamy spots over the withers and faint white stripes over the loins. His neat twisted horns were erect, his tarnlike eyes deep and innocent; all sinew and grace, he melted gently as a ghost into his dappled element. Then we rode on our way.

That was my first visit. I have just made my last. Some things are still the same. Behind Mount Kenya's sloping black shoulder the sun still leaps into a gold-and-saffron sky to tinge flamingo pink the pure, smooth glaciers under peaks so immemorial they look like the charred bones of weary, indestructible old men. Yet the swelling mountain with its twin nipples stands as if lightly pencilled against the sky. Very soon after sunrise long, wispy clouds gather round the peak to shield it for the rest of the day. The sun floods the enormous plain below, lion-coloured and wind-swept and stretching to the dark ranges of Settima and Kinangop. Your eye dazzles, and reaches out towards the end of the world. A pair of francolins dart between two bushes, a martial eagle circles overhead, a flight of crested cranes goes honking by and the scent of *Lamuria* brushes the mountain air.

The rhino and the bushbuck have gone, and next month John, the owner, his wife, Molly, and their sons are going too. John came out when he was barely twenty, after World War I, and worked for others—the pay was ten pounds ($28) a month in those days—until he had saved enough to make a shoestring start on his own. He never bought the farm, he only leased it, and a friend put up nine tenths of the working capital. But he farmed Lamuria for twenty-five years.

When he took over he found the old cedar shack half tumbled down and lately occupied by pigs. There was a mud-and-wattle shed or two and that was all—no fences, water, buildings, cultivation, human beings, anything. Marketable timber had been worked out, the place abandoned; rhinos and buffalo, forest hogs and buck had the cold and misty mountain slopes to themselves.

Much of it is poor, time-eroded soil, badly drained, with a good deal of "black cotton," a viscous, obstinate clay that turns into bog in the rains. Nights are cold, there's a risk of hail, buffalo poach the crops and for years the nearest railway was a hundred miles off. Then a branch line approached and finally went by near at hand, and for the first time you could get a crop away.

It was about then that John moved in. He added to the cedar shack, ploughed the coarse, tufty turf with teams of sixteen small humped oxen; planted wheat and barley; bought some half-bred ewes and cows and started to breed up with Corriedale rams and pure-bred Ayrshire bulls. He had to clear and stump a lot of bush and forest—hard, expensive work; to fence against buffalo, build dips to keep the cattle free of disease-carrying ticks, make roads of a sort, and do all the other things you do when you turn a slice of raw Africa into a farm. Later he planted pyrethrum, lucerne and grass leys, sank a borehole and made dams, and built a homemade factory to manufacture dried milk powder and cheese. "Lamuria" was the brand name of his cheese. Altogether he kept busy and managed with a minimum of capital, ploughing all the profits back into the land.

I stayed several times with John and Molly over the years. On each occasion there was something new to see: a caterpillar tractor, the first combine-harvester, a pedigree bull, a milking bail, paddocks where the coarse natural pasture had done well, when John first came, to carry one beast to ten acres: last year, on sixty-five acres of lush Rhodes-Setaria grass leys, he fattened sixty-five good, cross-bred steers.

There were other things to see besides farming. Mount Kenya's rose-pink and violet peak at sunrise and dusk, rainbow trout in the stream, young plantations, a garden full of scent and colour, a tame oryx, francolins and touracos and sunbirds, and, at last, a stone-built living room for Molly. I was sorry when they had to abandon the veranda where we had often breakfasted on pawpaw, yoghourt and honey in the sunshine, with bougainvillaea blazing at us from the rotting posts. But jasmine-scented *Lamuria* still drenched the crisp air, and Molly made an excellent, rather tart jelly from its scarlet fruit.

Alan, the youngest of her three sons, trained for the Merchant Navy, but changed his mind and took an agricultural diploma instead. Desmond, the middle one, entertained no

doubts: he went to the local farming college and then helped
his father. The eldest took up part-time white hunting to earn
the cash to lease a farm of his own. They are large, energetic,
self-reliant young men and born farmers, every one.

John started to export his milk powder and his cheeses to
the Congo, Aden and the Persian Gulf, and to win prizes with
his Ayrshires at local shows. By this time he knew as much
as most and sat on committees to advise other farmers, but he
still took advice himself from experts who sowed experimental plots of grass, tested fertilizer rates, analyzed soil and
helped in other practical ways. Then they mapped out a farm
plan for the next six or seven years. John was to work up to
seven hundred acres of wheat and barley, and double that
acreage of grass leys. A milking herd of three hundred cows
plus followers, a thousand breeding ewes, a hundred steers
fattened annually and, to consume the skim, fifty breeding
sows turning out every year seven hundred and fifty baconers.
And so on. Quite an output from land that had not supported
a single domestic animal, blade of corn or human being a
quarter of a century ago.

John was about halfway through his farm plan, and had
worked up the value of his annual output to nearly twenty
thousand pounds, when the first Lancaster House Conference
was held. He has never seen that handsome building in St.
James's with its gilded cornices, its chandeliers and big reception rooms, but those two words ring in his ears. The bell
tolled for Lamuria as it was, but rang out for the Lamuria
that is to be. The million-acre scheme began.

The Government made John a fair offer—enough for the
down payment on a South African farm. At sixty he sails this
month with Molly to make a new start in a new land. With
them go the car, five dogs, an arthritic cat, a couple of rams
and an assortment of farm implements. Desmond has gone

ahead to start things going in the Cape. Alan remains behind for the time being as a Settlement Officer employed by the Government. His job is to parcel out the farms, including his father's, into plots varying in size from eight acres to fifty or sixty.

On Alan's section of the scheme there are now half a dozen empty farmhouses whose owners have been bought out and have gone away. Already gardens are overgrown, roofs leak, termites are getting in. An irrigated market garden, about twenty acres, is going to seed; onions and feathery asparagus are waist high. Everywhere you hear the crack of axes as trees come down, and smell the aromatic scent of fires burning bush and branches as land is cleared.

In place of wheat, and grasses bred to thrive in these conditions, the Kikuyu are planting potatoes and maize. John's ex-tractor driver has a ten-acre plot on his ex-employer's farm. Alan said to him: "You know we tried maize here and it failed. The same with potatoes. But you've seen our wheat— you've helped to harvest it. You know it thrives. So why maize?"

Gichau, the tractor driver, rested on his hoe while his wife went on pecking at the stubble. "How can I plant a plot of one acre? Wouldn't all the birds in the forest come to eat it? And what should *we* eat, without maize?" He was half right, anyway; the birds would defeat him. And, like an ancient Egyptian, he would have to thresh the wheat by hand. So he was planting maize doomed to failure and potatoes that might get the wilt, and would anyway be hard to sell. With borrowed money he will buy a cow. He might grow some cabbages and keep a goat. He feels his own soil under his feet and his wife cooks on her own three stones and they are content— for the time being.

Before breakfast I found a spike-choked, overgrown path

to Berkeley Cole's grave. The path had been partially re-opened by new settlers going down to take trout from the river and hang honey barrels in trees. The stone slab had vanished under a tangle of undergrowth, among whose branches was entwined a rambler rose. I heard the river's gurgle and the falling, melancholy cadence of a wood dove, and smelled the jasmine-scented *Lamuria*. Soon hoes will be tapping here like woodpeckers; maize plants, sickly from the chill and misty mornings, will sprout among the rocks; and goats, like Bahram's wild asses, will trample the stones but will not break the sleep of Berkeley Cole.

John wants to start another cheese factory in South Africa —he says you cannot buy a really good local cheese down there—but he shook his head when I asked him whether he would keep "Lamuria" as the brand name. His cattle, sheep and pigs have gone to auction, the combines and tractors have been sold, his last crop of wheat has been railed. All around, hoes are breaking up the rich, productive grass leys to make way for little pocket-handkerchief, irregular plots of maize. Molly has packed her glass and china, and draws on scraps of paper ground plans for a new house, which is to have a mod-ern kitchen. At some time during a strenuous life John strained his heart, and she thinks he will feel younger, and she hopes live longer, at a lower altitude. The new farm will grow pineapples and sheep, an odd combination.

John isn't bitter, but he doesn't talk about it much. When I was leaving after breakfast I handed him back his farm plan. "Keep it," he said. "I never want to see it again."

THE INHERITORS II

Lessos

To look only at schemes where now settlers are taking over from the old the most productive and developed farms would, as Mr. Storrar, the Director of Settlement, pointed out, give a false impression. Plenty of undeveloped land is also being taken over in the million-acre scheme, and here output is being raised, not lowered; there is nothing to go into reverse. If you start from zero, one bag of maize is a net gain.

So I went to Lessos, one of the earliest projects, and peopled by Nandi settlers, not Kikuyu, in a part of the fertile hills that rise above Lake Victoria's basin on the western scarp of the Rift Valley. Little of this area, which is far from rail and market, had been much developed until tea estates began to take an interest and erected a factory not far away. But to establish tea needs very large sums of capital, which few of the former settlers could raise. (It is reckoned that the new settlers, through government loans, are on average able to invest three times as much capital per acre as their white predecessors.) Only one of the eleven farmers bought out in this particular project had got as far as making a tea nursery; he became the Settlement Officer, and has been in charge since the start.

Most of the plots at Lessos—a low-density scheme—are

around fifty acres, and the soil is rich, rainfall excellent, everything is lush and green. The Nandi, a non-Bantu people allied to the Masai but less tradition-bound, are a race of cattle
owners. They enjoy a reputation for being pleasant, cour-
teous, idle, intelligent, bibulous people, whose young men
enlist in large numbers in the army and police and whose
handsome women, less subservient to the men than the Kikuyu, are said to make the most sought-after prostitutes.

Many Nandi have grown rich by improving and exploiting
(in the virtuous sense) their cattle, and now they will become
even richer by growing tea. Between them the World Bank
and the Commonwealth Development Corporation are providing the capital, and the nearby factory is already buying
green leaf from its first Nandi producers, collecting and transporting it, processing, packing and sending it to world markets, and handing the proceeds back to the growers after
deducting their costs. All the Nandi producer has to do is to
bring his green leaf to the roadside at nine o'clock in the
morning when the truck passes by. Tea growing made easy:
and there seems no reason why a reasonably industrious settler, or at any rate one who employs others to be industrious,
shouldn't make an income of at least £1,000 ($2800) a year,
and more if he really tries.

"Lessos is a scheme for rich men," said the Settlement Officer. No one is admitted unless he can produce at least £150
($420) in hard cash, not in promises. After that he can draw
on government loans.

There is another scheme for even richer men who aspire
to become "yeomen farmers" and must put up the first £500
($1,400) of their own. For this they may count in all their
assets, such as cattle, implements and cars. The Settlement
Officer told me of two men whose hopes were dashed by a
shortfall of £100 ($280) in the necessary minimum. No argu-

ment could change the valuation of their assets, and they left thwarted and downcast.

In an hour or so they were back, smiling happily, to re-apply. "But you're still short by a hundred pounds." "No, we had forgotten something. Each of us has a daughter." "Daughters," the Settlement Officer pointed out, "are not cattle." "These are *marriageable* daughters, worth at least two heifers each, plus sheep and goats. . . ." Their arguments convinced the Settlement Officer, and the girls went in among the assets, valued at £50 ($140) each. The Nandi fathers got their farm.

Nandi Settlers

Kimitau arap Suret has built himself a five-room wooden house, European style, on a knoll overlooking about a hun-dred acres which he and three brothers jointly farm. There's an air of prosperity: a concrete well and piped water, a maize crib full of cobs, a tractor and a car and a sleek herd of about twenty good dairy cows, a cross between the native and the European breeds which give respectable yields of milk. This Kimitau separates, and sells the butterfat to a creamery through the co-operative society. It pays well.

His wife was in the kitchen, smoky from the usual fire be-neath three stones, suckling the latest infant while a cloud of tots clustered round, ready to scuttle to her protection like crabs darting down their holes. She and a paid hand milk the cows. The milker said his wages amounted to half the official minimum and he was well satisfied. "There's plenty of food."

Kimitau was out in his car, and so was the next man we called on: a settler living in a house taken over from a Euro-pean. It was a simple little creeper-smothered bungalow made

of posts and slats, not a grand affair of cut stone and tiles, and
so less intimidating; few ordinary Westerners, after all, would
care to move from a council house into Chatsworth or Blen-
heim.

The owner's wife showed us round. Her bungalow looked
barren with no furniture beyond one bare table, a few chairs
and an iron single bed, but each room displayed a poster with
the Annigoni portrait of the Queen. The larder accommo-
dated broody hens. Everything smelled of wood smoke and
was acquiring gradually that dark patina, like varnish on an
uncleaned old master, that the ever-smouldering pivotal
kitchen fire disseminates throughout all African houses. Ironically, perhaps, the bungalow's former owner is a descendant
of that van Rensburg who led a trek of Afrikaner families
from the Transvaal to the Uasin Gishu Plateau in 1908, and
established there the first white settlements.

His successor has inherited, besides the house and fifty
acres, an irrigated orange orchard whose fruit he sells locally
for twenty shillings ($2.80) a sack. Surely he could make more
than that? "Yes, of course, if he organized the marketing, but
he doesn't bother. That's plenty for him. He's satisfied." As
a Christian he can't buy another wife, so his wants are few.
On the erstwhile lawn stood the usual platform made of poles
on which a teapot and a set of mugs and cups are always to be
found. Sarah gave us tea, preceded by prayers. "Yes, it's good
here, there's plenty of food." She has a large family to eat it.
Cash in the bank, corn in the crib, cows in the paddock, fat
in the land: hers is a path of contentment. Satisfied with her
lot, she doesn't nag her husband for a bigger car, an inside
lavatory, a race week in Nairobi.

Will the Western world succeed in puncturing her contentment? Bring her to the belief that life is incomplete without
shoes and stockings, an electric cooker, a bath, a washing

machine? It will try. On our way home we met an eager, slippery-tongued young European selling something highly desirable—cattle medicines, I think, and mineral supplements, altogether good. Others will follow offering kitchen equipment, bedroom suites, carpets, encyclopaedias, brushes, nylons, all sorts of things just as commendable—steppingstones to those higher living standards extolled by all. Their price is contentment. Are they worth it? And will the Nandi, and others like them, pay?

Koma Rock

"Another scheme for rich men." The Settlement Officer at Koma Rock, about thirty miles east of Nairobi, was a small, tough, wiry Czech with fifteen years' ranching experience and a lifetime's knowledge of cattle, a quiet manner and a resolute eye. He had a tough task on hand: to establish on these dry plains below the hills belonging to the Kamba people an effective ranching proposition, and then to hand it over to a newly formed co-operative. To set up the ranch is one thing, a technical matter. To set up the co-operative is much harder. The Kamba, like the Kikuyu (to whom they are allied) are not co-operators by nature. The whole co-operative concept is alien to them, something imposed from outside.

We met the committee members in the Settlement Officer's house. This was, in its small way, a historic occasion. The assets of the Koma Rock Co-operative were being formally handed over to the society. Cameras clicked, signatures were appended to documents of some complexity. Henceforward the society with its assets—several thousand cattle and eighty thousand acres of plain—belonged to these eighty Kamba citizens who had paid their membership fees and contributed assets in the shape of cattle. Each member is required to put in not more than thirty head, to a minimum value of £350 ($630), which become the society's property. The society then buys an equal number of cattle, so that half its assets will come directly from its members, half from purchases financed by government loans. The Settlement Officer is to run the ranch on behalf of its members for two years, and then hand it over to the committee and depart. The chairman is a heavy, solid-looking citizen called Paulo, who owns, in addition to a lot of cattle, two thousand coffee trees and a transport business: a capitalist whose business experience will be valued, for the ranch must make money and repay its considerable loans.

"Most of our members," said the deputy Commissioner for Co-operative Development, "are coffee barons who now want to become beef barons as well. I'm afraid they're simply out to make money. The idealistic content of co-operation is wholly alien."

Without some thought of pulling together and pooling resources for the good of all, will they be able to run co-operatively a highly skilled ranching outfit when, after two years, the Settlement Officer withdraws? Or will the ranch split into individual holdings, to the detriment of the land? For these Kambas are sturdy, not to say prickly, individualists. They are the people who lay down in front of bulldozers that were clearing bush to combat the tsetse fly, and who marched en masse to Government House to protest against proposals to reduce the numbers of their overcrowded cattle.

This is dry, hot, marginal country, with a carrying capacity of at best one beast to ten acres. Water is scarce, pastures can be very quickly ruined by overgrazing and cease to support any beasts at all. Central direction and control are a necessity. Relax the rules, and you have a desert on your hands.

Probably the scheme's future depends on the society's continuing to employ as manager a skilled, experienced rancher, giving him complete authority and following his advice. The Kamba, like others, are not always ready to accept advice, especially when it concerns their cattle. Perhaps they will change.

> *Slowly responds the mind to what is told,*
> *That which the eye reveals takes surer hold.*

The co-operative officer quoted hopefully this couplet designed by Horace Plunkett to enshrine one of the major precepts of his great ideal.

That which the eye revealed to us was an open, sun-filled, wind-swept tawny plain rolling away towards the hills. Rain had fallen, and we saw the plains at their best, green-tinged and with grass that looks more nourishing than it is, mostly of a genus called *Themeda*. The cattle which the members had contributed to the common pool were far from impressive: tiny little bags of bones. One might call them miniatures were it not for the overtones of elegance and beauty attached to this word, and wholly inapplicable to these skeletal, disease-ridden objects.

"They've sent their *goi-gois,*" said the Settlement Officer, using that most expressive term for anything broken-down, halt, lame and useless. Even though good management will improve the *goi-gois,* they will never be acceptable for slaughter by the Meat Commission at its nearby packing plant, nor do they seem the best foundation stock to start a profitable herd. "The Kamba won't bring their best cattle. Those they leave at home. They don't trust the scheme; they're full of suspicions."

The cattle brought by the Settlement Officer on behalf of the co-operative were about twice the size and three times as heavy, and looked sleek and firm. The best cows will be kept to breed from, using bulls called Sahiwals, who hail from India. The members of the co-operative are now the owners of these proud beasts. Are they pleased? Paulo and his companions said so, but could not seem to free themselves from an undercurrent of distrust and reserve. Why was the Government doing all this? What was it up to? If this was really a scheme to benefit the Kamba, why couldn't each man fence off his own bit of land? Why all these rules and regulations, and what was the Settlement Officer doing here? The ranch had been taken over from Europeans, but there was still a European telling everyone what to do.

Perhaps he will be Africanized? "Africans are training as livestock officers, but not enough of them. Even when they get their diplomas, they've no practical experience." One or two now working on the scheme will perhaps take over its direction in two years' time. But they are young. "Will they carry the authority with the members? Will they be able to stand up to men like Paulo with seniority behind them, the local big guns, the rich and powerful?"

A Strawberry Martinet

Henry Kinoko grows strawberries and is very proud of them. Strawberry cultivation is highly skilled and full of trade secrets. "A friend showed me his methods," Mr. Kinoko said, "but warned me not to pass them on—this is a very competitive business. I've learned the hard way." (The friend was a European.)

At intervals you nip off buds to check the flowering and bring on the fruit at the right time. For three months of the year, at most, it goes by air to Covent Garden and commands enormous prices; this is the cream of the trade. Henry Kinoko looked sternly at his neat rows of plants, all mulched, all irrigated, weedless as a billiard table. "Now," he said, "these have my permission to flower." Any strawberry that bursts into bloom against his wishes, I felt, would have a thin time.

Erect, brisk, commanding, self-assured, Mr. Kinoko has something of a sergeant major's manner, although he has never been a soldier, but has made a lot of money as a salesman and in the secondhand clothing trade. He proved his toughness in the days of Mau Mau by defying the terrorists—it is said that he survived the Lari massacre by sheer luck. Now he has invested the profits of his secondhand clothing business, plus a loan from the Land Bank, in a farm formerly belonging to a European. He runs a small herd of high-grade Friesians and has bought a good pedigree bull; has five acres of potatoes and two under irrigated peas; is clearing land to plant tea. His hilly farm is a hive of activity.

Soon after he started, all his labourers went on strike. He sacked the lot, engaged new men and since then has had no trouble. "I treat them fairly, but they've got to work. Any argument, and out they go." They are all fellow Kikuyu.

Henry Kinoko is on his own—private enterprise. He has nothing to do with any of the settlement schemes and thinks very little of them. "It's wrong to break up the big, efficient units, and people won't make a decent living on these small holdings. They're better off working for an employer. And they prefer it. We need to build up bigger units, use machinery and modern ideas, not go back to small plots and hoes. Now I have this farm, I'm not content; I'm going to take over the next one from a European, five hundred acres and a herd of Ayrshires, walk in, walk out. . . ." Mr. Kinoko is ambitious. The Land Bank has given him another loan.

He's a realist, too. "I'm just starting here, and many things can go wrong. Come back in three years' time and then see.

I may have failed." I doubt this. Henry Kinoko is too good
a businessman.

The End of a Dream

There used to be a rule, if not a law, against the transfer
of land from race to race. If you lived in the white highlands
you couldn't sell to an African or an Asian; if you lived in
the black highlands you couldn't transfer your land to an
Asian or a European.

Lancaster House, 1960, swept away the first part of this
ban, though not the second; it would still be impossible,
practically if not legally, for an African living in a tribal area
to sell to a non-African—or, indeed, to a member of another
tribe. He'd get lynched if he tried. Kikuyu men have (though
rarely) married non-Kikuyu women, but have never, so far
as I know, sold a square yard of land, outside the townships,
to a member of another race or tribe.

Quite a number of white farmers are selling privately to
Africans like Henry Kinoko or—more frequently—to syndicates and groups. On the Uasin Gishu Plateau a descendant
of the Transvaal trekkers said: "Now I've an African on each
side. One's leasing a thousand-acre farm, the other's got six
hundred acres. They're keen enough, but their weakness is,
they don't know how to organize. And no good with machinery. I set their ploughs and help repair their tractors. And I
have to fill in their forms. They all employ far too much
labour, but most of it's unpaid—relatives, glad to be fed. I
hope they'll make out, but they've a lot to learn."

The farmers they displaced have gone south. Out of the
frying pan into the fire? "They're not South Africans, they're
Kenyans, like me; but down south the Government does
everything to help them. Why did they quit? Stock thefts,

mainly. Thefts of all kinds. It's got out of hand. I keep guards night and day on my maize and cattle, and even then you never know, every morning, what will have gone in the night. What sort of life is that?"

These Afrikaners hold to their creed, community and faith with a tenacity alien to the compromising British—much as Africans hold to their tribe. Soon after the Lancaster House conference they met in Eldoret, their local town, to consider the future. The intention of the British Goverment to hand over to a wholly African government was now plain. (No doubt it should have been before, but the universal human reluctance to accept unpalatable facts had been reinforced by assurances and pledges to the whites which the British Ministers who made them must have known could not possibly be honoured.)

These Afrikaner farmers knew land hunger when they saw it. They knew the Africans wanted their land and believed they would get it, once they had control. And many could not stomach the idea of African rule. Yet this feeling was not universal among Kenya-born Afrikaners. One, who takes time off from farming to hunt crocodiles, needed a permit from a district officer, and found that a young African had taken over the job. The Afrikaner returned to report: "I had more help and courtesy from him, man, than I've had from any white D.O. in all these years." He is staying on.

The grandfathers of nearly all these Afrikaners reached the Uasin Gishu Plateau in one of several organized treks between 1908 and 1912. Now most of their descendants decided to trek back again. Once more they gathered up their possessions: tractors, cars, implements, dogs, household goods, everything. The exodus started in mid-1961. Like the northward treks of fifty or sixty years earlier, these were carefully planned. The Dutch Reformed Church on the Uasin Gishu

is divided into three branches, and each branch organized
its own group, headed by the predikant. They went south
overland in a procession of cars, trucks, tractors and trailers.
One man built a caravan to take all his possessions; it caught
fire and everything was burned, including his money, which
he'd taken in currency notes.

This southward trek didn't make a clean sweep of the
Afrikaner community. The farmers agreed amongst themselves that some would stay behind to work the land. No
farm land on the Uasin Gishu was abandoned or allowed to
go out of cultivation. Those who stayed leased it, at fair
rentals, from those who went. Since 1961, seasons have been
kind and farming, by and large, profitable. Most of the leases
run for three or four years. After that what will happen?

"We have a tale about two men who were ploughing. God
appeared to one and called him to become an angel, the other
was left trudging on. Here if your farm is in the right place,
the Government will buy it and you become an angel; if it's
in the wrong place, you're left trudging on. Is that fair?
Either the Government should make an offer for our land
or it should find money for Africans to buy it." (This, through
the Land Bank, the Kenya Government is attempting to do.)

The Afrikaner who voiced these opinions, a man of fifty,
was still farming his inherited land. Going or staying?

"At first I thought I'd stay despite the risks; I'm Kenya-
born, I get on with the people. And I don't believe they want
us to go. The other day I was in the bank in Eldoret, drawing
South African currency—I went down south to have a look
round. A Nandi chief I know was standing next to me.
'What's that money for?' he asked. 'I'm clearing out,' I told
him. 'You can't do that!' he said. 'I can. I'm fed up with all
of you, all the *matata*, all the politics. You don't want us here.
I'm off.' 'You can't do that!' he repeated. 'How can you leave

us? We don't want you to go.' I believe that was genuine.
There's no personal ill-will." Mr. Kenyatta, the Prime Minister, has since publicly stated the same view.

Then why did this Afrikaner change his mind? He hesi-
tated, searching for words. "Farming's a creative thing. You
can't farm without thinking of the future. You go round,
you think: 'There might be water here, a new borehole; I'd
like to try this new grass they're recommending for leys; I
might rest that bit of cultivation next year. . . .' You farm
for your sons.

"Now I hate to ride over my land. I know I'll never sink
a new borehole; it won't be my cattle that'll graze the leys.
My sons won't come after me. All the creativeness is cut
away."

When the Afrikaner trekkers reached the Uasin Gishu
Plateau they found rolling, open, unstocked pastures, clear
rivers, lush grass and tall timber, herds and herds of game—
it was like a dream, a vision of the Promised Land. They
settled, shot, built, ploughed and made it all productive—
wheat and cattle, butterfat and maize. It is a smiling, sweeping countryside, golden when the corn is ripening, green
after rain. Now that dream is over, and from the hills that
ring the plateau its African inheritors are moving down to
claim their estate.

A View from a Pedestal

From a traffic circle opposite the New Stanley Hotel the hawk-nosed countenance of the late Lord Delamere, in bronze, used to gaze pensively towards what was the bar of Torr's Hotel, in his day a rendezvous for airline pilots, white hunters and the remnants, getting rather tatty even then, of the current occupants of the Happy Valley. Now it is the Ottoman Bank, and it seems unlikely that the white settlers' *m'zee* [1] will enjoy his view of it much longer: statues of the father figures of colonialism don't, as a rule, long survive *uhuru,* and the portlier figure of Mr. Jomo Kenyatta, the black settlers' *m'zee,* perhaps will soon be gazing down what used to be Delamere Avenue.

If he were to look the other way, at the Thorn Tree, the trellis-shaded pavement café attached to the New Stanley Hotel, he would see in an hour citizens of half the world's nations and more than half its races. Package tours from Frankfurt pour in as deputations from Somalia depart; Japanese trade missions brush shoulders with Brazilian coffee delegations or Yugoslavian advisers on industrial planning; trade unionists from Zanzibar consort with educationists from Indonesia. Twelve French-speaking Chinese students from

[1] "The old one," a term of respect imputing wisdom, like elder or senator.

Mauritius study at the Royal College, down the way. Tourists embarking on a day flight to a game park, and hung about with cameras, high-powered lenses, tripods, meters and binoculars like a medieval knight in armour all aclank with breastplates, visors and greaves, refresh themselves next to duskier French-speaking pan-Africanists shuttling between Addis Ababa and Dar es Salaam to hammer a few more nails into the coffin of the ancient empire of Portugal. Languid Indian girls in pastel-shaded tinsel-bordered saris adjoin weather-beaten English gardening ladies, bringing to mind secateurs and deadheads, fresh from chilly uplands, where they successfully cultivate crocuses, jonquils and daffodils.

Nairobi used to be one of the nastiest capitals in the world: dirty, dusty, squalid and at the same time pretentious, a frontier town whose sprinkling of flashily overdressed safari visitors, minor film stars and local glamour types, imitating celluloid white hunters, gave it an air of bogus Hollywood or failed St.-Tropez. Now it has become one of the most attractive and certainly the most flowery of capitals. Those banks of cherry-red and flaming orange bougainvillaeas, of ramping golden shower and other flowering shrubs and trees, which you pass through as you drive along Princess Elizabeth Way, must present one of the finest approaches to any city in the world, or at any rate on this continent.

Nairobi teems with bluebell-flowering jacarandas; hibiscuses and beds of succulents lurk in every spare corner. Most of the former stuffy little wooden rabbit-hutchlike buildings with rusty corrugated-iron roofs have been replaced by glittering modern concrete towers of dubious merit but a good deal of dash, inventiveness and often colour, which go well in this bright and brittle montane atmosphere.

The streets are lined with sun-reflecting, eye-assaulting parked cars and at rush hours choked with opulent-looking traffic; every empty lot is a parking lot crammed with vehicles and is the scene of savage encounters around eight in the morning, when offices open, among converging commuters in search of parking space. In places segments of empty lots have been fenced off, for some reason; and here, overshadowed by off-white or light grey or speckled concrete towers, little plots of maize have sprung up, tended by barefoot Kikuyu women in their shapeless cotton dresses, bent industriously over their hoes among the modern buildings.

Living Space

There's still, of course, plenty of squalor. Just off centre, those grubby narrow streets lined with Asian shops smelling of spices, secondhand clothing and sweating humanity, and the narrow alleys, designed as sanitary lanes for night-soil collecting and smelling of urine, haven't changed; and on the perimeter there's still a vast, ever-growing, subsistence-level African population packed into accommodations that remain, for the most part, depressingly sordid—ugly little bare boxes dumped down on a hot, flat, treeless kind of wasteland, spattered with sentry-box latrines.

The City Council keeps rehousing people as fast as its taxpayers can, and all sorts of benefactors are weighing in with aid; but Nairobi is a magnet drawing Africans from the Ethiopian border to the shores of Lake Nyasa, from Zanzibar to the Mountains of the Moon, and the Council keeps pounding along behind the population statistics like a Kafka-type figure trying to catch a train that's perpetually just pulling out of the station.

Nairobi started as a centre where men came to work, leaving their families at home, and all that had to be provided was "bed space" for single men. Hence the region known as

Kariokor—from Carrier Corps, that great African army of foot porters of World War I. Rows of barracklike little rooms seemed, in that day and age, thoroughly progressive: iron-roofed instead of thatched, in straight rows instead of scattered higgledy-piggledy, furnished with water from stand-pipes instead of hauled by women in old four-gallon paraffin tins.

Soon the families arrived and, such was the degree of over-crowding, two or three broods often crammed themselves into the stable-like accommodations meant for a single man. Kariokor became a slum. Others built their own shelters out of rusty gasoline tins beaten flat and bits of sacking, minus floors, windows or sanitation—the epitome of squalor. Eventually the city fathers faced the reality that Nairobi's Africans were no longer country folk come to town for a spell, each to return to his tribal arcady, but permanent city dwellers in need of family homes. So there arose new housing estates grouped round central halls, and schools and shops and clinics, not to mention beer halls, and equipped with the basic urban services: still, to the eye, bare and stark and ugly, but at least relatively decent and planned, and planted with caged trees. So Kariokor has gone, bulldozed out, and greatly superior houses are to arise on its flattened ruins.

Apartments and houses for white-collar workers reflect an almost wholly Westernized style of living. Almost but not quite, because so many wives have halted so much lower down the educational ladder than their spouses; some have barely had a chance to climb at all. That is one of Africa's tragedies: there just aren't enough educated girls to go round. A tragedy that's deep and wide, causes much frustration and can be resolved only by time.

These are neat little houses, each with a small front patch of garden and a larger patch behind, where tenants grow vegetables in a bleak, intractable, fine grey soil. There's a sitting room, a small dining room and a kitchen where a charcoal fire burns, a stew simmers and tots and babies cluster when they're not outside sitting in the sun, perhaps cared for by a wrinkle-faced grandmother or great-aunt, moved for keeps into some corner with her blanket and bowl.

I spoke to the wife of a clerk in the City Hall, clad in the inevitable head scarf and clean but washed-out, shapeless cotton dress, with a baby never far from the breast. She spoke no English, but welcomed her visitors with self-possession, calm and poise. The unheralded invasion of her home by pink-faced strangers she appeared neither to acclaim nor resent, nor did she allow it to interrupt the gentle rhythm of routine; it simply happened, and must be taken not so much in her stride as in her amble, as she might step round a plant or over a stone.

Yes, she said, she liked the house very much, there was room in it for everyone, food in the larder and a school close by, and a clinic where she took the baby every month to be weighed. She liked the city. She liked water in a tap. She liked having plenty of neighbours.

African good manners preclude the grousing with which a British housewife might greet an uninvited visitor, but here did appear to be a satisfied customer. Her soft chocolate, glowing skin seemed almost to exude, with its ripe and earthy bloom, a sort of fullness and contentment. To her sisters dwelling at home, off every morning very soon after sunrise to hoe and dig all day long, returning at dusk bent under a heavy load of firewood or water, I suppose she was living like a princess in a fairy story—water springing forth at her touch, a larder filled as if by magic, well-clad children mastering the mystery of letters, a husband on a bicycle—the whole family, above all, enfolded in an aura of *heshima*. She basked in the glow of that *heshima,* and smiled gently as she stirred the meaty stew.

We called next on a housewife who had been a teacher, spoke good English and was probably as well educated as her husband, a fellow teacher—they had met at their training college—who had gone into business. He was a Tanganyikan, she a Luo; a portent, maybe, of the coming Africa, where one day tribes and races will blend.

Small, relatively skinny, alert, she showed us with pride round her apartment with its cheap but well-polished furniture, its parlour table with a cloth embroidered by her pupils; family photographs on the walls, a few paperbacks on a shelf; white bread, drippings and a pot of jam in the larder, a bicycle and a battered baby carriage amid the charcoal in the shed—the seeds of Western life in its material aspects.

All these new apartments and houses are wired for electricity, and some already have their cookers. Sales of electric kettles, irons, hot plates and the rest of the gadgets rise year by year. The spin-drier, the dishwasher and the keeping up with the Kamaus are well on the way. A richer life, or the death of contentment? Both, perhaps.

Bougainvillaea Town

Well within living memory a sergeant of the Royal Engineers, George Ellis, built a depot for stores needed by Captain Sclater, who was making a road of sorts from the Masai plain over the Kikuyu hills. Unknowingly he gave birth to Nairobi, which was chosen in 1898 as a site for the railway's workshops because it was the last flat place where locomotives could manoeuvre before their steep haul began. So an ugly, sprawling collection of huts and tents and corrugated-iron sheds arose on the shadeless plain where lions hunted, and rhinos fell an easy prey to bearded engineers.

In 1947 a Mr. Peter Greensmith, equipped with no more horticultural training than wartime service in the Royal Navy could afford, walked with mounting gloom from the station along Government Road. Dusty, shadeless, unkempt and filthy—he remembers human excreta and a dead dog—the place stank.

Mr. Greensmith's disgusted inclination was to take the next train back to Mombasa and never set foot in the place again. But he had the promise of a job with a firm of nurserymen. Some years later he answered an advertisement, secured a junior municipal post and, remembering his dreadful first impression, resolved to do his utmost to brighten up the city.

Before long he found himself in charge of its all but non-existent parks. I don't know when he started on the bougainvillaeas, which today give Nairobi half its character, these and the jacarandas and hibiscuses: horticulturally it's a bougainvillaea town. And now he revealed not only the greenest of fingers, but a talent for making plants play tricks. Bougainvillaeas and bignonias are creepers, and before that had always crept, or climbed rather, clinging to veranda posts, trees, roofs, walls, anything. Mr. Greensmith obliged bougainvillaeas to stand on their own feet, like standard roses, and bignonias to creep about on the ground like a vetch; hence the glories of Princess Elizabeth Way. The idea of turning bougainvillaeas into standards came to him, he says, in a flash one day when he noticed a creeper that had been snapped off in a storm.

How he bullies or persuades them never to go into eclipse is something of a mystery. Those that show signs of flagging are whisked away, possibly in the dead of night, and replaced by others waiting in his ample nurseries. "The secret," he said, "is to grow everything on until it's very large and strong, then to move it quickly with a gang; every year we must move hundreds of tons of soil."

Besides the major city park, umbrageous and set with flowering trees, little parks have sprung up in odd corners; every traffic circle bulges with creepers and succulents, every verge with trained, obedient shrubs. No wonder the Mayor, Alderman Charles Rubia, and his Councillors are proud of what has been done. It isn't easy to find money anywhere for beauty when the bare necessities go short; in continuing to do so the City Council has shown a degree of courage and imagination rare among the elected rulers of frontier townships grown into commercial capitals.

Teutonic Aid

Help for Nairobi's development comes nowadays from unexpected quarters. American aid is taken perhaps too much for granted, but why are the Germans weighing in? Keeping up with the Americans, a form of *heshima*? Afraid of letting in the Russians? Hoping to reap a commercial harvest?

The spokesman of the Federal German Republic to whom I put these queries might have been chosen as a kind of Mr. West Germany: he was handsome, blond, dynamic, energetic, outspoken, fluent, with a mordant kind of humour that might congeal, one felt, into a purpose too inflexible to admit the lighter touch.

"The German objective," he briskly said, "is to help relieve the U.K. of part of the burden of fitting her colonies for independence. The U.K. is our ally in NATO: we mean to relieve her burden, not to take advantage of her position. A stable and prosperous West will be impossible if Africa's disturbed. Kenya's a potential trouble spot. We mean to help raise living standards and bring contentment to the people, and so checkmate unrest."

To this end, Germany is backing many schemes: the extension of Nairobi's water supplies; scholarships for students; development of the Royal College; and three quarters of the total is going into resettlement schemes. "We don't advertise ourselves, there's nothing to be pointed to as 'done by Germany'—all the money goes into development that will help the people help themselves. We Germans are not going to throw away our money. What we spend will go to the objects we decided to spend it on, not into the pockets of politicians. Not a penny shall we give to any party or to any individual.

"We have the advantage here of a clean sheet," he frankly added. "Africans do not hate us Germans. They do hate the British—not as individuals, as colonialists. Shall I tell you one reason? Your English language, which of course reflects your English character, is a root cause. It's ambiguous, vague, apologetic; no one knows what you mean. You reply with phrases which can be taken either way. In fact, you use the language as a smoke screen to hide your intentions, you advance crabwise, as if you were afraid of direct speech."

Launched on what was evidently a favourite theme, he gave an example. "*A*," he said, "rings up *B* to inquire after the health of *B*'s wife, who has just died. 'Well, actually, she's no better.' And there she is, lying dead on the couch. Knowing that already, *A* replies: 'Sorry to hear that, old man. A worry . . . this weather . . . perhaps a change of air. . . .' 'I'm afraid not. Kind of you to inquire. . . .' At no point does anyone say nakedly: 'She's dead.' "

This critic added: "A dose of our blunt, direct German speech is good for Africans. They know where they stand. That, they prefer."

As director of a cultural offensive he was distributing, free of charge, forty of the best German televisions sets to African schools and community centres. The Americans were hitting back with two hundred sets, but these were secondhand. The Africans were sitting tight on the receiving end, like a damsel in her hut, importuned by suitors offering herds and flocks of fat cattle, sheep and goats.

The Asian Squeeze

Nairobi's Royal College started as a polytechnic, and is therefore in the heart of the city, squeezed in among commercial buildings like Oxford or Manchester, not set apart on some arcadian rural site like Sussex or Norwich or, on this continent, Dar es Salaam. Its architects have had to make the best of cramped conditions and, by and large, have done so; its new buildings are varied, lively and sometimes imaginative—although it is a pity so many British architects seem always to be haunted by the gable, which crops up here, in muted form, on the library façade. But it is surely right, in these sunlit places, to have plenty of glitter and bravura, and occasional gimmicks like the mushroom-shaped water tower of the engineering laboratory and its wavy roof, or the V-shaped pillars of the science building patterned with grey chips of local marble, or the forest of globular light fittings, like a fistful of balloons, that fill the upper reaches of the library's big central hall.

Out of every hundred students at this college one of the three components of the University of East Africa, forty are Asian and ten—or slightly less—European, the rest African. All over East Africa, Asians are getting anxious. By and large their young are clever, hard-working, ambitious and meek; at this college many qualify as engineers. Yet, when they graduate, few find local jobs; some have failed to do so here and succeeded in Britain.

Africanization is the reason. Railways and harbours, electricity supply, public works and private industry, all need qualified engineers but for political reasons want them to be black, not brown.

The irony of it is that there are very, very few African engineers, not nearly enough to go round; nor can there be for many years. So public services especially go short of engineers and qualified practitioners go jobless. Promoting untrained or ill-trained people to fill the gap may lead to trouble. It's true that the arcane aspect of modern expertise is often overstressed; professional skills are elevated into mysteries comparable with those of the ancient Egyptian priesthood. (One thinks of the Suez Canal and its pilots.) Nevertheless, if there are two occupations in which a proper professional training seems desirable they are medicine and engineering. Most of us would feel reluctant to have a hole in our heart mended by a laboratory assistant or to work in a power station designed by apprentices.

Women Students

About fifteen out of every hundred students are girls. Their halls of residence, gleaming with newness, are luxurious by any standard; by the standards of most British universities, right out of this world.

Each student has her own room, decorated in dusky pink, pale blue or primrose yellow; her built-in desk, her study light and bedside light and window with a view through eucalyptus trees over a park to the roofs or, at night, the twinkling lights of the city. Tiled white bathrooms, laundry with racks for drying, ironing boards, constant hot water;

common rooms with gay modern curtains, deep armchairs, carpets, reading lights, a television set; a graceful dining hall in the shape of a crescent, set with tables for four or six; behind the scenes, all-electric kitchens with everything up-to-the-minute; a corps of cooks headed by a Goan; excellent meals designed by a professional caterer.

As I looked at this handsome hall full of trim, decorous, quiet-voiced girls in scarlet gowns, like bedded-out poinsettias, there was no reason to marvel because they were Africans. Yet marvel, a little, I did. Even today many of these girls come from round thatched peasant huts shared with sheep fattening under the bed and goats walking in and out; their sisters are still beasts of burden, who undergo circumcision, marry at fourteen and give birth to babies in old, crude and primitive conditions. Even those from what are called superior homes, maintained by teachers, parsons and civil servants, may return in the holidays to share a poky room with eight or ten children, study by smoky paraffin lamps, revert to stodgy meals of maize meal and beans.

So wide and deep is this gulf across which they are continually being shuttled that one would expect them to develop split personalities. To live at once in two worlds so wholly dissimilar—has this ever been asked before of adolescent humans quite so abruptly? And do others always realize what this day and age demand of these young? It's a wonder to me that they are sane, rather than that some are, on occasion, awkward, difficult and unpredictable.

I met some of these students over coffee after dinner. Most of them were Asians. Perhaps because they feel protected from uncertainties by their own ancient culture and traditions, like a grub in its cocoon, these girls seemed more at ease, poised and forthcoming than their African colleagues, more free from shoulder chips. Their manners were soft and charming like their saris, their movements graceful and controlled, their intelligence sensitive and fluid. It is said that Asian women are more repressed than Africans, more family-ridden, more subservient to custom and religion. And it is, I believe, a fact that there are virtually no Asian prostitutes.

African girls equipped with a sixth-form education who can therefore sit for university entrance examinations are almost as rare. Most girls at the Royal College are students of domestic science, whose academic demands are lighter than those needed to sit for a degree.

One of these students came from a kingdom called Ankole and from its ruling race, the Bahima, who emerged from the north several hundred years ago to conquer the Bantu people of the Lake Victoria basin. It was among the Bahima that the strange and cruel custom of bride-fattening was followed. Imprisoned in their huts, the girls were forcibly fed through long reeds on milk, milk and more milk, until they grew so fat they couldn't walk, and crawled about on the floor. The first Europeans to see them described how their flesh hung down from their elbows like huge boiled puddings.

It is hard to imagine why this gross obesity became associated in Bahima eyes with beauty, value and breeding, but apparently it did, and many years passed before they could be persuaded to abandon the custom. It has not been practiced for at least a generation and perhaps Chloe, the student from Ankole (slim as a model), had scarcely heard of it, but she deplored other practices that still prevail. One was the bride price. "It's become a racket," she said. "In my part of Uganda the man must pay five thousand shillings [seven hundred dollars]. Who can afford that? It means debt from the start. Everyone knows it can never be paid, so it becomes a kind of blackmail.

"And then everyone must have a Christian wedding. At a

Christian wedding you must have bought food—mainly bread and jam—but at a pagan wedding you can have beer and meat. You don't have to pay for this; relations make the beer and bring sheep. But no one dares to have a pagan wedding these days. It's all bread and jam, and expensive cakes."

When the Royal College started, two women's halls were built side by side, but separate. One was to be for Europeans, the other for Africans and Asians. No one could envisage the races living together under one roof. This was less than six years ago. Now the two halls have been linked by a bridge, and have become one unit. All races share them, and no one can envisage anything else. So quickly has opinion changed.

Do these students realize how lucky they are, by the standards of almost any other country—certainly of Britain—to have everything laid on, such comfort and luxury, so much attention (a teaching ratio of roughly one to five), nothing to pay, a choice of jobs, the world at their feet? Of course not; whoever does? They take it all as their right. The danger is that they will grow arrogant, careless and frustrated when gainsaid. There are always dangers. These girls are confronted by a formidable prospect of leadership. They are so few, those without opportunities so many. By their very existence they are setting standards, raising questions, propagating doubts.

Kenya's Benenden

A good many of them received their earlier training at the African Girls' High School, about fifteen miles out of the city: Kenya's oldest girls' secondary school, the first to introduce a sixth form and to pioneer in science teaching. Yet it was only at the end of 1963 that the first of its pupils sat for their Cambridge Higher School Certificate, which matches the British A-level and opens the doors of universities to the successful candidates.

I arrived at a dramatic moment, at the same time as the ordinary School Certificate results. The teachers were gathered for tea in the house of Miss Mary Bruce, the headmistress, a forceful, down-to-earth, exceedingly competent Highland Scot from Caithness, who in any company would stand out as a personality to be reckoned with. All her staff are Europeans; there is not, as yet, a single African graduate woman teacher in the country. Miss Bruce read the results to a staff whose members could scarcely have been more excited had they been listening to news of, let's say, the destruction of all the nuclear weapons in the world. Had Rhoda really passed in physics? Could Kisia have failed in French? Wanjui —how had she scraped through in chemistry? Alas, poor Phoebe, undone by geography. . . . Only two, I think, had failed completely.

Miss Bruce grapples with a chronic shortage of money for everything. The money goes to the boys; girls' education stands and begs at the bottom of the queue. Pupils must be fed for one shilling (fourteen cents) a day. (It costs about two shillings a day to feed an Alsatian dog.) Still, I saw a satisfying stew heaped on the plates of three girls living in an old-style African hut, untraditional in that it had a window and a concrete floor, otherwise of the normal bush pattern. All the girls take it in turn to live for a week in this hut, in trios, to apply domestic science to the peasant conditions into which they nearly all plunge back during the holidays, and which most of their relatives will never quit.

Here is this gap again, this dichotomy between the peasant hut and the academy of Western learning. It does, in the opinion of their teachers, cause among the girls tensions and psychological upsets. These girls quite often suffer from mysterious complaints almost certainly of psychosomatic origin.

What about circumcision? "My guess is," said Miss Bruce, "that the majority haven't been circumcised. Most of them come from Christian homes, and all have been to schools run by missions. But I don't know. I've had several come to me and tell me that in the holidays they've been forcibly circumcised."

On average, about one pupil a term leaves because of pregnancy. No doubt this is a higher proportion than would be found at Benenden, but then the senior girls here are considerably older. It is almost certainly a lower proportion than would be common in many American high schools, and probably some British comprehensive ones. One third of all British brides, after all, now reach the altar in the family way.

Are these girls beginning to rebel against their immemorial subjection? Yes, the teachers think, a change is coming slowly, very slowly. Only that week two girls had written to one of the Nairobi newspapers to deplore the use of women as beasts of burden; men, they sensibly suggested, should build wheelbarrows. And a few question the bride price. But these critical shoots have just started to thrust up through the heavy clay of custom, consolidated by the feet of so many centuries.

Politics seldom touch off sparks in their minds. They are encouraged to discuss such matters in debates and in classes on current affairs. To them, conformity makes more sense than freedom of opinion. The principle of free speech found few supporters in a recent debate. They considered that opposition to the ruling party shouldn't be allowed.

"Miss Bruce," the teacher pointed out, "is a Presbyterian. Suppose she were to say: 'Anyone here who isn't a Presbyterian will be expelled.' Would that be right?" Cries of "Yes, yes, of course that is right," greeted this. The idea of tolerating views you disagree with is an alien one. "We're trying to drub it in," the teachers added. Will it stick? They shook their heads. "Here and there, perhaps, a little. But it won't go deep."

It may be poor, Miss Bruce's school, but the setting is lovely. Tall trees cast long shadows over fresh green lawns, sunlight sparkles, there are blue and mauve and golden creepers, brilliant shrubs, simple whitewashed buildings—simplest of all, a little chapel built from local wood and stone by local carpenters and masons, as plain and honest as homespun cloth. The girls wear simple blue dresses. In a form room, with plain and scarred old desks, a bare scrubbed floor, charts tacked to walls in need of paint, sixth-formers were poring over the works of Blake, Milton and Cowper. They had been acting *She Stoops to Conquer.* One of them assured me that Jane Austen was her favourite author. These are the chosen ones, mounted on a cloud of *heshima,* savouring the strange fruit of the tree of knowledge: the destined brides of future Ministers, Permanent Secretaries, judges, generals and ambassadors. Even if Milton, Blake and Cowper wielded flaming swords, for the sake of the treasure that they guard these obdurate angels would be worth overcoming.

Special Centre

The phrase "Special Centre" might mean anything. In fact, it means a tall, gentle, dedicated Irish scholar called Charles O'Hagan, and his centre is a couple of rooms opening off a long corridor on the top storey of Nairobi's City Hall.

After a career spent in the Indian educational service, where he became deeply versed in several Asian languages, he retired to continue his studies on methods of teaching English—not just its vocabulary and grammar, but the *tongue,* the phrases as tongue and mind unite to shape them, alive and colloquial, into the instrument of meaning. A lifetime of experience had convinced him that the only way to do this was to begin at the beginning, and the beginning was the very small child; not a child already literate in his own tongue, who would thenceforward always translate the words into English. His amazingly bold intention was that the child should *think* in English, and learn from the outset to express the sounds in symbols on paper in a foreign tongue.

Then he emerged from his retirement, enlisted in the Kenya educational service and set to work, with the help of three disciples, to train teachers to apply these revolutionary ideas in Asian primary schools. The methods worked, and now are spreading like a bush fire in African schools.

If these teaching methods take root, spread and become universal, as they surely must, I believe that Mr. Charles O'Hagan will have done more than any other living individual to overcome the biggest single obstacle to the intellectual advancement of those Africans inhabiting the former British dependencies. This obstacle is an imperfect knowledge of English, due not to an incapacity to learn it but to bad teaching.

This bad teaching takes place in the primary schools where the foundations of knowledge are laid. It is not really anyone's fault, it is simply that the great majority of primary school teachers have themselves learned poor English from teachers indifferently trained. Not until they reach a secondary school, as few manage to, can most Africans learn English from an English teacher—one, that is, to whom English is the mother tongue.

No wonder the standard of spoken English among all but the most highly educated is, by and large, atrocious. The great majority of African pupils, including university students, lack the comprehension of English needed to grasp ideas which lie within the range of their minds. The intelligence is there, ready to receive the concept; the concept is there, ready for conveyance; between the two, lines of communication—the language—have broken down.

Not only is English badly taught in most primary schools, but—and this is the nub of Mr. O'Hagan's thesis—it is the wrong kind of English: the written, not the spoken, word. A stiff, awkward form of English the pen may shape but the mind will never use to clothe a living thought. Symbols arranged upon a sheet of paper may enable children to pass examinations but never to pass on an unpremeditated thought, capture a half-formed notion or bridge the tantalizing gap between mind and human mind.

In schools which follow Special Centre methods, English is spoken before it is written, and spoken from the day the six-year-old arrives to start his school career in Standard I. And everything is taught in English. This, not the vernacular, is the language of instruction from the start.

Two of the Special Centre's teaching staff of three, Miss Crowhurst and Miss Honey, took me to a school at Pumwani, one of Nairobi's African townships. To the wall was pinned a chart covered with red triangles, blue circles and yellow squares. The teacher—a young, sturdy Luo woman with two or three children of her own—was taking Standard I.

"Show me a triangle." A forest of hands shot up. "You, Kamau." Taking the pointer, the chosen boy walked over to the chart and tapped the right design. "This is a triangle." "Yes, that is a triangle," the teacher agreed; and all the class echoed, forming each word carefully and fully: "That is a triangle."

"Is it a blue triangle?" "No, it is a red triangle." "That's right, it is a red triangle." And the class pronounced: "That is not a blue triangle, it is a red triangle." Next it was the turn of Kimotho to demonstrate a yellow square, then of Otieno to select a blue circle, and so on, through the class. All the pupils take up the words. Everyone is involved, no one is left out.

Stage by stage they proceed to more advanced exercises. Fresh pictures appear on the walls, depicting common objects: a clock, an elephant, a coat, a rose, a fish, a table, a pair of scissors, a ladder, a bicycle. There is something slightly wrong with each brightly coloured picture. Where is the fault? Who will spot that the clock has one digit missing, the elephant's tusks are in the wrong place, the coat has lost a sleeve, one of the table legs is crooked, there's a rung out of the ladder and the cycle has one round and one square wheel?

"Special Centre methods," my guides explained, "create a completely different relationship between teacher and child. The teacher doesn't just stand there telling her pupils, she takes part *with* the children; it's a joint activity, they're all finding things out together. The effect on the teacher is every bit as great as on the pupils. Her mind seems to wake up. She behaves quite differently, and there's no problem of discipline."

No child is stationary for long; he spends the morning walking about, picking up and putting down pencils, tins, oranges, books, anything he can see; touching doors, windows, walls, chairs, to identify them; drawing with chalks; modelling with plasticine. His whole body is at work, not just his mind.

In Standard II the children were acting a spontaneous little play—all, of course, in English; almost the only strict rule is that no word of any other language may be spoken.

A heap of old clothes lay in one corner. A boy put on a tattered coat, grinning; everyone tittered, and boy gravely announced: "This is the father." A girl detached herself and found a dress. "This is the mother." Two others came forward to be the children, and one the baby, stationed in another corner of the room.

The first boy walked across to the table. "This is the dining room. Mother, is it time for tea?" From the girl: "I am in the kitchen, getting the tea. Yes, it's time for tea." The boy calls out: "Come in, children, it's time for our tea." And so the mime continues: the children wash their hands and faces, the girl helps her mother to bake some cakes, the boy brings the baby, they sit down and begin to eat an imaginary repast, they stir in milk and sugar, the children finish and go out to play.

Nothing much to it, perhaps; and yet it was impressive; the children were so patently enjoying themselves in the use of their imaginations and sense of mimicry, and their English was remarkable for its clarity, simplicity and force. It was unlikely that any one of these children had ever heard an English sentence spoken by an Englishman. They came from a dozen different tribes, from poor homes and overcrowded lodgings, but they spoke with an air, acted with spirit and moved with speed and bounce.

In a few years, when these children have worked their way up through the schools, there will be a generation accustomed to speak and understand and *think* in English in a wholly new way. This must affect profoundly the children's own self-confidence and therefore happiness, and the understanding between man and man across racial and tribal barriers. It is a tragedy that all this did not take place twenty years ago.

There is one danger. In the flush of pride that fills all new nations when they gain their independence, symbols become cardinal. Language is a symbol of freedom. As free men, you naturally want to use your own tongue, not someone else's, least of all that of the departed rulers.

Tanganyika has adopted Swahili as the national language, making it compulsory in all schools. Will Kenya follow suit? There is less reason. Swahili has for long been more widely spoken in Tanganyika than anywhere else in Africa except Zanzibar. It is nobody's native language in Kenya except at the Coast. But it is a Bantu language, easier on the tongue than English; above all, it is African. Since nationalists for long opposed the use of Swahili as part of a colonialist plot to hold them back and prevent them from understanding English, it will be ironic if they now swing round to support it as an expression of the African personality. But such ironies abound.

Nationalism is a Janus. One face looks towards a radical, egalitarian, industrialized and Westernized future; the other back towards a dignified, traditional, harmonious and culturally creative past. Another dichotomy. One of the nationalists' hardest tasks will be to reconcile the two.

NEW MEN

The M'Zee

Modern Africa is a land of fairy stories come true: of Dick Whittingtons walking barefoot to the city without even a bundle of belongings, let alone a cat, to become its venerated mayor; of woodcutters' sons transmuted into princes, foundlings into Prime Ministers, Cinderellas from a round mud hut into ambassadors' wives. Anything can happen; there is magic in the air.

Can there be a more extraordinary story than Mr. Jomo Kenyatta's? Can any man before him, throughout all recorded history, have spanned such changes in a single lifetime? Most nationalist leaders grew to manhood in a world already brought within the ambit of the West. Mr. Kenyatta, now probably over seventy, was born into an Africa whose tribal pattern had remained essentially unchanged for centuries. It is said that he was ten before he ever saw a white man; when he did, that white man was a Scots missionary, Dr. Arthur, who may have saved his life by operating on his spine. His name was then Kamau wa Ngengi. This was probably in 1902 or 1903.

He stayed on at the mission near Kikuyu, went to its little Bible school, was baptized and took the name of Johnstone. One of the earliest literates, he found a clerical post in the nearby capital and made no mark until the birth of the Young Kikuyu Association, formed soon after World War I by Harry Thuku. Here was the conception in Kenya of the nationalist movement, an embryo that came to birth as an independent nation on December 12, 1963, rather more than forty years later.

Mr. Kenyatta was in the movement from the start. Harry Thuku's prototype became the Kikuyu Central Association, then the Kenya African Union, and finally there emerged KANU, with Jomo Kenyatta as its president. And so the boy born into a crude Kikuyu hut, nurtured in pagan lore, clad in goatskins, taught to hurl a spear and use a bow, cleansed of tabus by drinking concoctions made of the undigested contents of a sacrificed goat, unaware even that men could record their speech in symbols or ease their burdens by such devices as the wheel or pump or plough, oblivious of all the cities and ships and kingdoms of the outer world: this boy became the venerated head of an independent modern state, commander in chief of a mechanized army, master of a nation trading with the nations of the world, walking with his fly whisk and shrewd eye through the courtyards of a mansion built for the proconsuls, lord of its spacious rooms and splendid gardens, its white-gloved attendants and family portraits and glass and silver on the polished tables and all the pomp. Goatherd into governor: a true story as fabulous as any fantasy invented by the most imaginative teller of tales.

I met him first in 1936, when we were fellow students at the London School of Economics, attending seminars on anthropology conducted by Professor Malinowski and Dr. Raymond Firth. In the discussions he was fluent, alert, cogent and authoritative—one of the stars. Already in his mid-forties, he was preparing his monograph on his own Kikuyu people, *Facing Mount Kenya,* to which Professor Malinowski gave

171

high praise. He dedicated his book to the mythical ancestors of his tribe, believed to have originated from an Eve called Mumbi, whose nine sons founded its nine clans, "in the firm faith that the dead, the living and the unborn will unite to rebuild the destroyed shrines."

There was the Janus look of nationalism: the old, destroyed and sacred shrines exercising their magic to unite the people, evict the conqueror and then (still using magic) create a bustling modern nation with an international airport, a nuclear-weaponed army, a favourable balance of payments, a seat at the United Nations and health, wealth and happiness for all.

Now and again we lunched together at a Chinese restaurant, where he was a genial, loquacious and sometimes evasive companion, whose conversation hinted at the tortuosity masked by humour common to almost every intelligent man of his tribe. The spark of oratory was always smouldering, but a crowd provided the bellows; then he could become as compelling as a modern Savonarola or Mark Antony, riveting by devious subtlety an African audience.

He was always a showman. Even in his London days, which lasted for fifteen years, he wore the now familiar heavy ring with its dark stone—a garnet, is it, or carnelian?—and carried an ebony walking stick, although I cannot remember whether it had an elephant's head, like today's, or whether, like the fly whisk and beaded cap, that came later. To aid the cause of what was then called subversion, but now the struggle against colonialism, he would be photographed in a leopard skin, gripping tribal weapons, above the caption "Burning Spear."

He was bearded, thickset, dressed with style, deep-voiced, affable and active. During this period he twice visited Russia; made friends with such Labour stalwarts as Mr. Fenner

Brockway, Mr. Hale and Mr. Creech Jones; shared a flat with
Peter Abrahams and Paul Robeson; lectured for the Workers'
Educational Association and worked in a nursery garden;
married an English schoolteacher and begot a son. After the
war he joined with George Padmore, Dr. Nkrumah, the
American Negro writer Dr. W. E. Du Bois and others to form
a Pan-African federation centred on Manchester. It was not
until 1946 that he returned to Nairobi.

Then came Mau Mau. On October 20, 1952, the Government declared a state of emergency and arrested Jomo Kenyatta, among many others. The rest of the story is as well
known as it is controversial. Mr. Kenyatta and five of his as-
sociates were charged with managing a proscribed society.
Defended by a team of distinguished lawyers headed by Mr.
D. N. Pritt, Q.C., he was convicted and sentenced to seven
years' hard labour. Excused from the hard labour, he occupied his time by acting as cook—an excellent one, I believe—
to his companions at Lokitaung, an outpost in the lava
deserts of the Northern Province. A hard penance in that
scorching climate braced him for his time of triumph. When
released from the detention imposed upon him after his sentence had expired, he returned amid the acclamation of his
people first to his farm at Gatundu, outside Nairobi; next to
join Kenya's first African government; and then, after
KANU's victory at the elections of May, 1963, to become his
country's first Prime Minister.

Earlier in this year of triumph we had shared a fleshpot in
the restaurant of Parliament Buildings. More jovial now
than ever, mellow as vintage port, an orator still but shorn
of prickles, no longer so watchful and so wary, relishing the
sweets of office, he had put on weight, his features were flesh-
ier, his eyes a little bloodshot, but his mind was still alert
and sinewy. A bead cap on the back of his head, his elephant-

headed walking stick hitched on to one wrist, the big ring in evidence, fly whisk on broad knee, napkin tucked in Gallic-wise, the *m'zee* looked every inch the father figure poised to usher in the age of plenty—a dark Silenus, redolent of feasts and vine leaves and sunlit song.

A few months later Jomo Kenyatta was to hold out an olive branch to the white farmers with such grace and candour that even those who, believing him to be the fount of Mau Mau, had sworn never to become a citizen of a Kenya of which he was Prime Minister were at the least shaken, at the most converted to faith in his sincerity. "If I have done a mistake to you in the past, it is for you to forgive me. If you have done a mistake to me, it is for me to forgive you. The Africans cannot say the Europeans have done all the wrong and the Europeans cannot say the Africans have done all the wrong." Let bygones be bygones.

His white audience rose and joined with him in the shout of *"Harambee!"*, that rather mysterious catchword introduced by KANU to signify: "Let's pull together." A transformation scene indeed. Thus can high office reveal qualities of toler-ance, goodwill and statesmanship not previously discerned, except by the most perceptive, under the nationalist's cloak. "I'd never have believed," commented a departing expatriate, "that we'd all be saying: 'I hope to God nothing happens to Jomo!' "

It is pleasant to see ripe fruit mellowing, not rotting, on the bough—though menaced now by wasps in the shape of Youth Wing Kikuyu thugs taking oaths, amazingly, *against* the *m'zee*. But he goes on his way, genial and unconcerned, for relaxation inspecting his cows and orange crop at Ga-tundu—"a farmer like yourselves"—benign, adroit, subtle and outwardly temperate.

With him at our luncheon was his whiskered colleague,

Mr. Bruce McKenzie, the Minister of Agriculture: almost as generous in build, as mellow in manner, as astute in politics. By birth a white South African, an ex-R.A.F. pilot several times decorated, arm in arm with the Kikuyu ex-agitator and idol of the Pan-Africanists—companions and colleagues, not only political allies but personal friends. When such unlikely things can happen, no one should either despair of or try to foresee human behaviour.

Victor and Vanquished

The popular image of the Luo among non-Luo peoples is that of a slow-witted, exceedingly obstinate fish eater with protruding teeth. Nothing could be less like this than Kenya's Minister of Justice. Mr. Tom Mboya is exceedingly nimble-witted, and while he may be stubborn as regards his ultimate objectives, he will consider a reasonable compromise in his approach towards them. He is a negotiator, as much at home in London, Bonn or New York as in Nairobi, and more at home in these cities and in a club-room atmosphere of iced drinks and tobacco than he would be in the small fishing village on one of Lake Victoria's islands, where he originated.

He began his working career in 1951 as a sanitary inspector in Nairobi. After an interlude at Ruskin College, Oxford, he became a founder of the local Government Workers' Union and then secretary-general of the Kenya Federation of Labour. Thence he moved into politics and, after a year as an ordinary member, became Minister of Labour in 1962—just ten years after he had inspected his first drain. After the 1963 general election he took over the Ministry of Justice. Another meteoric career, and only beginning: he is in his early thirties still.

Self-reliant, well informed, retentive in memory, exceed-ingly eloquent, he commands nearly all the qualities that go to make an outstanding politician except perhaps one: the quality of inspiring loyalty and healing breaches rather than confirming them. He does not always suffer fools gladly, and has a lot of fools to suffer. Sometimes he can be jovial, amus-ing and approachable, but sometimes also graceless and what his enemies call arrogant—he can wound with a thrust where a greater politician would parry with a smile.

In other newly independent nations the wings of the trade unions have been severely clipped; the new rulers will tol-erate no rivalry and very little answering back. Some hope that Mr. Mboya, for old times' sake, will prove less severe; but when I asked him about the future of the opposition he replied: "There's no room for an opposition on the West-minster model in our African states. There must be one-party government, and all discussion must take place within the party." The Nyerere line.

That will leave Mr. Ronald Ngala, the opposition leader, out on a limb, if not (like his counterparts elsewhere) in jail. At the elections his party, KADU—the Kenya African Demo-cratic Union—polled six hundred thousand votes against KANU's one million. These were cast mainly by members of the smaller, poorer, on the whole more backward tribes of the Kalenjin group, including such peoples as the Masai, Nandi and Kipsigis, who deeply distrust the Kikuyu-Luo al-liance which controls KANU.

As a party leader Mr. Ngala has been a sort of African Baldwin, only more energetic and less adroit. He has a pipe (one of those heavy, crinkled ones) and an air of wisdom, pa-tience and calm. He is a Christian, with a family of ten; comes from a fairly small tribe on the Coast, the Giriama; went to Makerere; spent most of his working life as a teacher and has never been much of a firebrand or tub-thumper; an almost perfect image of the good shepherd.

As an architect of *majimbo*, the principle of as much autonomy as possible for Kenya's regions, at first built into the agreed constitution and then repudiated by KANU, Mr. Ngala has had a brief and apparently superficial impact on the course of destiny. But his very moderation may have saved the country from civil strife. Some of his henchmen thundered of sharpened spears, loaded muskets and poisoned arrows, of blowing whistles for the start of civil war. Several of the tribes then controlled by KADU are by tradition warrior-like, and by nature belligerent and excitable. Ronald Ngala acted to reduce the pressure. Had he forced it up, there would have been serious trouble.

"It's quite untrue," he told me, puffing at his pipe—a small, tubby man with an open face and a mild, pleasing manner, "that *majimbo* encourages tribalism. The truth is just the opposite. Only if each group can feel secure in its own homeland, only if it doesn't fear the tyranny of other groups, will it be ready to co-operate. We must get rid of tribalism, grow towards unity. But this can't come overnight—it must come by agreement. Each group must feel secure."

Security—another Snark in modern Africa, no less elusive. So is *majimbo*. Those who back a loser in this modern race are lucky if they only lose their shirts, and not their liberties.

An Able Trio

For a country so newly independent, Kenya has a remarkably able team of Ministers. The Kikuyu trio in charge of finance and industry could make their mark in any country.

The senior, Mr. James Gichuru, a graduate of Makerere, taught for five years at the Alliance High school, Kenya's foremost secondary school, where many of its present leaders got their start. After ten years as a successful headmaster for the Church of Scotland, he gave up teaching to become president first of the Kenya African Union, then of KANU, handing over in both cases to Mr. Kenyatta. Then he became Minister of Finance in the first African government. His speeches have been moderate in tone and well considered, his financial policies sober and constructive, his persuasive powers with the holders of foreign purse strings, whether in government or banking, compelling. At fifty he is by the standards of modern African politics almost a *m'zee,* but now he has as his number two Mr. Mwai Kibaki, freshly back from the London School of Economics with his degree: a young man of much promise.

Dr. Julius Kiano has not one degree, but several, the first from Makerere and subsequent awards from universities in the United States, where he studied economics and political science for eight years, returning to Kenya to be ome the first African lecturer on the staff of the Royal College.

"To restore confidence," he said, "that's our problem in a nutshell. Once we do that, investment and expansion will follow. Of course we need outside capital. And we shall get it. You've read the reports of the World Bank? . . . This is Mr. Kariuki, who is in charge of the tea." He broke off to introduce a middle-aged man with a delightful smile who rose from a dreamy stance near the door to shake hands. "You'd like some tea? Mr. Kariuki will bring it. . . . But if we're to restore confidence we mustn't let production fall. I'm worried about the settlement schemes. It's wrong to break up the big units and liquidate the going concerns. We must investigate the possibilities of collective farming. . . ."

His grasp is quick, his mind well informed, his confidence robust. All these qualities and more will be needed to get these countries to what is known in economic jargon, I believe, as the point of "take-off," where they can start to generate their own capital and develop themselves. There is some way to go before this heavier-than-air machine leaves the ground.

Business Tycoon

Today the lure of politics brings down all the hawks from the sky with offers of money, power, patronage and their attendant *heshima*. Now and again one of the birds is successfully tempted by big business, whose controllers, anxious to Africanize both staff and boards as quickly as they can, diligently seek the raw material of future tycoons.

An apprentice tycoon gave me lunch at the New Stanley. A Muganda in origin, but for ten years in a senior branch of Kenya's civil service, he was an obvious candidate for high office in the KANU government, but chose commerce instead. Still in his early thirties, he is already a director of several companies, and flies in and out of Kampala, Dar es Salaam and Nairobi to attend meetings and advise on labour relations, has a car and a house at his disposal, and a generous expense account. His keen interest in his work does not preclude an interest in politics.

"For the next ten years," he said, "all African countries need a strong, stable, perhaps a dictatorial central government. The problem is how to prevent the leaders from abusing their powers. There must be ways. . . . But the two-party system isn't suitable."

Everyone is chasing hares running in opposite directions. Strong central authority, but no abuse of power (benevolent Hitlers) . . . trade unions, but no strikes. . . . European capital and expertise, but no Europeans . . . free universal education, but lower taxes . . . land parcelled out to small holders, but more, not less, production. . . . The bun and the penny.

"The British Government," said my host, "is like a father who builds a big, expensive house with many rooms and says to his son: 'Now you have come of age and must take over this house, but I won't give you anything to pay for the up-keep.' The British Government should give us the money to keep up this big house of Kenya."

Mustn't a son who comes of age earn his own keep? If he continues to be supported by his father, isn't his independence a fake?

With his mind my host agreed, but in his heart felt betrayed by a paternalism that when it was there he hated, but now that it has been withdrawn fears that he may need, and at the same time resents that need—a complicated state of mind, and not a happy one. In one breath he says—and means: "We don't want to get rid of Europeans, we need their help and skill. In the new Kenya all who mean to help us forward will find a place." And in the next, with equal sincerity: "What will be the point of independence if we're still governed by expatriates?" In one breath: "Our trouble is, we've no one qualified to become Permanent Secretaries"; in the next: "I blame the British Government for being slow to Africanize."

When I suggested that many Europeans were Africanizing themselves, largely because they feared that standards of education would fall and that their children would have no future here, he asked: "Why don't Europeans send their children to Makerere and the Royal College? If they are Kenyans, why should they have no future here?"

Because there'll be no openings for them, for one thing, with the civil service, commerce and industry all hell-bent on Africanizing. Thousands of African students now at the universities, or moving towards them, will soon be back with their degrees. "Naturally, we must look after our own students, the people we've trained for these jobs—we must have an African civil service and government." Well then, what future for expatriates? "But we don't intend to *discriminate. . . ."*

This dichotomy is too deep to be easily healed. Often the African personality is a split personality.

Tomorrow's Rulers

Green lawns, flowering jacarandas, clipped shrubs, edged paths, clean new buildings of dressed stone with bright, airy rooms and pastel-shaded tiles; a spacious dining hall done in polished local timbers; a flag fluttering from the mast; everything is spick-and-span, well ordered, smart and on parade.

Stalwart young men stroll about the paths and lawns with their jackets over their arms, displaying freshly pressed shirts —no beatnik stuff or patched trousers; their shoes gleam. Exuding an alert self-confidence, they pile into coaches and speed along the tarmac to Nairobi, to reappear in time for their glass of sherry or tankard of beer before dinner. On mess night, smartly attired, they spread starched napkins folded into shapes of boats, fans and bishops' mitres, and white-coated waiters serve them with the soup, the fish, the meat, the sweet, the savoury and with the right wine to match; then come the port, the toasts, raised glasses, a scraping of chairs. "Gentlemen, you may smoke."

In this time and place it all seems unreal: the graces of a dead regime and vanished age transplanted to this training ground for new rulers. Here at the Kenya Institute of Administration at Kabete, district commissioners are created out of district clerks, civil secretaries from assistant storekeepers, finance officers from junior accountants. Here the consul at sunset is handing on his baton with a clap on the shoulder and an "Over to you, old chap."

If it all seems more related to a past privilege and tradition, to Edwardian house parties, butlers who press the daily newspapers to iron out the creases, cricket on the lawn and a far-flung empire than to the harsher scene of contemporary Africa, the defence is: "Don't forget we're training here not just district officers or chief accountants, but our future ambassadors in Paris and London, our representatives at the United Nations, our Permanent Secretaries and Ministers. They've got to hold their own in foreign countries. If they feel awkward and uncouth, they'll develop great big chips on their shoulders, or fail to grow out of the chips they already have." So they are instructed in the manners of English gentlemen as well as in the right drill for handling files. Perhaps ironically, it is partially financed by the Americans.

How can you teach anything so multisided, uncodified and vague as "administration"? What *is* it, anyway? The two senior district commissioners in charge, both expatriates on the way out, explained about *shauri* day. (*Shauri* means business, discussion, affair, lawsuit, trouble, arrangement—almost anything.)

A student takes the part of a District Officer. He sits at his desk, ready for what the day may bring. First it brings a heap of files made up by the instructors. The first deals with an application by an Asian, Mr. Patel, for a licence to operate a maize mill, which has been turned down once or twice already—the district has enough maize mills, mostly African-owned. This time the application is supported by a strong recommendation from the junior officer in whose subdistrict Mr. Patel resides. And here also, on the file, is a note from this same young officer inviting the D.O. and his wife to a

Christmas party. "I can promise you good refreshment; I
have some whisky kindly sent with the compliments of the
season by Mr. Patel which I am keeping for the occasion. . . ."
The exercise is to draft a reply at once firm and tactful.

More files follow, and the morning's peace is shattered by
one of the instructors, Mr. Alan Simmance—an amateur actor
of note—who storms into the office in the guise of an infuriated farmer who's just had twenty steers stolen, and demands
redress; he thumps the table, accusing the Government of a
breakdown of law and order. A special branch detective enters
with a security crisis—should permission be given to hold a
meeting that could lead to a breach of the peace? The telephone rings: a flustered bureaucrat from Nairobi queries a
recent return of stores. Another Nairobi call comes through
to say the Minister of Health wants to inspect a pure-water
scheme, to have the latest figures on a hookworm campaign,
will need a night's accommodation. . . . All this must be dealt
with calmly, sensibly and simultaneously. The main point is
that to give a clear-cut decision, even a wrong one, is better
than none. The whole class discusses each question.

What happened to the angry farmer? Thrown out, after a
struggle—Mr. Simmance is a proficient wrestler too, *and* a
barrister—to be charged later with resisting arrest. Was this
the right treatment?

"The whole class thought so, but we explained that it
wasn't. They're too brusque. We plug the line of patience,
restraint, the use of reason in preference to force—they see
the point, but . . ." They are all young men—their average
age is twenty-seven—tasting authority for the first time and
thoroughly enjoying it.

Everyone agrees that these new rulers, unlike colonialists,
are not afraid of their own shadows or troubled by qualms
of guilt. They are there to rule, and intend to do so with few

holds barred. A Nairobi businessman told me of an incident to illustrate this. His company owns a timber mill in Uganda. This had been plagued by strikes so irresponsible that the directors were considering its closure. Yet one more strike was threatened, and after weeks of negotiation, concession and leaning over backwards by the European manager, the African trade union leaders called off the talks and fixed the strike for the following Monday.

That weekend the District Officer—an African—arrived and called for all the records and minutes of the negotiations. He read until late into the night and then gave his verdict. "These trade union people only want to make trouble and positions for themselves. They're not considering the good of the country. The company's terms are reasonable. Strikes are bad for our economy. Leave this to me."

On Sunday morning the police arrived, arrested the trade union leaders and charged them with a variety of offences, including nonpayment of taxes. On Monday morning all the men turned up to work, and since then the mill has had no strikes.

"Under the old regime," commented the director, "we should have been forced to close. The British administration backed the African employees automatically in every dispute and never even listened to our side of the case. They didn't dare go against the unions. The African D.O. didn't care twopence, and got the necessary backing. If this is *uhuru* . . ."

How to Administer

There is no doubt of the *esprit de corps* of these picked young men of Kabete. (Kenya's civil service has four thousand Africans, apart from manual workers; at Kabete are the chosen three hundred.) This could get out of hand. One of the lessons the Institute tries to instil is that other valid points of view exist besides the official one.

To this end "problem-solving seminars" are held jointly between Kabete students and their opposite numbers in commerce, industry and the professions. Small groups discuss and report on actual situations and needs—nothing wholly theoretical—such as developing the Nairobi Stock Exchange, how to attract more overseas investment, what industries can be successfully established, what markets explored for Kenya products—and the freedom of the press. "They support this in theory, but come down hard against it when there's any actual issue involved."

Kabete doesn't train only district commissioners, those showpieces of the civil service glamorized in films, plays and literature from *Sanders of the River* down to Gerald Hanley's gloomier and harder-drinking consuls lowering their flags. Out of the limelight there toil a throng of executive officers, accountants and local government officials, of establishment experts, registrars, treasurers, community development officers and scores of other specialists in different branches of bureaucracy. Men in all these categories are to be found at Kabete, either learning how to do their jobs better, or preparing to step into higher grades and to replace departing expatriates.

All budding administrators of senior rank who are physically fit and under thirty-two spend three weeks at the Outward Bound school, where latent qualities of character, will power and endurance are coaxed into the open by tests of resolution and stamina. Most of these young adults lack enthusiasm for climbing Mount Kilimanjaro and camping in the snow, for cold baths, athletic sports and exercises in map reading. Yet *heshima* has been successfully involved. One who failed to pass the necessary medical tests slid "more and more off the beam; his work went to pieces; he grew truculent and nonco-operative; we had to send him to a psychiatrist. She diagnosed the trouble as his *not* having been on the course—a feeling of rejection and inferiority. So we had to get round the doctor, the student took the course and came back cured."

After mountain climbing, three weeks at the nearby College of Social Studies, which is all theory, stretches the intellectual sinews. A "language laboratory" sent from the United States is said to teach fluent English in a few months by means of tape recorders which play the student's own speech back to him over and over again.

Are these young men anti-European? "Yes, but as a rule with good humour—partly to needle us. They say a lot of provocative and silly things. The trick is never to answer back. Then they get tired of the game. We think that here at Kabete a lot of shoulder chips at least get reduced in size. What we aim at is a professional pride in the service, to cut across tribalism." The students are by no means lost in admiration for their own leaders. "Politicians are spoiling Kenya" is a phrase often heard over beers and coffees—sometimes with the implied corollary that if politicians were to bungle things too badly men trained to govern would have to put them right. They want a single-party state—so long as their own party is the top dog.

Even among these sophisticated young men tribalism goes deep. A test designed to probe into prejudices and attitudes of mind—a series of short, sharp questions fired off quickly and answered off the cuff—has demonstrated that in the mind's instinctive layers tribal loyalties are as strong among Makerere graduates as among older and less educated men. The Kikuyu, above all, are gripped by them.

"Once I asked a Mau Mau hard-core detainee," one of the

instructors told me, "whether he was glad to be going home."
(This, of course, was not at Kabete; it was at Hola.) "He
looked at me with that curious, cold glint they have in their
eyes, picked up a handful of earth and said: 'This is the soil
of Kenya; all Kenya is my home.' The other tribes know this
and that's why they fear and often hate the Kikuyu. At this
level people try to overcome it, but it's in them still."

Love and Marriage

It is, I think, a tragedy that the wives of these young men
receive no parallel training. How can the most sophisticated
Ambassador, perfectly *au fait* with the best vintage years for
claret and the use of finger bowls, happily entertain his guests
if his unfortunate wife sits there tongue-tied, awkward and
humiliated—or, more likely, if she's left behind in Africa
precisely because she's not presentable? The breakup of family life seems a heavy price to pay for easy manners.

The whole relationship between the sexes is getting more
and more unbalanced as men draw away from women into a
different world. This must set up harmful and disruptive
tensions, and impose on the children yet one more damaging
dichotomy. A whole generation of children, or at any rate
the most important section of that generation, is being condemned to the condition of the psychologically broken home.

Many of the young men wish with an almost desperate passion to find educated brides. Some of these Kabete students
have paid to send their wives to Britain to take courses which
include "social behaviour" as well as practical skills like
cookery and homecraft.

But it is no good pretending that most Africans are any
more prepared than the colonialists were to press for wom-
en's equality. They share with the British a strong patrilineal,

male-dominated tradition. In African society the male decides, governs, judges everything. It is the father who is served first at meals; in some tribal societies no woman may eat in a masculine presence, or until every male has had his fill. The father disposes of his daughters' hands, and may beat his wife, if he so wishes, without infringing tribal law.

Among the young men this is changing, but very slowly. Some politicians have paid lip service to feminine equality; whether they will act to promote it remains to be seen. Two important changes will, in time, have their effects. Women have equal votes with men. And the prejudice against sending girls to school has all but died out. It is still the case that far more boys than girls stay the course, and this will probably continue; but the breach with tradition has been made.

But votes and literacy won't help much if women can no longer share the interests and the lives of their husbands as they once did, even if they had little say in the ordering of them. Under tribalism marriage was a partnership in the joint business of existing, cultivating and rearing a family. Education plus the money economy are rupturing that community of interest.

As for romantic love, this has never been the motive force in African marriage. It is only very recently that it has been regarded in the West as the main, indeed the only right and proper, basis of matrimony. African marriages, by and large, have stuck to the pre-romantic pattern so recently abandoned by Westerners. It is not, for them, primarily a way of satisfying the sexual urges of the young; it is a relationship designed to spread more widely the web of kinship that unites clan or tribe, to share out resources of land and livestock and, above all, to satisfy tribal ancestors by providing them with new human vessels in which to continue their spiritual existence. It is a contract between families and clans, not an exchange of promises between individuals. In all this there is little place for boy-meets-girl romance.

So must African marriages be loveless? Some are. African fathers, like other men, can be selfish and glad to give a girl of thirteen to a rich old man able to pay more generously than the father of the boy of her choice. I knew of a girl who hanged herself because her father parted her from her lover and forced her to become the fourth or fifth wife of a wrinkled elder.

Such cases are exceptions. More normally the young man and the girl choose each other and then the fathers are approached. If they agree, negotiations start, the bride price is settled, first instalments are paid and the pair set up house together. Dissolution of marriage is still rare, though less so than it used to be. Under the tribal system divorce was so complex a business, with all the livestock to be disentangled and handed back, and fraught with so many dangers of quarrelling, that it was generally avoided.

Matters, of course, did not always go smoothly. A young man whose father couldn't pay the bride price would not get his girl—it is not only in Africa that poverty thwarts desire, especially in matters of marriage. And ways could be found to get over this obstacle. A Kikuyu father, approached by a young man whose own father lacked resources, would sometimes take on his prospective son-in-law as a kind of tenant, and allow him to pay his bride-price instalments in the shape of produce and labour.

Young girls espoused to rich old men are not always brokenhearted. Some enjoy the attendant riches: the beads and bangles, expensive ornaments, full granaries. And there is always *heshima* attached to a plutocrat's establishment. Some girls would rather be the tenth wife of a rich, respected chief than the hard-worked bride of a poor man without land or prospects.

It is children that most husbands want, more than their wives' chastity. If, by reason of age or infirmity, they can't themselves beget them, some are prepared to let a substitute perform their office. Under African law the children will belong to the husband's family, and that is what really counts. Of course, if the matter comes to light the girl may get a beating, but that, in one form or another, is generally the penalty of being found out.

Polygamy

Polygamy raises many questions. Why is it the custom of some peoples and not of others? Does it reflect a fundamental difference in outlook, or is it merely a practical response to certain social or economic conditions? Why do Africans prefer and cling to it while Westerners make it a criminal offence? Is monogamy really a superior system, or do Westerners think so only because they follow it? Could Western women take to polygamy? Or are they naturally too jealous? What do women in polygamous households really think of it? No one knows.

Polygamy is on the wane, but for economic and not moral reasons. Few men can now afford the bride price for more than one wife, or the school fees for the progeny of several. All the same, leaving aside a minority of genuine Christians, probably most men would *like* to be polygamists if they could; and when they can afford it, they are.

For women, polygamy has a number of practical advantages. It spreads the burden of caring for a husband; enlarges the family circle; sets up a miniature welfare state in which you are sure to be cared for when sick or elderly; enriches that sense of community valued by almost every African, male or female, above everything else. And it provides, as you grow older, a permanent succession of mothers' help—and help that cannot give notice, demand a rise or go off on holiday. A senior wife holds an enviable position of authority over junior ones; the newest bride may get the shiniest bangles, but she must also willingly obey the senior wife's commands. The bullying of young wives by senior ones is probably the greatest single cause of unhappiness in polygamous households.

Jealousy would wreck polygamy among Westerners. Are African women less jealous by nature, are their sensibilities blunter or have they got their emotions under better control? Only African women with experience of polygamy could answer such questions. On the surface, certainly, in most polygamous households, contentment rules. Each wife must have her separate quarters, normally her own hut; in it are her own cooking stones, next to it her own granaries, nearby her own plot of land; by ensuring this minimum of privacy, custom reduces opportunities for friction and spite.

But that some remain is suggested by the sour Kikuyu proverb: "Two wives are two pots of poison." African women have no choice but to accept a custom made, like all customs, by men, to suit male convenience. If the shoe pinches, they may turn to witchcraft for a clandestine revenge on co-wives with whom they do not dare to quarrel openly.

A study of a tribe called the Bugisu, in Uganda, revealed examples of a jealousy which must often be stifled and concealed, but erupts now and then into violence and open hatred.[1] A rich man took a girl, Nambozo, as his fourth wife. When his senior wife died, her two surviving co-wives ac-

[1] "Witchcraft in Bugisu," by Jean la Fontaine, in *Witchcraft and Sorcery in East Africa*, ed. Middleton and Winter. Routledge and Kegan Paul, 1963.

cused Nambozo, the young and attractive newcomer, of killing the older one by witchcraft. Fearing for her own life,
Nambozo abandoned her child and fled to her father; the
child died; Nambozo's family accused her husband's family
of killing it. So began a bitter feud between the two families.
The Bugisu are great ones for feuds; this one may well be
rumbling on still, breaking out in slashed coffee trees, burned
huts, sabotaged trucks and a vicious war between coffee co-
operatives, whose germ may lie in the jealousy of two middle-
aged women, feeling the effects of time and toil, for the
young, attractive girl favoured by their mutual husband.

Westerners consider monogamy to be superior morally,
nearer to a spiritual idea and a fundamental Christian principle. But Africans have pointed out that Christ did not lay
down a clear rule. St. Paul, instructing Timothy in the qualities to be looked for in bishops and deacons, said they must
be "the husband of one wife," [2] thus implying that run-of-
the-mill, nonoffice-bearing Christians might be the husband
of several.

Christ, in his injunction to the Pharisees, directed that a
man should cleave to his wife: "And they twain shall be one
flesh: so then they are no more twain, but one flesh. What
therefore God hath joined together, let not man put asun-
der." [3] Christians maintain that this implies, if it does not
explicitly state, the union of one man with one woman and
no more. Many Africans do not accept the implication. Christians, they point out, may have as many wives as they like,
provided only one is living. As this is Christ's only recorded
statement on the topic, there is plenty of room for argument.

In one respect, at least, monogamy bears hardly on women.
It was the general tribal custom for mothers to suckle their

[2] I Timothy 3:2 and 12.
[3] Matthew 19:5 and 6. Mark 10:8 and 9.

young for between two and three years, and for husbands to abstain, during this period, from sexual intercourse. This resulted in a sensible form of family planning. With one wife out of action, in a polygamous household another would be fit to meet the master's needs. Not so for the monogamist, and to expect a normal husband to forgo the pleasures of the marriage bed for several years would obviously be unrealistic. So the custom has collapsed. Milk in the breast no longer makes a woman untouchable, and as a consequence most wives now have an annual baby instead of one every three or four years. This is one of several causes of the "population explosion." Contrary to a general belief, monogamy normally results in more babies than polygamy, not fewer.

Does it also, as its adherents claim, raise the level of marriage to a more spiritual plane? Most Africans, I think, would find this question pointless. It is not that they care nothing for spiritual matters; on the contrary, the world that has not been made manifest is very real to them. But those who inhabit it, ancestral ghosts, are concerned, in regard to marriage, with a single aim: the procreation of children to perpetuate and strengthen the clan. The spiritual aspect of marriage is therefore the same as its physical end, to create children; obviously, for that purpose, one man does not need to cleave to one wife only; and so monogamy has no superior merit.

I doubt if many Africans of either sex would accept the argument that the mystical aspect of union between the sexes is deepened or enhanced by the custom of exclusive pairing. Life must be created, the child cared for, loved and trained to take his place in the community; families must be strengthened and enlarged, no one left uncared for in sickness or old age—such are the social purposes of marriage, indissolubly linked with its spiritual ones.

In these respects the question of monogamy or polygamy is irrelevant. African peasants (if not politicians) are realists. Aware that few men's sexual appetite will be satisfied, from youth to age, by one woman, they consider it wiser to build society's institutions on this simple fact than to indulge in the elaborate pretence followed by Westerners and Christians that one man will cleave to one woman for a lifetime. When this (in their view false) assumption fails, Christians have only hypocrisy, censure or the violence of the *crime passionnel* to fall back on. No wonder, when monogamy (they think) is founded on an error of judgment.

Where does love come into all this—not the love of adolescents, but of married couples? Once again it is probably a question of meaning. Love in the romantic sense seems generally to absent itself from marriage, as from adolescent love affairs. Adultery leads to fines, not to the breakup of the marriage; it is an offence against property, not against trust. The world of an African man might be well lost for a plot of land, a brindled cow, for revenge and certainly for *heshima*, but never, I think, for a woman.

Yet love does grow. If, to the Westerner, love's symbol is Cupid's arrow—or perhaps a fork of lightning that strikes with blinding glory and can fuse into one the hearts and souls of two people—Africans, I think, might see it rather as vegetable. You plant the seed with marriage and, if the soil is fertile and the seasons kindly, it germinates and roots—slowly perhaps, with setbacks possibly; some seeds do not grow at all, and some develop into sickly plants and some plants are scorched or drowned. But most grow, in their fashion, and so does the seed planted with marriage grow into mutual respect, interdependence and a shared experience. And ultimately is love more, or less, than this?

TSAVO PARK

On a Voi Veranda

The first to appear on the veranda was the dwarf mongoose: fat, sleek, brown, furry, about eight inches long, with a shrew face and yellow eyes, it sniffed my feet and then sat on my lap. Not for long, because Uppity, the zebra foal, mounted the steps: a ridiculous toy creature, so obviously hand-painted, a sort of natural joke, it nudged and butted until I got up just in time to greet Rufus, a two-and-a-half-year-old rhino, standing about three feet at the shoulder, who licked my hand with a purple tongue and nuzzled with a long, prehensile upper lip. He had been wallowing in tractor grease, which encrusted his sides, and followed me about, licking my hand until he was stayed with bananas and peppermint rings.

The senior warden of the Tsavo National Park, David Sheldrick, and his wife share their house at Voi with a great many animals and birds. Both Sheldricks belong to that small company born with an instinctive understanding of their fellow creatures and with the patience which goes with these queer, unsought talents. Such individuals are gentle, quiet in motion, slow-spoken, unassuming, in a sense absorbent; they have a tranquil, indrawn quality. People who are taut, jerky, sparklike and aggressive seldom draw from an animal the trust and feeling of security it needs.

Few people would really like to share their garden with four young buffalo and two elephants, one almost full grown. It is a miracle that there is any garden left to share. This is dry gardening, with an average annual rainfall of ten inches; but averages mean little here: one year 7.24 inches fell, another 47.27 inches. Lawns are kept green with sprinklers, and beyond them, except soon after rain, everything is ash grey and biscuit brown. The steep hills that rise just behind the house are clothed with thorn scrub and resound with the harsh bark of baboons. Everything is dense and spiky: you cannot push a way through the scrub. In amongst it are acacia trees haunted by clumsy-flying banded hoopoes and by those miraculously coloured, brilliant blue or soft violet rollers. Each roller seems solitary and independent and, at this time of year, sits alone on the end of a branch.

All day you hear the melancholy, plaintive hooting of the emerald-spotted wood dove, a small bird to make so much fuss, dropping its rounded notes like pebbles falling softly from a narrow-necked gourd. From the garden comes the bubbling note of black-headed orioles with canary-coloured plumage; a flash of scarlet betrays a pair of redheaded weavers in a tree by the veranda steps.

The Sheldricks' elephants walk right up to the veranda, but fortunately stay outside. Sometimes one of them will wind his trunk round David Sheldrick's arm and the two will wrestle, the elephant at first pretending to give ground and then pushing his playmate backwards into a tree. After that he strolls off to uproot a few shrubs and trample the petunias.

Four buffalo stand with lowered heads to have their backs scratched. Rufus nudges everyone till he gets more peppermint, and strolls off for a siesta in the tractor shed, where he has located a useful pool of sump oil. When he was about a day old he wandered unaccompanied into the kitchen. His mother was never found, and had certainly been killed by poachers. Rufus is now a sturdy, placid child, lacking in the least desire to return to the wilds. No animal here is put under restraint, although those vulnerable to lions must be shut up at night.

A Warden's Problems

The life of a game park warden seems idyllic; but, like other men, he has problems.

One is poaching: how to keep out of five thousand square miles of bush and scrub and craggy mountain, with very few roads, not a single aircraft and a mere handful of rangers, the mobile, leather-footed hunters with their poison-tipped arrows and bush lore skills, and the organized gangs whose trucks wait on the park boundaries to take meat, horn and ivory to the coastal towns, where the merchants who control this racket smuggle out the ivory and horn in dhows.

Rhinos are the worst hit. The reason is, of course, that a lot of middlemen make enormous profits. The African poacher gets about three shillings (forty-two cents) a pound for the horn—to him, good money. The Asian trader at the Coast gets eighty to a hundred shillings ($11.20 to $14)—a three-thousand-per-cent profit. The consumer in Asia pays £70 to £80 ($196 to $224) a pound. In between, the only costs are those of transport. The gap between the three shillings (forty-two cents) received by, as it were, the producer and the fifteen hundred shillings ($210) paid by the consumer must surely be the widest in the world. So rhinos go on dying and merchants thrive.

Elephants are poached too, but from the point of view of statistics this does not matter. (From the point of view of cruelty, of course, it does.) The problem of the elephants is that there are too many of them in and around the Tsavo Park.

For this the basic reason is that age-old migratory movements which kept animals in balance with their habitat have been disrupted. Eleplants can no longer trek, as they once did, hundreds of miles in search of fresh woods; they are boxed up in one area, and must go on eating what it will provide until they have eaten it bare. If they stray outside the Park and its immediate surroundings, they are destroyed. So they stay inside and destroy their own sustenance.

You have only to drive a few miles to see evidence of this. Dead recumbent grey-white tree trunks and shattered branches lie about like toppled ninepins on the ashy soil—a graveyard of trees. Some have been knocked over, some have died first on their feet after elephants have stripped their bark to find the nutrients stored there. Baobabs, in particular, have suffered because the silvery-grey glistening bark of these queer-shaped, thick-boled trees is rich in calcium, and elephants—not surprisingly, when you think what big teeth they have—need a great deal of this mineral.

The trees go, and at first grass replaces them—the wiry, coarse and mainly unnutritious grasses of these arid lands with a marginal and fickle rainfall. (The only reason five thousand square miles have been set aside for animals is that no humans can live there.) The death of trees exposes the soil to a heat so fierce that even grasses barely survive, and the earth gets baked and sterile. Then along comes a fire which sweeps across the tinder-dry country, consuming everything—surviving trees, bush, the struggling grasses, insects, reptiles, even birds and beasts—and leaves behind a blackened desert.

It is true that after rain, up will come green shoots again, and a deceptive smile of verdancy will spread over the land, but this *is* deceptive: many of the trees have gone for good, the grass has been weakened, the soil scorched. While elephants can and do eat grass, here the rainfall is insufficient to sustain a grass cover in its turn robust enough to support large herds of elephants.

What these elephants need are trees; between them, fires and hungry pachyderms are wiping them out. And how can you control fires in an area without inhabitants, almost as large as Wales, where everything is as dry as wood shavings? A tourist's cigarette end, a poacher's campfire, a spark from a locomotive, even sun striking through a piece of broken glass, will start one. What the vegetation map describes as "desert grass-bush" is regressing by way of open grassland into unadorned desert. All this, in turn, is changing the fauna of the Park.

The worst year anyone can remember was 1961. No rain fell until October. Everything became denuded, bare, desiccated; hot winds swirled dust devils across the plain; grasses withered; rivers shrank into dry, sandy gullies; every day the sun rose into a hard, unpitying sky; big, hollow rolls of cumulus cloud mocked thirsty creatures with their emptiness, like the heavy breasts of childless women; only vultures thrived, too gorged to move more than a few reluctant paces from carcasses whose stench polluted the air.

Elephants, who can walk farther and are very adaptable, had most of what little sustenance there was, rhinos least. Along a forty-mile stretch of the Galana River, and close to its banks, the Park's wardens and rangers counted the carcasses of 282 rhinos who had starved to death. Some, too weak to stir, were being pecked by the vultures before they were dead. In the Nairobi Park and its environs, no more than about two hundred square miles, perhaps ten thousand animals perished, despite all the efforts made by devoted wardens to save them, and the distribution of bales of hay which they were too weak, or too set in their habits, to tackle.

Tsavo wardens were puzzled by the black, wet appearance of some of the rhinos still on their feet—as if they were literally sweating blood. And they were. The blood had been drawn by millions of tiny flies. (It is quite untrue, Mr. Sheldrick told me, that rhinos have thick skins; their blood vessels lie close to the surface and their hides are sensitive.) Further researches showed that these flies breed in the rhino's dung. In normal conditions rhinos are fond of wallowing and coat themselves with mud—that is why they more often look red than black; and this coat protects them from flies. In the drought there was no mud, hence no protection; flies smothered and tormented them, weakened their resistance and so hastened their ends.

"There's always something new to find out," David Sheldrick said. While I was at Tsavo reports of a new, or at any rate unidentified, disease of elephants were coming in. The Africans knew about it, and called it *garabogoya,* but it lacked a scientific name, and neither they nor anyone else could specify the cause. Elephants are not afflicted by many diseases. A few die of anthrax, and rather more of babesiasis, an ailment carried by ticks.

Too Many Elephants

As part of an attempt to break this vicious circle of overcrowding, destruction of habitat and the consequently dwindling capacity of the Park to support any animals at all, a great deal is now being found out about the behaviour of elephants. If a way to break the circle can't be found, the Park will turn into a desert, everything will go except a few desert-loving creatures, Kenya will lose one of its major tour-

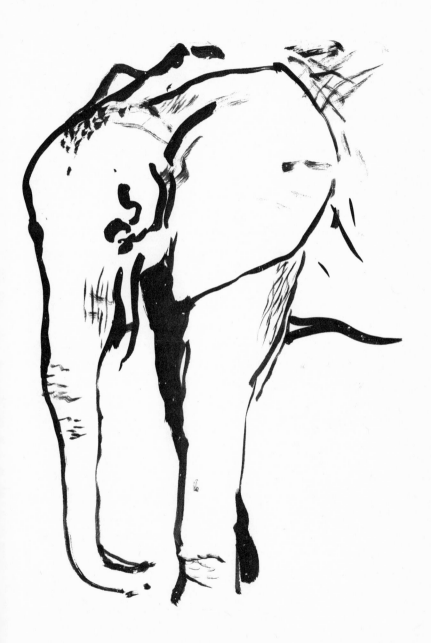

ist attractions and the world one of its last surviving wildlife
sanctuaries.

A year or two ago things looked black. Rough estimates
put the elephant population of the Park and its surrounding
areas at sixteen thousand and its carrying capacity at about
ten or eleven thousand beasts. The Park's director, Mr.
Mervyn Cowie, and his staff were therefore faced with the
prospect of culling five or six thousand elephants.

The prospect appalled them. To begin with, were you to
shoot animals in large numbers within its boundaries, you
would destroy the two main objects of a national park, which
are to provide sanctuary and to enable visitors to enjoy the
creatures who avail themselves of it. No one could expect
hunted elephants to pose placidly for photographers; nor,
indeed, could photographers be allowed to come, since no
one could shoot elephants in thousands without allowing a
proportion of wounded and therefore dangerous beasts to escape. Skilled hunters do not exist in numbers sufficient to
tackle such a task; unskilled ones would spread havoc; carcasses could only be left to rot. To create a morgue of dead
and dying creatures for the benefit of vultures and hyenas
cannot be the answer to the problem of too many elephants
in a national park.

To find out just how many elephants really were in occu-
pation of the area was clearly a prerequisite to any serious
plan of campaign. An aerial count was needed. Lacking any
aircraft themselves, the Park's authorities turned to the commander in chief of the armed forces, Sir Richard Goodwin,
who willingly sent observers in light aircraft and helicopters
to carry out a full-scale count in 1962. The first accurate
mapping revealed 10,799 elephants actually within the Park,
another 3,282 in an area across the Galana River, and a further 1,522 in other adjacent regions: in the whole ecological

unit which includes the Park, a total of 15,603 elephants. So the wardens' guess of sixteen thousand had not been far out.

More than this, the airborne observers mapped the units into which this population was split. They found over eleven hundred separate herds, ranging from solitary bulls to groups of thirty or forty. The commonest size was between five and fifteen animals—family parties consisting of cows, their calves and two or three bulls, with an average of just under eight young to every ten mature cows. A cow elephant reaches maturity in about twelve years; after that, barring accidents, she will breed for about half a century, and die between the ages of sixty and sixty-five. Calf mortality is high. A statistical analysis of the data concluded that of every 10,000 elephants, 775 cows bred annually some 700 living calves, of which only 300 survived to maturity.

The next stage was to estimate the Park's carrying capacity in terms of elephants. For this it was first necessary to discover exactly what these Tsavo herds feed on. Elephants do not eat anything that comes along; they select, and their diet varies with their habitat.

So David Sheldrick and a biologist, Mr. Napier-Bax, spent every hour they could squeeze from routine duties with their field glasses, watching elephants eat. As soon as each animal moved on, they took specimens of the plants it had been feeding on and sent them to the Coryndon Museum, in Nairobi, to be identified. This done, they returned to the bush and took samples of each plant—over a hundred species were collected—for chemical analysis by Dr. H. W. Dougall at the plant research station at Kitale. Thus has been assembled a card index not merely of which plants these Tsavo elephants eat, and when, but to some extent of why: of the mineral content, for instance, of each species, which in its turn varies according to the time of year.

Only a botanist could appreciate a list of the species included in what is clearly a well-mixed, varied food supply, derived from four sources: trees, grasses, bushes and creepers. These the elephants favour at different seasons. The leaves of the shrub *Cordia gharaf*, for instance, are eaten only when they begin to shrivel; of *Dobera glabra* and *Anisotes ukambensis* only in times of drought; the bark of baobabs seldom in the rains, when grasses are favoured above shrubs or trees. There are minor mysteries. Why do elephants in the deserts lying several hundred miles to the north eat with apparent enjoyment the fruits of the doum palm (*Hyphaene coriacea*), while these Tsavo pachyderms reject them? All elephants are wasteful feeders, and will often knock a whole tree over to get at the bark, and spit out the fibre.

Whatever the nature of their appetites, one thing remains clear: there are too many elephants. And especially too many in the eastern sector of the Park, the driest sector, which suffers most from overstocking. Here, in round figures, seven thousand elephants are attempting to live in an area which at best can support five thousand. Dead or mutilated trees, broken branches, trampled bush and general desiccation are the consequence. This is a dying countryside, carrying at least two thousand surplus elephants.

To cull them is too difficult. The only remaining palliative is to increase the carrying capacity of the region. For this no weapons are needed: only more water and fewer fires.[1]

[1] Since my visit Dr. Glover has written: "I flew over the area only last week, and the devastation is truly appalling. There are large areas of bare red soil with only a sparse grass cover in the dry season. Obviously something immediate and drastic must be done to reduce the number of elephants in the Park. . . . What we most urgently need are aeroplanes and money for trained men to study this fascinating problem while there is still time before the population crash occurs."

Water for Wild Animals

Elephants seldom travel more than twelve or fifteen miles from water, and so whole stretches of this eastern sector of the Park which lack water also lack elephants. If water could be provided, the elephants would be presented with a new range of feeding grounds to relieve pressure on the old.

During the 1961 drought Mr. Cowie and his Park trustees started a Water for Wild Animals Fund, which saved many lives. One of his best moments, Mr. Cowie told me, occurred when the Nairobi manager of a firm selling tent and camp equipment walked into his office to say: "My boss has authorized me to bring you this check. It's for ten thousand." Taking this to mean shillings, the currency of the country, Mr. Cowie began to thank his caller warmly. "Not shillings, pounds." A condition was that the donor should remain anonymous. Later, however, the name of Mr. Herbert Bonar, the head of the firm, became known.

When the drought ended, plans were made to lay on water, with the money that was over, to some of the drier regions of the Park. I watched pipes being laid from a pumping station on the Galana River to concrete tanks on hilltops, whence water was to be reticulated to drinking troughs installed in the bush at five-mile intervals. The birds and beasts who have since, no doubt, discovered these thirst-quenching stations and the tourists who enjoy the birds and beasts will alike have cause for gratitude. A satisfactory thing, it seemed to me, on which to spend one's money.

The more dried-up and denuded this zone becomes, the more trees give way to open grassland, the more unmanageable do fires become and the more damage do they inflict on a sick countryside. The only practical means of control known at present is to make, and maintain, firebreaks—corridors kept free of vegetation, too wide for flames to leap—across the direction of prevailing winds.

So the art of park management gradually takes shape: in essence, the art of the rancher applied to a three-million-acre estate—itself an enclave in a zone six times as large—to elephants and other wild creatures which cannot be rounded up and sent to market, instead of to cattle, which can.

Culling in the Park

There still remains the nub of management, control of numbers. Stopping fires and laying on water can help to spread out and support the existing elephants; but this population, like that of humans elsewhere, will go on increasing up to the limit of its food supplies, tightening the spirals of the vicious circle until disaster comes. Birth control for elephants—is that the only solution? What can be done?

Scientists are groping for an answer. A few slender lines along which it might be sought, mere threads, are emerging; but it is still too early to say which are, and which are not, sound enough to grip. There is far too little money to pay for the few explorers of this new field, and some of the keenest can do this work only in their meagre spare time, for no reward but their own satisfaction.

One such, Mr. James Glover, was until recently statistician at Muguga, the East African Common Services research centre, near Nairobi. Applying his statistical technique to an analysis of the aerial counts made in the Park, and their breakdown into herds, sex ratios and ages, he concluded that by culling every year for six years only a hundred and forty young cows in the twelve- to fifteen-year age group, plus a similar number of young bulls to balance the sexes, you would reduce a "resident population" of seven thousand ele-

phants in the eastern sector of the Park to five thousand, a
level which could be held indefinitely by even lighter culling.
Two hundred culled annually from a herd of ten thousand
would reduce the numbers in five years to seventy-five hundred elephants. This modest annual slaughter of young females would arrest the replacement of natural wastage and
would, if continued, halve the original numbers in seventeen
years. Such are the miracles statistics can suggest.

Objections remain to shooting even a few animals in a national park. But there are more ways to kill an elephant than
to plug it with bullets. There is darting. Normally hunters
discharge their drugged darts merely to immobilize their
quarry, but an overdose will put it out for good—safely, silently and humanely. Two scientists working for the Nature
Conservation Department of the Kruger National Park, in
South Africa, recently fired from a crossbow a dart containing
succinylcholine chloride into a young bull elephant, who,
quite oblivious of their presence, collapsed within five minutes and died within thirty, while his companions went on
eating, undisturbed.[2]

This technique is still experimental, and leaves unanswered
the question of how to dispose of carcasses. At present Mr.
Cowie says there is no intention of destroying any elephants
in the Tsavo Park. The whole ecological zone of which it
forms only about one sixth must be tackled as a single unit.
And for that a lot of money must be found.

2 See *Oryx* (Journal of the Fauna Preservation Society) for April, 1963, U.
de V. Pienaar and J. W. van Niekerk. An indication of the capacity of elephants (like all other species) to multiply when released from the normal
balance of nature is provided by the increase of a nucleus herd of ten in
1905 to 1,750 in 1962, in the Kruger Park, where grave dangers of overstocking loom ahead.

The Galana River Scheme

Northwards and eastwards of the Park, and outside its borders, lies an area of about three thousand square miles where a small tribe of hunters called the Waliangulu live, mainly by poaching elephants. Poaching, of course, is here purely a European term. The Waliangulu have always lived off elephants, and they simply go on doing so, oblivious of rules and regulations invented by distant bureaucrats in cities they have never seen to collect money for purposes of which they know nothing.

When the Tsavo Park was set up, these Waliangulu hunters became not merely tax dodgers but a threat to the Park, since they strayed across its borders to slay its elephants with poisoned arrows. Poaching became so serious a menace—the Park at one time was strewn with carcasses and hundreds of young ones starved to death after the demise of their mothers —that a major anti-poaching campaign was mounted. To the extent that this succeeded, it deprived the Waliangulu of their living. They are not adaptable enough to change their ways; schools, literacy, even for the most part trousers, have passed them by.

If nothing would stop them killing elephants, it was argued, then the killing might as well be legalized, controlled and used to benefit everyone concerned. A dead elephant is valuable: mainly for its ivory, but also for its meat and other by-products; let the profits be shared out fairly among the tribe, numbering only about three thousand souls. The Nuffield Foundation backed an experiment begun in 1960 and planned to last three years.

It would be impossible to imagine anyone more unlike the popular image of the brawny, tough, hairy-chested elephant hunter, a Hemingway figure if ever there was one, than Mr.

Ian Parker, the young man in charge. If asked to place Mr. Parker, I would have put him down as a rather frail city-dwelling office worker of about nineteen, economizing on buns and instant coffee and interested perhaps in music or photography. And there he is, dwelling among the doum palms on the scorching banks of the Galana River, hunting over a vast area of trackless bush and shooting an average of about three elephants a week. He lives among primitive tribesmen, every one of whom is armed with poisoned arrows that can kill in five minutes, and is responsible not merely for dispatching the elephants but also for loading their carcasses into brine tanks on trucks, getting them back to camp, drying the flesh and then transporting it across a hundred miles or so of roadless bush to the railway before the meat putrefies. All this, and a lot more, he has done with the help of one English colleague and a small band of Waliangulu tribesmen.

Both young men had wives and babies, and their camps were separated by the brown and turgid river from a Land-Rover track on which they jolted, now and again, sixty miles to Voi, to buy fresh vegetables and watch trains go by. During the floods of 1961, when the river became a savage torrent and stayed so for three months, their supplies were dropped by air.

The essence of the scheme was to share out all the profits from the elephants, ivory included, among the Waliangulu, so as to demonstrate that legal hunting paid them better than illegal poaching. But the Treasury in Nairobi took the line that the Government, not the Waliangulu, were entitled to the ivory. A paper battle over this continued for two years and resulted in a draw satisfactory to neither party.

Then came trouble with the Giriama, the Waliangulu's eastern neighbours: a tribe of cultivators. They infiltrated

into the area set aside for the scheme and not only poached elephants, but started fires which drove the beasts away by consuming their food supplies. The Giriama tribesmen also stripped the region of its trees to make charcoal. Their object was to settle in and claim the land as their own.

After much negotiation representatives of the Giriama reached agreement with agents of the Government to withdraw from Waliangulu territory if, in return, they were allowed an uninhabited region to the north. This agreement had to be ratified in London, whence no decision emerged for two years. Meanwhile more Giriama infiltrated and more fires raged. When a reply did percolate the bureaucratic filter, it was to the effect that the Giriama could have the northern area but mustn't be ejected from the Waliangulu scheme.

Despite all this, the scheme achieved a limited success in its short life of three years. In the first year it showed a loss, as was expected. In the second, although much of the country was under water for four months and the tracks were eradicated, it made a tiny profit. In the third year it made a considerably larger, if still not handsome, profit.

Every bit of elephant was used. The ivory was auctioned, the dried meat sold for about tenpence a pound, the feet went to Rowland Ward's to be turned into umbrella stands, the ears were split into four and became handbags and wallets, an order came from New York for one million bracelets made from tail hairs, and Mr. Parker sold seventy-five skulls for fifteen shillings ($2.10) each to a film company wishing to depict an elephant cemetery. (These are wholly mythical.) The experiment proved that elephants *can* be cropped at a profit under very difficult conditions; further, that the scheme could provide permanent employment for some, if not many, of the Waliangulu. But Mr. Parker would like to see cattle brought in. These would justify a canning factory to deal with the meat on the spot. Elephants could then be processed, too, and the ranching of pachyderms and bovines combined.

Mr. Ian Parker has bold ideas for developing this region of arid, unused land. These need capital, and control over the Giriama, whose present depredations are placing in jeopardy the region's capacity to support cattle, elephants or anything else. Neither aim is impossible. There is capital waiting for sound investment if political stability can be ensured; and independent governments do not have to wait two years to get their agreements ratified, or wrecked, by London authorities.

Mudanda Rock

David Sheldrick pointed out a small shrub called *Sericomomopsis* growing in profusion. It was, he said, a favourite food of rhinos. Before the drought of 1961 we should have seen very little of it; now the shrub's unbrowsed abundance testified to the paucity of rhinos. That day we must have driven a hundred and fifty miles and we saw only one, so well known he was semi-tame. Rhinos seldom travel long distances, and he appeared to be condemned to permanent celibacy; at least no one had seen him with a mate. Can numbers build up again? It seems doubtful.

In fact, we encountered few animals: a couple of giraffe-necked gerenuk, three lesser kudu, some oryx with their look of unicorns, one solitary, distant buffalo, a herd of Peters' gazelle, a tortoise and a hare. But we saw an Africa empty of humans—hard, bare, spiky and magnificent, its trees stripped and bashed about by elephants. The whole countryside has had a triple bashing—poachers, drought, fire.

At Aruba Lodge we sat beside the big dam. A strong wind roughened its brownish waters. On a pale, denuded farther shore some zebra and a herd of waterbuck were drinking when along came four lions—the parents and two half-grown cubs. At a stately and deliberate pace, as if performing the measure of a dance, they advanced across the shore. Zebra and waterbuck raised their heads, but made no move; when lions are not hunting, other beasts are wary but display no overt fear. All four lions lay down and lapped the water. Then the cubs had a gambol, cuffing each other while the parents, outstretched to cool themselves, looked on indulgently.

Evening at Mudanda Rock. From a smooth grey saddle that hugs the sun's heat you look down across the dam to all Africa beyond, speckled with thorn trees, beguiling with birdsong, beckening with the harebell haze of distance and threatening with indifference. Crumpled hills lie over the horizon, immemorially old—the oldest rocks, some say, in the world, pre-Cambrian granite, formed perhaps six or seven hundred million years ago. Has this immense antiquity, stretching back even beyond the first life on this planet, instilled into the very atmosphere a brooding feel of total unconcern, the very core of stillness? So have things been since before creation, so will they always be. We saw Africa as the first hunter saw it before he learned to rub fire into being: unmarred, unsullied and primeval; animals at peace with one another, balanced and harmonious. No rifles, no arrows, no snares, no discontent and discordancy—no men.

From bush and wide-stretched plain the elephants converged upon the dam in small parties: slowly, majestically, unhurried, mellow, red in the slanting sunlight with dust or mud coating their skins. As they paced on they swung their trunks gently to and fro and flapped their ears. (This is to cool the blood; a cluster of blood vessels lies behind each ear, and the flapping acts like the agitation of a fan.) In turn, each group halted a little way from the dam to wait for members of the preceding herd to drink, cool their limbs and complete their ablutions. Some sucked from the shallows, some waded out until they were belly-deep, some wallowed and rolled over. These, the wallowers, are bulls; cows are more timid and stay close to the margin. We must have seen at least three or four hundred elephants, and not one was impatient, bad-tempered or ill behaved. "The only harmless great thing," as Donne described them.

Many birds came to the dam. A pair of Egyptian geese circled round, and a flock of whistling tree ducks with white-ringed ears. White egrets and ibis perched on the branches of half-submerged trees. Storks came, and herons.

The sun sank behind the Teita hills, which rise in ridges, black against a sky of apricot and orange. The jagged edges of the hills looked as if they had been slashed decisively from plywood: everything was hard and clear, splendid and eternal. A misty blue seemed to enfold among those distant hills a phantom sadness; and day was over, light gone, and there were the first stars, soft pricks in a sky of dark lilac, or the deepest delphinium.

More elephants were coming down to drink. As the light died they started to trumpet to the stars. A flock of white egrets settled among black branches. Frogs croaked, a tree duck whistled, elephants splashed. We drove away, disturbing on the road many grasshopper owls crouching in wait for small rodents. And so home.

THE BLAZING NORTH

Isiolo to Wajir

The road from Isiolo to Wajir runs straight for many miles across a waste of shale and rock and scrub, twisting now and then to traverse a dry watercourse, moistened only after rain, where bush grows a bit thicker and a few stunted thorns are hung with weavers' nests. Their fevered building of surplus nests, the work of males, seems a pointless waste of energy, but may—or so a naturalist suggested—be a ruse intended to confuse predators. These birds, searching the nests for fledglings, may—or so the weavers apparently hope—fly off in disgust before they come upon an occupied habitation.

I travelled in a truck whose diesel engine stoked up like a fiery furnace as the day went on, my feet resting on a sack containing, I was told, eighty thousand shillings ($11,200). At long intervals we passed police posts, defiant in their isolation and barrenness, each with a flag dropping from a pole above a shining iron roof, and beside each, shadeless on the plain, one or two rectangular huts, the *dukas,* whose owners sell a few bare necessities and trade illegally, in some cases, in rhino horn and giraffe hide. Each *duka* shelters in its poky depths a refrigerator and a supply of ice-cold orange squash or Pepsi-Cola. It seems impossible that this enterprise can pay, but the cold drink was like the milk of paradise.

On this flat desert you are never out of sight of hills. These are not like hills in temperate countries, rounded and eye-enticing; they are jagged, harsh and queer-shaped, jutting up like cones, pillars, pyramids or teeth—hard and angular, as if some mighty hand had hurled them down like dice in a fit of cosmic fury.

Habaswein means the place of dust, and so it is; round it lies the Lorian swamp, in which the Uaso Nyiro River peters out, never reaching the sea. When I crossed its doum-fringed course it was reduced to a string of muddy pools, their verges trampled into caked mud by cattle and donkeys; but water lay in them, and the Lorian was swampy. This is not always so.

Elephants, since time immemorial, have used it in years of shortage, when other water sources fail. In the savage and prolonged drought of the early thirties they assembled here from hundreds of miles around. But the swamp shrank and shrivelled. At first the elephants were able to survive by digging mudholes which they shared with hippos; then even these failed them; the Lorian became an expanse of caked black soil and choking dust, swept by scorching gales. Hippos and elephants died in their thousands. Some, I was told, were trapped in mud which hardened to the consistency of cement, too weak to struggle free. For years afterwards the area was strewn with bleached bones. Since then floods have washed away most of these grisly relics.

A Desert Hero

At Habaswein we left the river and struck northeast towards Wajir, along a road made by Vincent Glenday. In colonial days this region with its proud, quarrelsome, nomadic peoples, resistant alike to what we call progress and to alien rule,

needed to control it a special kind of man, possessed of at least some of the qualities of the legendary hero of the Western tradition, from Theseus and Achilles by way of Roland and Richard Coeur de Lion to Roger Keyes, Wingate and Lawrence of Arabia. Qualities, that is to say, of personal courage, independence of mind, an ability to make quick and firm decisions; integrity, physical toughness and a mental toughness, too, that will enable a man to thrive on solitude.

General Wavell, writing on the attributes of great commanders, placed highest on his list robustness, which he compared with the robustness of weapons buried in mud for a prolonged period to test their reliability. Rifles, commanders and administrators on Kenya's Northern Frontier all share a need for this trait. The names of those who have possessed it are remembered here from the days of Kittermaster, a giant of a man and the first Englishman to be seen by most of these nomads, by way of Glenday and Gerald Reece, down to Sir Richard Turnbull, the last in this tradition to wind up the colonial epoch. The indefinable quality of leadership was theirs, and they loved the land and its peoples with that peculiar kind of love that some men feel for deserts, ships and mountains. Essentially the love of challenge, I suppose, to a man's own character, combined with the instinct of the gambler who needs danger as the human frame needs salt.

Not that Vincent Glenday, as I remember him, would strike anyone as a gambler; a rather stocky, foursquare, grave-looking, dependable individual with a quiet manner and a directness which won him the respect of the tortuous-minded Somalis. Common sense seemed more his mark than any hint of recklessness or flamboyance; he dressed soberly, and did not speak when he had nothing to say. He shunned women, and selected bachelors as his lieutenants; but married in the end.

The romantic, T. E. Lawrence approach to deserts, solitudes and nomads irritated him. Mr. Eric Dutton, who shared some of his journeys and wrote a book of which he was a joint hero, recorded that he once remarked: "The North is the victim of romance: campfires, sheikhs and the rest. Cut all that out and what is left: my job; and that is as clear as day—to maintain law and order, to keep the wells open and to improve the conditions of the people. You can titivate that any way you like; it is enough for me as it is." [1] Enough, indeed, for anyone; and too much for some.

Wells at Wajir

Wajir is a Beau Geste kind of place, with white crenellated battlements, sentries with neck flaps on their peaked caps, and bugles that sound reveille and the last post at the day's start and ending. It stands in the eye of a ruthless sun, among sparse thorn scrub and baked grit on a plain whose spiky little trees cast no noon shadows, at the junction of three roads and beside wells that account for its existence. It is the Somali headquarters of the North.

As you approach Wajir you pass long strings of camels looking, in the distance, like some tawny serpent undulating across the plain. They are converging on the wells that have for centuries drawn men and beasts to this bleak spot. For here is no oasis, grove or even hill; the water, trapped by limestone, reposes at the bottom of several hundred separate wells, each forty or fifty feet deep, and every drop must be hauled by hand in soft, round bags made from goatskin or calfhide.

Why couldn't pumps be installed? "Because they'd very

---

[1] *Lillibullero, or the Golden Road,* by E. A. T. Dutton. Privately printed, Zanzibar, 1944.

soon exhaust the water." These wells replenish slowly, as you'd expect in a region whose mean rainfall is under ten inches. In fact, it seems a miracle there is any water in the wells at all. "And with less to do," the D.C. added, "the Somalis would spend even more time quarrelling."

The Somalis' reputation for discord and feuding is widespread and justified. Their lives revolve round water, especially round access to wells. There is never enough water, and its enjoyment is a matter of life and death. Quarrels that are bitter, deep and worth dying for constantly arise.

If more water could be provided, would the quarrelling die down? "No, because their herds and flocks will always increase to the limit that the country can support. That limit's already been passed in many places, thanks to veterinary science; and now the people are increasing, thanks to medicine. But no one can increase the rainfall, therefore the water or the pasturage. The pressure's building up."

About two hundred thousand people live in this Northern Frontier District, which covers over one hundred thousand square miles. Even a population density of a couple of humans to the square mile, having regard to the livestock they own, is too high. There are years in which virtually no rain falls at all. Men often do without water for two days, cattle normally for three. When they travel between wells, perhaps fifty or sixty miles apart, during the *jilal,* that four- or five-month drought between the two periods when people hope for rain, men will squeeze moisture from the roots of a red-flowering plant called *Buta worabesa* and live on bark, berries and air.

From the District Commissioner's veranda you can see camels at the wells and stroll out to watch them queueing up like patient British housewives at the fruit and vegetable market to take their turn at the troughs into which the water haulers empty their buckets. Each batch has a turn, retreats, waits an hour or so and then comes back for more, repeating this several times until replete. Flocks of doves swoop in to sip the puddles, and women fill their wooden or goatskin vessels from the shallow troughs. They are strong and tall but, in times of relative plenty, tend to store fat round the hips, as sheep do in their tails, in contrast to the men, who have the slimmest hips imaginable, spidery legs and thin wrists and ankles.

Water hauling goes on all round the clock. All night long the low-pitched, gentle roaring of camels, the clattering click-clack of their wooden bells and the rhythmic, plangent chanting of the haulers rise towards a deep velvet sky and hard, unshrouded stars. These sounds are of the essence of Wajir, as much part of it as the heat, the glare, the smell of dried dung and goats and cattle.

The mosque's white phallic minaret was built by Italian prisoners of war after its predecessor had been bombed. Five times a day an elderly imam climbs the steep, narrow steps to summon the faithful; an even more elderly imam, who has made three pilgrimages to Mecca, conducts prayers.

Out in the scrub, bush and desert itinerant holy men travel from nomad *boma* to *boma,* each with his rosary and tattered Koran and long strips of wood, rather like cricket bats, on which sacred texts are inscribed. Islam here may be attenuated and impure in doctrine, but it is a real and living faith that unites all the Somalis and many others they have half absorbed, conquered or proselytized.

Somali Pressure

Some of the leading Somali chiefs had come to Wajir for a meeting. They were tall, erect, wily old men—one was seventy-five—with wiry beards, fine heads, clever faces and with pride, cunning and authority written all over them. Dressed in brick-red and gentian-blue woollen shawls and checkered woven *kikois* (striped wrap-over skirts, one might say), they looked like so many Old Testament prophets come to testify. They had come, however, not to testify but (as usual) to argue, mainly about the boundaries of their tribal grazing grounds, perennially overstocked. The only hope of saving these from total destruction lies in closing certain areas, at certain times of year, to all livestock, and so operating a rough system of rotational grazing. This control is exercised through the tribes and subtribes into which the Somali people are divided. There are six major groups, sometimes called confederacies, each composed of many different subtribes or sections. A general rivalry of pride and ancestry between confederacies such as the Ishaak, Darod and Hawiya is reinforced by a specific rivalry for grazing grounds between subtribes. Chiefs reach their position mainly by personality and prowess in war.

Although they have lived a long time in the Horn of Africa and intermarried for centuries with its native peoples, the Somalis reject their African blood and trace their lineage back to a descendant of the prophet who landed on the North African coast about the time of the Norman Conquest, married a local princess and founded one of the confederacies. Myth reflects fact; the Somalis spring from Arab settlers on the Red Sea coast. With remarkable tenacity they have kept alive their Moslem faith, their cast of feature and most of their customs and qualities, especially those of hardihood, ferocity, intrigue and contempt for Bantu and Negro peoples. The political subjection of a race of Moslem nomads, fantastically proud of their descent from the prophet and of

their Arab blood to the blacks of Nairobi they regard as mon-
strous.

Somali men wear loosely wound turbans of scarlet, tomato
and sky blue, and shawls of garishly dyed wool. Their hair is
fuzzy. The women go about swathed in black, but unveiled,
their eyes limned with kohl, looking like Rebecca at the well.
They dwell in low, round human birds' nests, whose interiors
are hung with cloths of gay design—all Somalis love colour—
and are scrupulously clean. Camel's milk (rich in calcium)
sustains them so effectively that they can walk all day on a
single swig of it through blinding heat and over gritty, boul-
der-strewn, shadeless desert. Most Europeans who have lived
among them at once esteem and distrust them; admire their
courage and regret their ferocity; respect their hardihood
and deplore their duplicity; know them at once as brave and
treacherous, frugal and arrogant, proud and unreliable.

The Somali Line

The history of Kenya's Northern Frontier is one of a steady
southward and westward pressure from Somali tribes who
have for centuries been infiltrating, deceiving, sometimes
conquering and eventually absorbing everyone in their path.
This process was arrested by the short-lived colonial spell
which froze all the fluctuating tribes and races of Africa in
the position they happened to occupy at the moment, like the
children's game of grandmother's steps.

Fixed frontiers—a wholly alien, artificial concept in this
land of nomads—were drawn on maps which quite ignored
traditional grazing grounds, water holes and seasonal movements of camels and cattle. The Somalis found themselves
parcelled out, without any attempt to consult them, between
four powers all nominally Christian—Ethiopia, Italy, Britain

and France. Ever since, they have been striving to reunite in a Moslem world of their own, free of the infidels' authority.

The boundary fixing was a rum affair in places. For years a dotted line on a wholly inaccurate map, agreed in 1897 between the British Minister in Addis Ababa and a reluctant and evasive Emperor, represented the Ethiopian-British frontier. In 1906 Philip Zaphiro, a Greek, was taken on at £200 ($560) a year to patrol it. Clad in an admiral's full-dress uniform hired from a theatrical costumer, he rode about the foothills of the Ethiopian *massif* on a mule, arguing with proud, suspicious Amharic barons who lived largely on raw meat and a fiery wine called *tej,* with cupbearers and concubines, in a barbaric sort of splendour unknown elsewhere since medieval days. By sheer bluff he managed to restrain their southward pressure against those remnants of the Galla people they had not yet conquered.

When, in 1895, the British established an East African protectorate, away in the far and unknown north the Somalis had not long started to infiltrate and push against the non-Somali Boran and Rendille. They were pushing hard, and in 1892 a spearhead of their forces got as far south as Mount Kenya, where a warrior of the Ogaden tribe, Abdi Ibrahim, fought the Meru people on its northern slopes. He was defeated, and himself slain while kneeling on his prayer mat with his pistol arm supported by retainers; but his was only the first probe of a general advance. "There is no doubt," Sir Richard Turnbull has written, "that had it not been for European intervention the Somalis . . . would have swept through Kenya; the local Bantu and Nilotes could scarcely have held them for a day." When the first District Commissioner set up his post at Wajir in 1912, he wrote that "Wajir was occupied to prevent the Boran from being driven from the wells which originally belonged to them." It was by then too late; the Ogaden Somalis had moved in from the east and driven out the Boran.

The British checked but did not stifle this unrelenting pressure, and in 1934 Vincent Glenday drew the Somali line from the Daua River, on the Ethiopian border, to Garissa, on the Tana River, in a renewed attempt to contain it. All the country east of this line was conceded to the Somalis. They were forbidden to penetrate west of it to use the watering places and grazing grounds of the Boran, the Rendille and other non-Somali tribes.

The Somali line existed only in the minds of its creator and his lieutenants on the one hand, and of the Somali chiefs, each one a born intriguer, on the other. It had no patrols, forts, walls or fences, and traversed well over three hundred miles of desert. For thirty years it held back the Somalis, largely through the bluff and personality of a few men whom the Somalis respected.

They respected Vincent Glenday. For three years, during World War I, he lived as one of them among the Gurre branch, in the northeastern corner of the district, intent on arresting the southward surge of the powerful Degodia and Aulihan tribes. With about seventy askaris, one machine gun and some Gurre recruits he repulsed a massive Degodia attack which had it succeeded would have enabled the victors to thrust into the undefended Kenya highlands, avenge the defeat of Abdi Ibrahim and lay waste the countryside while Allied forces were chasing General von Lettow-Vorbeck and his men all over what was then German East Africa.

Still with his small band of Gurre irregulars, Glenday continued so to harry and hustle the Degodia and Aulihan that he prevented them from mounting another organized attack, although at one time Wajir had been evacuated and his lines of communication had been all but severed. Riding about on a white stallion, he earned the name of Faras Adi and an almost legendary fame among the Somalis. Eventually he bullied and bluffed them into surrendering their rifles. On a smaller, less important scale it was a feat of the order of T. E. Lawrence's, without any of the glamour and publicity. Sir Vincent Glenday has spoken seldom and written nothing of this episode. Now, in his early seventies, after a term as Speaker of the Central Legislative Assembly, he lives quietly near Eldoret, in Kenya, cultivates his garden and keeps himself to himself and to his family.

Secession

Towards the end of 1962 a Canadian general and a Nigerian barrister toured the Northern Frontier District to assess the strength of public opinion in favor of breaking away from Kenya and joining the independent Republic of Somalia. They concluded that opinion east of the Somali line was almost unanimously in favour of secession. West of the line, it was mixed; all the Somalis, the so-called half-Somalis and those who had adopted a Somali way of life, wanted to join their brethren; the Boran and other non-Somali tribes, with equal fervour, did not.

These conclusions surprised no one. The KANU government in Nairobi has made clear beyond the least shadow of doubt that the Somalis are not to join their brothers. The borders of Kenya as colonialists drew them at the end of the nineteenth century are to remain sacrosanct; the blood of Kenya's last man will be shed before an inch of sacred soil is surrendered.

It is, of course, ironic in the extreme that one of the first acts of a nationalist government which has just shaken off the colonial yoke should be to reject a perfectly reasonable de-

mand by fellow nationalists to do the same thing. In principle, the KANU government hasn't a leg to stand on: less of a
leg even than Ethiopia, the most imperialist of nations, whose
royalist rulers are aligned with Kenya's democratic ones in
the "not an inch" policy. It is not even as if the region is of
the slightest use to anyone; on the contrary, it remains an
economic burden. Hitherto the British have paid for its expensive, unproductive policing, and now a hard-pressed African government will have to take it on. The chances of
finding oil, very slender ones, are scarcely worth all this.

But the KANU line also has some strong arguments. Once
you start this process of disintegration, where does it end?
Everyone would agitate to rearrange boundaries, which, as
President Nyerere has remarked, "are so nonsensical that
without our sense of unity they would be a cause of friction;
we have no alternative but to start from the position we inherited after the colonial partition." [2] To fall out over boundaries, he added, would be to play into the hands of those who
want to see Africa weak and divided rather than united and
strong.

And so, politically, all is in ferment; an African District
Commissioner at Isiolo has been assassinated; but at Wajir
the camels roar gently at the wells, their wooden bells clatter
and an ancient chant accompanies the rise and tipping of the
leather buckets; flocks of doves sip at puddles; life is basically
unchanged.

So it must remain. This country is in the grip of forces
stronger than those of politics: the elemental forces of sun
and rain. Where grass (of a kind) springs up and scrub un-
folds its tight leaves, there must the cattle and the camels go,
and the people with them, loading their pots and hides and

[2] "A United States of Africa," in *The Journal of Modern African Studies,*
Vol. 1, No. 1, March, 1963.

mats on to their camels and donkeys, whether they live under a government that is democratic or tyrannical, congenial or harsh, alien or native, good, bad or indifferent. Despite all mankind's rocketry, no government has learned the trick of Moses to strike water from the barren rock.

Marsabit Mountain

At Marsabit, the centre of territory still retained by the Boran, the police superintendent with whom I was staying had his after-dinner rest broken by a radio signal from North Horr, an isolated police post three hundred miles to the northwest, reporting that a party of armed Gelubba raiders had crossed the frontier from the Ethiopian side. This was serious because, not long before, Gelubba raiders from Ethiopia had slaughtered a hundred and fifty unarmed people on the Kenya side and driven their livestock away.

My host was well equipped to deal with this, or any other, crisis. A tough, decisive and unruffled man, wearing a gold ring in one ear, he had fought both Jews and Arabs in Palestine and then the Mau Mau in Kenya, with a wartime interlude in the Navy, and enjoyed all the active moments of it. With relish he wrote out and handed to the corporal his terse instruction: "Shoot to kill."

At the receiving end, at North Horr, the askaris carry water bottles, a little biltong and a rifle, but wear no boots; barefoot men can always outpace booted ones on these wastes of jagged lava rock and shale. Once a month a truck takes out rations from Marsabit, a three-day journey, but supplies are dropped by air when rain falls. The sole purpose of this and other posts is to intercept Ethiopian raiding parties whenever possible and, when it is not, to give chase. They are a long way from agreements reached in Addis Ababa.

On the way to Marsabit we passed herds of camels, Samburu women in wide ruffs of copper wire and heavy bead earrings, angular and crooked hills, herdsmen spare and long as herons, bone-dry watercourses, weaver-nested thorns, two giraffes and, when we reached the foothills of this strange mountain that rises straight out of the plain to an altitude of over five thousand feet, half a dozen greater kudu grazing on a slope drenched in a most dramatic, claret-coloured evening light such as I have never seen before or since.

The mountain of Marsabit is a very small national reserve, the remnant of a much larger game reserve now abolished because there was virtually no game left to preserve. It is the old story, with a variation: African poachers began on the animals and then British and South African soldiers, stationed here during the war, took over with much greater efficiency. A favourite sport was to go out in trucks with automatic weapons and wipe out everything in sight; carcasses of zebra, giraffes, hartebeest and gazelle lay about in thousands (the wounded dragged themselves away to die), and all vultures were gorged. No doubt time at Marsabit hung heavily on the soldiers' hands, but they made a clean sweep of the animals.

The game on the plains and in the foothills has never recovered, and never will. On the mountain itself plenty of elephants and buffalo live in a cedar forest that clothes the slopes and surrounds a crater lake near the summit, which the American couple Martin and Osa Johnson—an earlier Armand and Michaela Denis—publicized in the thirties and named Lake Paradise. A small and pleasant lodge has been built on the edge, from which, in theory, you can watch elephants, buffalo and smaller animals drinking in the lake. But we saw a lake shrunken to a reedy puddle attractive only to water birds.

Comparisons between the Martin Johnsons' photographs

and the situation today show how severely Marsabit has, ecologically speaking, degenerated in the last thirty years. Not only has the lake shrivelled, but the forest appears to be dying on its feet. Many of the cedars are old; their stark grey skeletonlike branches are festooned with long beards of grey-green lichen which look eerie and romantic, somehow reminding one of druids, but are a sign of morbidity. Young trees are few. If present tendencies persist, the forest of Marsabit will perish slowly, and with it will perish the streams on which the pastoral people of the plain, Samburu and Rendille, depend.

Changes in rainfall and climate are commonly blamed, and fires started by honey hunters have certainly contributed. The whole mountain area seems to be getting drier than it was, in the grip of an ecological change.

Nature, of course, could reverse this, and no sooner had we reached Marsabit than it began to look as if she intended to try. Rain bucketed down all one night, all next day and the day after. Mist shrouded the forests and it was bitterly cold. We heard elephants and smelled buffalo, but never saw them. Tracks through the forest became impassable, and even our policeman's Land-Rover, driven with the skill and dash one would expect, stuck in the mud. In a few brief interludes of sunshine a host of brilliant-hued butterflies hovered round vermilion poinsettias on his lawn. All roads leading off the mountain were closed, and it appeared that we should over-stay our welcome, possibly by weeks. Minimal as the rainfall is on the surrounding desert, here on the mountain it rises to respectable proportions. The elephants, it seemed, had gone down below to get away from the drips, but we, bound like slaves to our mechanical galleys, were unable to follow.

A Magic Motorcar

It is a rule of the district that all travellers must proceed in convoy with at least one other vehicle. On the way to Marsabit our mate had been a Volkswagen driven by Miss A, who was conducting an English visitor on a round of game parks. Volkswagens are small cars, and both its occupants were fairly bulky, but the amount of equipment stowed in that vehicle was remarkable.

We were put to shame, at lunchtime on the road, by plates, knives and forks, napkins and glasses, a table spread with a cloth, chairs with cushions and a splendid repast, while we munched our sandwiches sitting by the trackside on the hot brown sand. Even more were we impressed when our companions generously invited us to dinner at the game lodge. The roadside luncheon paled before the meal our hostess, clearly a *cordon bleu* cook, served us: she had brought her own utensils, including a chafing dish and spirit lamp, not to mention cutlery and china and such extras as a can of the best olive oil, a canister of herbs and spices and a coffee percolator; we drank sherry and had a choice of red or white wine; both she and her client, who had quite a lot of luggage of his own, appeared immaculately dressed, and so far as I could make out, a good deal of furniture seemed to have come along in the Volkswagen into the bargain. It was like one of those tricks when the conjurer pulls an inexhaustible supply of handkerchiefs, flags, bunches of flowers and eventually birds and rabbits out of a plainly empty plywood cylinder.

The District Commissioner's mother-in-law, marooned like ourselves in the forest by the mud, celebrated a birthday during our visit; and Miss A offered to bake her a cake, having, apparently, all the ingredients handy. We heard that it was excellent. In a facetious spirit I remarked to its creator: "I suppose you had some birthday cake candles with you?" She replied: "As a matter of fact, I had." After that we found it hard to envisage any situation for which Miss A had come unprepared into this wilderness.

When we travelled back along the road to Isiolo, the Kaisut desert, which had been a vast expanse of tawny barren sand and boulders only a week before, had become miraculously carpeted, as far as eye could see, with a yellow-flowered creeping plant of the genus *Tribulus*. It was like a field of buttercups stretching for thirty or forty miles. Cocoa-coloured water was racing down the *wadis,* but had subsided just enough to give us passage. The Volkswagen appeared to leap from boulder to boulder with its magical load. At Isiolo we parted company with our companion, who was due next day at the Amboseli safari lodge to cook a George Washington dinner, involving roast turkey, cranberry sauce and cherry pie, for twenty-four Americans. No doubt enough cherries were tucked away behind the seat.

The Adamsons at Isiolo

Isiolo, the capital of the N.F.D., will for me always be associated with the world's most famous lioness and her foster parents, Joy and George Adamson.

I first saw Elsa as a cub playing with an old tire hung from a tree in the Adamsons' garden, and renewed acquaintance at several stages of her growth until not long before the Adamsons attempted to settle her in the Meru game reserve, where she mated with a wild lion and reared her scarcely less famous cubs. And of course I shall not attempt to add to all that has been written with such felicity of Elsa's story. Her charm and grace were undeniable, and even more remarkable the love, care and patience devoted to her by both her foster parents in their very different ways: Joy with the intensity, passion and taut-nerved concentration of a high-strung, single-minded woman of exceptional talent (she is also a first-rate botanist and skilful painter) without children, George with the unruffled calm, keen observation, quiet humour and aloof and yet companionable reserve of the born naturalist, sportsman and nomad.

Joy herself became more and more leonine as she and Elsa developed their extraordinary relationship. Her colouring is tawny, her figure sinewy and her eyes, although pure blue instead of agate, harbour that pinpointed, hard-packed intensity you can also see in those of a lion. Perhaps it was only in the beholder's imagination that these qualities seemed to grow more pronounced.

Often Joy would withdraw at about six o'clock into Elsa's apartment—you couldn't use the word cage, for she was never confined—and sit with her for the rest of the evening, oblivious of a meal, talking, sketching and sometimes just sitting and watching her companion. They understood each other better than many human pairs do. Joy, as we know from photographs, had complete trust in Elsa, and would put a hand in her mouth or roll and wrestle with her on the floor. But Joy was terrified of elephants, and sometimes in the Land-Rover would shout to George to go no closer to a herd, or to turn quickly and drive away. George would pay no attention. Joy feared the elephants might injure Elsa, who sometimes teased them, leaping off her seat on the Land-Rover's roof to gallop up to them and practice stalking. The elephants paid no attention. Elsa was an obsession. You cannot rear and tame an animal unless you allow it to possess you.

As guests, we saw more of Pati-Pati, the rock hyrax, than

of Elsa; she was always around, whereas Elsa was normally excluded from the bungalow when visitors occupied it, in case they did not like a lioness inviting them to rough games at all hours or jumping on their beds. Pati-Pati, with her thick furry pelt, her purposeful actions, strong will and beady eye, had great charm; also a marked ruthlessness of character. She knew exactly what she wanted, and allowed nothing to stand in her way.

One of the things she wanted was to curl herself round the neck of anyone who occupied Joy's bed. Generously Joy would surrender her own room to her guest and retreat to a camp bed in the office. Pati-Pati went with the room. My mother, deeply flattered by this mark of trust from Pati-Pati, struggled through her first night with the furry hyrax encircling her neck; but Isiolo can be very hot, and during the second night she attempted gently to disengage Pati-Pati and persuade her to sleep at the foot of the bed.

This move was ill received. After a good deal of argument Pati-Pati turned and bit, quite savagely. An unfortunate scene ended with Pati-Pati chattering furiously on the veranda and Tilly dabbing iodine on her neck.

In the morning both felt ashamed. Tilly apologized to Joy, but Pati-Pati did better; she apologized to Tilly. With the early morning tea she entered the room, approached the bed and rolled over on her back with all her feet in the air. Her meaning could not have been plainer. All the same, Isiolo was not getting any cooler and it was fortunate for both parties that we left later in the day.

Pati-Pati liked to share anything that was going at mealtimes, but tobacco was her favourite food, and she would tear cigarettes to pieces or delve into George's pouch. She also liked whisky and, given half a chance, would pull off the top and tip the bottle to get at it. Her other habits were rigid.

Hyraxes are accustomed to expel their droppings over the side of a rock. Droppings, therefore, must literally be dropped, and if this was impossible Pati-Pati would call her bowels out on strike.

It took the Adamsons a little time to discover that whenever they were on safari Pati-Pati grew more and more uncomfortable. While they themselves, when on the move, made use of the bush, Pati-Pati stood firm: no rocks, no droppings. She nearly burst herself before the Adamsons divined her trouble. After that they never travelled without a sort of perch which they rigged up in the bush for her at every camp.

In the house they cut a little hatchway through the base of the door to give her free access to the water closet. A notice on the door asked visitors to leave the seat tipped up for her convenience, as she found it difficult to get a grip on polished wood. Sometimes one would see her squatting there, her toes clasping the edge of the porcelain bowl, in an attitude of deep contemplation; disturbed, she would cast a baleful look at the intruder, give a throaty chuckle and waddle through the hatch in her purposeful way. It was tragic to hear that she had died of heat stroke when taken for a seaside holiday.

TWIN THORNS

Dragons on Twigs

Two thorn trees link horizontal branches across the track to form a natural gateway at the last bend before you climb steeply to the house at Njoro. They haven't changed for forty years—longer, I expect, but that is as long as I remember them. They always seem to welcome you.

The house hasn't changed much either, except to retreat behind a screen of creepers, like a Victorian elder muffling his face in whiskers. Whether the house holds up the creepers or the creepers support the house is a moot point. It is a rust-coloured little bungalow made of mud rammed into wire netting and roofed with corrugated iron—far from beautiful, but cozy. You walk straight into a small, square, dog-filled sitting room whose walls are, surprisingly, sheathed in dark panelling designed thirty years ago by a visiting aunt and copied from a room in Hampton Court, together with a garland of fruit carved over the fireplace. You need a good fire every night and sometimes in the daytime, when mists roll down from the mountains. I have seen the lawn white with hail. A honeysuckle hedge which never seems to cease flowering guards the door.

Generally we breakfast off fresh fruit under a very old olive tree, with white orchids in its branches, near this sweet-smelling hedge, and watch visitors to the bird table. Starlings are the boldest; they have a self-assertiveness and greed which puts one off despite their handsome royal-blue plumage that glistens in the sunshine like a satin armour. They always look immaculate, well preened. Much more attractive is the white-browed robin chat, often called the Kenya robin, whose slate-grey plumage is faced by a rufous rump and breast and whose fluting song is perhaps the sweetest note in the dawn chorus. And they are excellent mimics. Tiny, precise and chubby, little waxbills in pale turquoise and rich plum purple come in small bands; the golden orioles keep their distance; sun-birds thrust slender sickle beaks into the throats of the orange bignonias, penetrating the base of each trumpet to reach the nectar, while their wings vibrate like pulsometers.

Goodness knows how many kinds of sunbirds there are— dozens, scores. Here the commonest is the bronzy sunbird— as its name tells you, a metallic bronze all over with a hint of olive green, not as spectacular as some, but very beautiful. A pair is busy every morning among the bignonias. Almost certainly they have a nest nearby. Their breeding habits display a restraint humans might well copy; only one egg as a rule, never more than two, in basket-shaped nests hitched on to twigs. Probably if I asked Nanga, the gardener, or the old man with the crippled foot who does odd jobs, they would find the sunbirds' nest, for they are far more observant than I am. Annoyingly, they can discover chameleons in the bushes in a few minutes, whereas I peer in vain. They seem to know exactly where to look.

When either has located a chameleon he will not touch the creature, but manoeuvre it on to the end of a long stick, and then carry it held as far as possible from his body. Superstition about chameleons extends all over Africa to unrelated peo-ples who share a common legend. There are many variants,

but the basis is the same—the chameleon is to blame for death. God created man immune to death, but one day sent a messenger to proclaim the edict of mortality; then, relenting, he dispatched the chameleon to cancel his proclamation. The chameleon dallied, and arrived too late. And so chameleons are the emblem of death, untouchable.

Modern Kikuyu half believe the legend and half don't, laugh at themselves for these childish notions, yet won't relinquish them entirely, just as Europeans behave about new moons, ladders and touching wood. Karanja called me one day and said: "Look, here's a chameleon who's telephoning." He pointed out one that had attached itself to a wire supporting the telegraph pole. Its tail was coiled above its back in a neat spiral. "He wants to make a call to Nakuru."

Chameleons have an air half ludicrous and half tragic. Is it their slow, jerky pace, their defencelessness, their expression of stoical anxiety? Their dry, papery claws grip your finger nervously but firmly. They never bite or scratch, and are totally harmless, except to flies. To glimpse that long, thin tongue—much longer than the body—dart out like a whiplash to nip a fly off a twig fascinates; the motion is so quick you can barely detect it, which is no doubt why Shelley believed chameleons to feed on light and air.

They eat prodigious quantities of flies and nothing else, so are wholly beneficial creatures. Miniature dragons, they are rough-skinned with a saw-edged back, appear to test each step with a front foot before they move a single pace forward and are endowed with eyes which can swivel round in all directions, independently of each other, just like a ball and socket joint.

When Mr. Ionides, the renowned herpetologist, paid a visit to the farm in search of the Njoro horned viper, he called for a rally of chameleons, and twelve or fifteen were collected from the bushes in and around the garden. Tilly supposed him to be looking for some rare species, or conducting a census to estimate their population density. After providing him with his frugal meal of a slice of biltong, she inquired after the chameleons, and was deeply distressed to hear that every one had perished. "They're all pickled by now," said Mr. Ionides. A massacre of innocents.

By the time of my visit the population had built up again. I doubt if these chameleons have many predators, other than Mr. Ionides. Since few Africans will touch them, they are safe from man, the savagest of all, and generally stay deep enough in the heart of bushes to avoid the eyes of hawks and eagles. When attacked, they swell up to twice their normal size, flap their ears, hiss and literally turn black with fury, in the hope of frightening off their enemy—all bluff, and hawks probably pay no attention. Endearing creatures, whom no one (even Mr. Ionides?) could fail to like.

Old Retainers

Old Karanja wa M'Kono has known me since I was a small child, and sometimes dredges up alarming recollections. "Do you remember," he inquired the other day, "chopping off the heads of maize stalks with a knife and saying: 'This is what my father is doing to the Germans'?" That must have been in World War I. "Do you remember falling off a white pony that shied at a python?"

Karanja is tall and lean and light in colour, an indication of his Masai blood, which comes out also in a passion for cattle. Formerly the senior herdsman, he descended to a single Jersey house cow, and when the house cow went he retired, being well past seventy, only to mooch about so miserably, with nothing ungulate to care for, that Tilly bought a pair of goats, of some superior breed, to occupy him. He has the manners of a polite aristocrat and a very upright carriage, except when his rheumatics are bad. He was once so crippled that Tilly wrote to ask if I could find in England some long woollen combinations to comfort him on cold nights. At first I failed; they are no longer stocked. But a reference to the problem in a radio programme brought several generous offers from daughters who had kept their late fathers' underwear put away in mothballs, and one from a firm in Suffolk which still carried the line. Now Karanja's rheumatism troubles him less than it used to.

He is the sole male survivor of those Kikuyu who came here forty years ago from Thika and walked from the station, their wives carrying their belongings, with Tilly in the lead. Not a living soul was to be seen then in the forest and bush, unless it might be a wandering Dorobo hunter; buffalo and antelope were plentiful. They and the bush have gone, and nearly all the trees except the big thorns which Tilly has insisted on preserving. Almost every inch is cultivated, and at the school shared between three adjoining farms—not very big ones—nearly three hundred Kikuyu children receive instruction.

Mbugwa, son of Njombo (the first headman) was a baby when the pioneer column moved into these hills. His welcome is the warmest, his smile the broadest and most spontaneous of all the Kikuyu. He must have been fourteen or fifteen when I first remember him as the kitchen *toto,* the cook's skivvy. We took him with us on a short safari and, one evening, pitched camp in the dark. Mbugwa went forth to gather firewood and returned with an armful of excellent dry sticks. Next morning a posse of tall, infuriated men carrying spears, and swords in vermilion leather scabbards, invaded the camp. They were Meru warriors, and practically marched us away to their shambas, which were enclosed in a neat fence of split cedar posts. At least partially enclosed: Mbugwa, in the darkness, had removed most of them for our fire. In those days he stuttered badly and fright so paralyzed him that he was unable to explain. Luckily, five shillings (seventy cents) appeased the warriors and we went on our way.

Another memory of Mbugwa concerns a variation of the three-card trick, done with little bells. Two rang, and one didn't; but when you tried to spot the silent one you never could—all three tinkled. This fascinated Mbugwa. He would beg for the trick to be performed and lean over the bells and try again and again, looking more baffled and incredulous at each failure.

At last the secret was revealed. I thought Mbugwa would explode. He swelled like one of the chameleons, and then laughter shook him as a gale shakes a tree; he staggered about the room in ecstasy and finally collapsed on the floor. After that he was chuckling, and now and then guffawing, for days, if not weeks, and at intervals would split his face in two, strike his thigh and cry: "The bells! The sorcerer's bells! The bells of magic! Eeeeeee! The bells!"

As well as being one of the best-natured and most hard-working of men—you never see him dawdling, and he often runs—Mbugwa is also one of the most considerate. He is always thinking of other people's comfort, trying to anticipate their needs and remembering their preferences. There came to lunch a friend of Tilly's, well known to Mbugwa—he has several times accompanied Tilly to this friend's house near Nairobi. Would she, he asked, be kind enough to take a small bag of maize back with her and keep it until called for? It was for "someone who helped me once many years ago; I want to send a small present to show that I have not forgotten him."

One day Tilly happened to express a mild regret that she never tasted sweet potatoes these days; they didn't grow at Njoro, and seemed to have vanished from the market. On Christmas Day, some months later, Mbugwa called her, as usual, sharp at six, with tea and a beaming smile and, on this occasion, a basket which he placed on her bed. "Your Christmas present": a basketful of sweet potatoes, sent for specially to Nairobi, and decorated with a red ribbon tied in a bow.

Mbugwa's wife, alas, is lazy, and something of a scold. Almost every afternoon he goes to his shamba with a hoe to do what, by Kikuyu custom, is her work. But she has given him six children, so far, and he is back in time to listen to the news in Swahili, which always attracts a crowd.

Despite a lifetime's acquaintance with European houses, Mbugwa prefers to live in an old-style Kikuyu round hut with its cooking stones and smoke-blackened beams. His hut is full of souvenirs. When he came with us to the Murchison

Falls, he stuffed his pockets full of stones "to edge the path with, by the door." From the coast he brought the shells of cowries and clams, and he is almost as fond as Tilly is of collecting garden seeds.

Mbugwa has never learned to read, although I am sure he could if he tried, but his English, which he practices on guests, is fluent, if a little bumpy in accent and unpredictable in vocabulary. He can turn his hand to anything, from cleaning out a carburetor to ironing tender fabrics, from planting maize to whipping up an omelette, from mending the refrigerator to arranging flowers, at which his touch would not displease Constance Spry. The main thing is that he is always gay. Mbugwa is a rarity in any country, and in any age.

Newcomers

Most of Tilly's neighbours have been here almost as long as she has, except for newcomers who are now taking over a small, undeveloped farm—about a hundred acres—on the riverbank. They have built a temporary shelter and hired men to hack down bush, drag out stumps and get some land under cultivation. A small herd of in-calf Jersey heifers pick a living from the slopes.

These are the first Africans to buy land in this part of the former white highlands. There are two partners, both middle-aged men. One worked for a European farmer as his stockman, the other as his tractor driver. They are investing all their savings in this venture, their ex-employer has advanced some capital and they are getting a Land Bank development loan. Their immediate neighbour is a retired Indian Army cavalry officer, without doubt a pukka sahib. His reaction surprised me. "Not bad chaps at all," was his comment. "Very decent manners. They came to ask my permission to take their lorry across my land." Another white farmer said: "They're very amiable, and good workers. But they've got a stiff job ahead." Both neighbours are helping the newcomers in various practical ways.

It's never any good, of course, kicking against the pricks. Those who won't accept these drastic changes have departed. Those who remain do so in the full knowledge that they will live in an African country under African rule. But this revolution in relationships, surely one of the quickest and most drastic nonviolent reversals in the world's history, has come about with more good humour and restraint on both sides than most people would have thought possible. In a land where tempers can be violent and tensions run high, and where a bitter five-year civil war ended less than a decade ago, the relative serenity with which power has been taken over and surrendered is remarkable.

Of course there is friction sometimes; tactless speeches, fears, grumbles and resentment. But, by and large, most whites accept the inevitable with a fair grace, most blacks disarm by genuine friendliness. A friend of Tilly's, employed at a luxurious upcountry hotel, found herself in conversation with one of the first African customers. "Are you," she inquired, "a traveller passing through?" "No, madam, I am a gentleman of this town." A pause. "And you, madam, you are perhaps a traveller?" "No, I'm the cook." No pause this time. "It is because I have not yet visited the kitchen that we have not met before." Then they all shook hands.

Njoro Students

Until October, 1961, Egerton College, at Njoro, had no African students, only whites, for whose express benefit the college was founded by a rich eccentric English peer. In October, 1963, out of 220 students all but 38 were African, and only 6 European (the balance Asian). Though it was designed originally to teach both local lads and new settlers from Europe how to farm in Kenya, its main function is now to train young Africans who will man the Government's agricultural and cognate services. So it has changed its direction as well as its colour.

Everything about Egerton College is expanding. Money is pouring in—perhaps it would be more accurate to say it is being sucked and persuaded in by its energetic, black-bearded principal, Mr. Barrett—from "the Outside." The Guildford and Farnham branch of the Feed the Hungry campaign is financing research on the manufacture of milk products: the Dulverton Trust is putting up a students' hall; now Egerton has been "adopted" by the University of West Virginia.

Every American university and college now has, or wants to have, an African or Asian "project," to bring aid to the undeveloped in a more direct and personal way than merely by paying taxes and subscribing to appeals. A "personal relationship" can then be formed between the two institutions.

Two West Virginia professors were scouting round, when I visited the college, to see what sort of aid they could recommend. For a start, they were awarding twelve scholarships to the best students. Egerton's top place went, last year, to a European, the second place to an Arab. Clearly these two bright young men should have been awarded the first scholarships. But their skins were the wrong colour. This is a scheme to aid Africans, not Europeans and Asians; so they were passed over. In view of past history, such a tipping of the scales the other way is to be expected. Still, it has its irony; and (as in all cases of racial discrimination) its wastage of talent.

Young men from almost every part of East Africa mix in

here. The Kikuyu supply the biggest element and also the brightest; nine out of ten of the most successful are Kikuyu. Is there resentment among the others? If so, it is suppressed; these educated young men know that in unity, *umoja*—together—lies their only hope of a modern future.

For two years these young men learn the scientific basis of the industry on which East Africa's whole future must be based. Their own future is equally in hazard. Examinations are to the modern youth what circumcision was to his father. Once he is over this ordeal, a future opens up bright with opportunity and hope of reward; failure brings total disaster. To the successful go the best jobs, well paid and full of *heshima,* in the higher ranks of the civil service; and a clear run through to the top for the luckiest and ablest; failures can look only for the second-best. No wonder, as their instructors report, they are keyed up, tense and work too hard. "Our trouble is to try to stop them overworking and reading books they lack the grounding to understand."

Once again—no women students. Some of the men are paying to get wives or fiancées into a Homecraft Centre at Njoro which provides a three-month course in strictly practical household affairs for those with little schooling—they needn't even be literate. In fact, the illiterate prove, on the whole, quicker to learn than readers, because they work harder and concentrate more.

The Centre is simple, clean and practical. Everything is done inexpensively because money for women's projects comes, if it comes at all, in dribbles, not in gushes. Across the way, at Egerton, they spend £15,000 ($42,000) on one new dining room; here the whole place has gone up for less than a fifth of this sum. There is fierce competition to get in. Male students write from Britain and from the United States, imploring admission for their wives, or future wives.

Laughter in the Clinic

I asked if instruction is given in family planning. Yes: a midwife explains it to each course. The reaction? "They roar with laughter. They think it's all a great joke. Why should anyone want to stop babies? They want as many as they possibly can."

If birth control is to come, it will be the men who will accept it, and for one reason—because they can't afford school fees for a dozen children. The most reactionary step that could possibly be taken in modern Africa, the step most fatal to hopes of progress, would be to abolish school fees.

Unfortunately, few African leaders agree. I think they are mistaken, and will one day recognize the truth of this. By then it will be too late, if things go on as they are. The mounting flood of babies will have swept away hopes of better living standards and of satisfied appetites; the gap between rich and poor will have widened; for mere bulk, the human race will have sacrificed quality. What is the object of feeding the hungry, who will breed even more and even hungrier offspring, to find standing room only on a depleted planet stripped of its resources, beauties, forests, of its very soil?

Pay through the nose for education; therein lies the only hope of averting disaster. Mr. Leslie Brown, former Deputy Director of Agriculture and authority on flamingoes and birds of prey, would pass three laws and scrap the rest. (1) Everyone to drink at least one litre of wine a day; object, to make people happy. (2) No tax on earned incomes over (say) £2,500 ($7,000) a year: object, to encourage and reward ability. (3) The first two children to be educated free and to qualify their parents for other benefits; after that all benefits to be forfeited and taxation to rise progressively, to crushing heights, on each successive child: object, to eliminate large

families. The only exception would be that those who qualify under rule (2) could have as many children as they liked:
object, to encourage breeding from the competent instead of,
as at present, mainly from the feckless and moronic. He reckons these three simple laws would enable the human race
to go on living for some time to come on this planet; otherwise things will explode.

"The glory, jest, and riddle of the world," Pope described
the human race. Julian Huxley has added another term: its
"cancer."

Meek Schoolboys

Njoro has a new secondary school—for boys only, all board-
ers. Although it is in the heart of a Kalenjin region, ninety-
five out of every hundred of its pupils are Kikuyu. And half
the graduate staff are Americans.

The greatest difference between American and African
schools observed by these visiting teachers lies in the discipline. In the United States much of the teachers' energy, capacity and effort goes in keeping order in class. A moment's
relaxation invites chaos and mayhem. By contrast, discipline
in Africa is no problem at all. "The kids here just *want* to
learn." This young American, spectacled and earnest and
gentle, sounded amazed. "The worst punishment you can inflict is to keep them out of class. It's teaching made easy."

A colleague agreed. "The energies we have to burn up
back home in keeping order we can give here to our real job,
teaching kids—and kids who want to learn. That's fine. All
the same, I don't feel I've gone as far with them as I should
have. They're intelligent and yet there's a real stubborn-
ness. . . ."

By this he seemed to mean conservatism. They were prepared to accept only the forms of teaching they were used to, nothing experimental. They preferred well-worn tracks.

"It's given me," this teacher said, "a wholly new conception of the primitive." Formerly he had thought backwardness due to a lower mental capacity. But now—"potentially these boys are just as bright as comparable Americans. There's something else holding them back." Just what, he couldn't say. After eighteen months his time was up, and he was leaving.

Another colleague found the boys' discipline a handicap, not an advantage. "Classes lack the stimulus of continual questioning, disagreement and inquiry. It's too easy for the teacher. We need tension to keep us on the *qui vive.*"

A young Irishman chipped in to say he *did* get questions, often careful and considered ones. He cited as an example the passage in *Julius Caesar* when, after Mark Antony has roused the rabble with his famous speech, the plebeians put four questions to Cinna, the last being: Is he a bachelor? Why, said the pupils, was this asked? What was the significance of bachelors? Was Cinna killed for being one? Such questions provide plenty of stimulus to the teacher.

All schools are now, in theory, multiracial, but this had only Africans. There are plenty of Asian families at Njoro. Why didn't any of their children attend? "They wouldn't be accepted," I was told, "by the Africans." Multiracialism is a one-way street here.

Secondary school fees are £20 ($56) a year, but the headmaster didn't think the father of a single pupil paid the fees. All enjoyed scholarships or bursaries, and any father whose son had failed to qualify for one of these awards could ask for a remission of fees on the grounds of hardship.

A European education officer in process of training an African to succeed him in his job told me of a Kikuyu who wrote to apply for such a remission. "I am old," ran the letter, "and I have thirteen children. My son is clever, but I cannot pay his fees. . . ." The African official drafted this crisp reply:

Dear Sir,

I have the honour to acknowledge your letter of the 10th instant. As you have thirteen children, you must have two wives and therefore be a rich man. I regret, therefore, that I cannot see my way to a remission of fees.

I have the honour, to be, Sir, your obedient servant. . . .

A few days later the education officer ran into the applicant's employer in the bank. "Who's the fellow who wrote that letter to my headman?" The official told him, fearing an outburst against obtuse African bureaucrats. "I'd like to shake him by the hand," said the farmer. "Would you like to see my headman's bankbook?" He had it with him; it showed a credit balance of £1,300 ($3,640).

"The old humbug's got three wives. On the last day of every month each of the wives and all the working children hand in their pay. He puts it in an envelope without counting it and hands it to me and says: 'Put it in the bank for me, *bwana*,' and I do. God knows how many children he's got, but most of them are working, only three at school. Remission of fees . . ."

When it was the European's job to waive or not to waive school fees, remissions were granted in between eight and nine per cent of the cases. Since the responsibility has been handed over to Africans, the percentage of remissions has fallen to one.

Lake Baringo

At Campi ya Samaki—the fish camp—we visited a bold young man who lives with his wife on the shores of Lake

Baringo with five small children (one a baby), runs a fishery and captures animals and birds for zoos. Marabout storks and crested cranes parade up and down the lake shore like street-walkers, or perch in the leafless branches of a tree killed when the lake rose high enough to flood the house and waves broke into the first-floor sitting room.

On the edge of the lawn bask crocodiles who, it seems, ignore the elder Roberts children when they come to bathe. Their father has a theory that crocodiles don't snap at people when they have enough fish to eat, and these are copiously supplied with offal from the factory. David Roberts should know. It was as a professional crocodile hunter that he first came to Lake Baringo, and he killed over a thousand of them here.

His method was to wade into the lake at night with a torch in one hand and in the other a flat wooden club made from a thorn branch. He would shine the torch into the crocodile's eyes and bash the reptile on the back of the head with his club. This would only stun it. With his African team he would haul it quickly to the shore, kill it with an axe and wade back for the next victim.

Didn't the smack of the club disturb the other saurians? Crocodiles have a night habit, Mr. Roberts said, of thumping the water with their tails, making a sound much like that of a club or axe. A rifle shot would have panicked them. He had to average at least five crocodiles every night to make a living.

Now he has given up hunting and gone to the other extreme. He tries to preserve the crocodiles; partly to supply their young to zoos, partly because he thinks they help, in their turn, to preserve the *Tilapia* he needs for his fishery. This they do by eating the *Tilapia*'s enemies, the catfish, and also by ripping the nets of fishermen who poach *Tilapia* in the shallows near the lake's edge. Poaching is now on such a scale that it threatens to exterminate virtually all the *Tilapia* in Lake Baringo. It has already almost done so in the infinitely larger Lake Victoria.

David Roberts started his officially backed fishery mainly to provide the Tugen, a poor tribe without resources save their stunted little cattle, with an industry and means of livelihood. The Tugen bring the fish early in the morning to the factory, where Mr. Roberts buys them at a fixed rate, freezes them and sends them off once a week, packed in dry ice, to bump and jolt over a track which any serious storm puts out of action, to the tarmac, about fifty miles away, and thence to Nakuru.

This worked well until the Luo arrived. Avid fish eaters, they have, despite endless entreaties and by-laws, overfished Lake Victoria almost to the point of no return. The average catch is now down to one fish to every two nets. The Luo established an illicit trade in sun-dried *Tilapia* with the Tugen. They paid less than Mr. Roberts, but the fishermen did not have to get up early to bring in their catch before the heat of the day. So now the factory at Campi ya Samaki can't fill its orders and its future is dubious. Although local by-laws forbid this Luo trade, the Tugen District Council, which is supposed to enforce these laws, takes the side of the poachers.

Don't they see that they will very soon kill their goose? Mr. Roberts shook his head. "The Luo didn't see it on Lake Victoria. The Tugen won't see it here. We had the senior fish warden down to address them, but he might as well have been talking to a brick wall." It is the story over again, in replica, of the blue whale, all but exterminated in the Antarctic by the greed and short-sightedness of international whaling fleets. The Tugen are no more and no less enlightened.

David Roberts can see only one chance of saving the fishery: to turn the business over to a co-operative owned by the Tugen. This might bring the dangers home to them. But they are an unreceptive people, suspicious of new ideas and with few educated leaders.

We lunched out of doors, under the eyes of openmouthed crocodiles. (They lie with their jaws locked apart.) A baby zebra butted us and a pair of monkeys got away with some of the ham. A frieze of storks and cranes was outlined against the satin-smooth blue waters, and a self-tamed fish eagle watched from a log with two almost full-grown children by her side. Although they were nearly as big as their mother they still insisted on being fed. Several eland and gazelle walked around, a peacock sat on a Land-Rover, two baby buffalo grazed a withered lawn.

This must be a bird watcher's paradise. The aviaries were full of an enormous variety, from the towering goliath heron, elongated as a modern sculpture, and big white pelicans to the small squacco heron, the Caspian plover and the tiny ruffs and stints. In one cage some wattled starlings, doomed to be experimented on for cancer research in the United States, flew about. In the breeding season these starlings sprout a big coxcomb on their heads. Scientists have advanced a theory that this growth may be in some way connected with the cellular mechanism that gives rise to cancer cells.

Baringo is about thirteen miles long and dotted with islands. Several Tugen families keep cattle on them and swim the beasts over to the mainland when they need a change of grazing, or for purposes of trade or bride price. One man is prosperous enough to load up his canoe with three or four cases of beer when he returns; others prefer the mead their wives make from wild honey. An old man who had clearly let himself go on this beverage waved us off so wildly from

the jetty that he had to be plucked back by his son. His legs
and back were terribly scarred. When returning from a cattle
raid in his youth, he had paused to adjust a sandal, and a
leopard had sprung on to his back. So bravely had he defended himself that he threw off the leopard, and his fellow
warriors had been able to rescue him, but his flesh had been
ripped from his bones. Sutures of antelope tendon threaded
through needles of thorn mended the gashes, and herbs over-
came septicemia. He is now well over seventy and lives largely
on mead.

Flamingoes

Baringo is a fresh-water lake. Flamingoes favour the alkaline waters of lakes like Hannington, Natron, Magadi, Man-
yara and Nakuru; on this last up to one and a half million of
the lesser variety have been seen together at one time. This
is probably about one third of all the lesser flamingoes in the
world. The sight takes the eye by storm and defies the pen.

You can approach to within about forty or fifty yards of
the nearest birds. They marshal in the shallows, heads down
to strain the water through bristles lining their hooked man-
dibles, and extract the algae on which they live. Sometimes
they strut about in display like country dancers, looking
slightly absurd with their long, thin red legs and their dip-
ping heads and skittish prancing. All the time they emit an
urgent, guggling, chuckling sound that rises in pitch as you
approach and then dies down, but never ceases.

The very young show little pink; their plumage is a creamy
grey. As they mature a red patch appears under the wing on
the shoulder, like a spot of blood. They grow pinker with
age until they assume that wonderful soft, rosy shade like a
sky at sunset, and when they take off reveal a vivid carmine

underside to their wings that fills the sky with flame. Against apple-green hills and an azure sky creamed with smoky cumulus cloud, above a white soda shore fringed with reeds, the sight dazzles and amazes. I doubt if the genius of any painter could encompass it.

On my previous visit at least half the birds had been immature, some not much bigger than the black-and-white stilts who mingled with them. It was a wonder they could have made the flight from Lake Natron, in the south, where they had hatched on sand castles, protected by a treacherous crust of soda from human interference, though not from marabout storks, which prey on chicks. Some of the older young, as might teenagers, were strutting to and fro in bunches like platoons, turning as if at a word of command to retrace their footsteps. Among them were groups of greater flamingoes, paler and longer in the neck—the birds the Red Queen used as croquet mallets.

Two months later hundreds of thousands more had arrived. They formed a pink crust far out into the lake, feeding, chuttering, rustling, flighting, always on the move. Nearby a party of pelicans sat on a bank of reeds, looking smugly sage and contemplative. At some unseen signal they took off one by one, with surprising agility for such heavy creatures, swept with outstretched necks towards the water and alighted with perfect judgment just like flying boats, braking with their great wings.

Although the greater and the lesser flamingoes mingle in the lake, they seek rather different foods. The greater will eat insects and larvae, whereas the lesser stick to plant food, mainly the blue-green algae, whose abundance in these viscous soda-impregnated shallows is astonishing. Mr. Leslie Brown has calculated that Lake Nakuru must yield at least two tons of algae per acre every three months,[1] and reckons he has seen over one and a quarter million flamingoes on the lake at one time.

Flamingoes do not nest on Lake Nakuru, or have not done so for many years; sometimes they vanish altogether; they are unpredictable birds, controlled in the ultimate, no doubt, like other creatures, by the availability of food.

In concentrations of such enormous size, hundreds of natural deaths must occur every day, and you might expect to find corpses littering the shore. You see none. Marabout storks eat them all. These are horrible birds, with beaks as sharp as razors, beady, glittering eyes and an expression of smug ferocity. In a dusky cloud they circulate above the abattoir, waiting for offal. Leslie Brown has described the attack of a marabout commando on thousands of incubating greater flamingoes on Lake Elmenteita. The storks prowled amongst them like storm troopers until the flamingoes panicked, fled and deserted. The marabouts gorged themselves with eggs and fledglings, but could not consume more than a fraction of the spoils.

Crested Cranes

The only birds that can compare for beauty with flamingoes are the crested cranes. Indeed, as an individual, a crane surpasses a flamingo; his feathery crest is like a golden halo, his steel-grey neck and wing coverts like a smart satin cloak contrasting with buff and chestnut below. He is above all an elegant bird, neat and well tailored, colourful and yet restrained.

I watched several flights of crested cranes coming in to roost beside a dam. They had been out all day robbing wheat

[1] See "The Mystery of the Flamingoes," *Country Life,* 1959.

fields. From behind the black ridge of the Mau Escarpment a dying sun had flooded with a golden lambency a bank of cloud along the eastern sky. The great cranes streamed with outstretched necks across the golden glow, honking with a high, sad, plangent note, their wide and powerful wings beating rhythmically, dark as witches.

Three or four parties followed and drifted silently to earth, settling like great leaves floating down to rest. Their golden crests exactly matched the colouring of the golden cloud above the forest. Crops replete, they strutted for a while beside the dam, their plumage blue-grey in the failing light.

We left them there and drove home up the hill, under a sky aglow with colours impossible to define: a luminous pearl, an apricot as soft as breath, a tender violet and, just above the skyline, a lustre one can describe only as being of the very essence of light itself, in all its purity. Against it blackly rose umbrella thorns, their horizontal tabletops as sharp and substantial as machinery. The air was pungent with the smoke of burning vegetation. Women were toiling up the hill with heavy water barrels on their backs, or loads of firewood. We passed between the two sentinel thorns and saw a light beyond the honeysuckle hedge, and were greeted by the frenzied welcome of the dogs, and Mbugwa advancing across the lawn with a lamp, at the double.

THE SILENT HYRAX

Farewell to Cedars

When you crossed the Njoro River, by a footbridge, you were in the ancient juniper and olive forest; dark, thick, tangled, only wild beasts could traverse it except along the tenuous traces made by Dorobo hunters. These led through open glades, treeless and sunlit, where coarse, slippery grass clumps tripped your feet and your eye was caught by shrubs like the purple-flowering *muthakwa* abuzz with bees, and by flame-flowered wild gladioli.

Finally you entered the region of the silent feathery bamboos, whose canopy filtered sunlight down to a crepuscular gloom. Bamboos clothed the crest of the Mau and spread down into Masailand, where you might encounter a long-legged, pig-tailed, red-ochre-smeared warrior standing on one leg, the other cocked against his knee, and always with a spear in his hand, herding cattle driven up for pasturage in dry seasons.

The bamboos are there still, but the native junipers and olives have yielded to regimented plantations of exotic cypress and pine. Firebreaks, roads, sawmills have replaced tortuous paths twisting through half darkness, lichens and creepers, a smell of leaf mould and cedar, the squawk of turacos and the chatter of monkeys, and the wild animals.

When Tilly settled at Njoro she called the farm Gikammeh, the Kikuyu word for tree hyrax; every night the air vibrated with their strident screams. There's not one left now. The nights are silent, save for human sounds, or frogs after rain.

All this had to be, of course; junipers and olives can't be kept as pets because of the wildlife they shelter; nor because, if you stood on a hill and looked down, you saw a many-toned green sea—greens brilliant from the bamboo's brightness, like new grass, or dark from the olive's sobriety, like yew; and on their surface, marching cloud shadows created an illusion of waves. All this was uneconomic, like the small Dorobo hunters with their cloaks of chestnut bushbuck skin or hyrax pelts, and quivers of arrows, and craving for tobaccco; like Colobus monkeys in their silky black and white, or buffalo drying their coats in the singing golden sunshine of early morning in the silver glades, or bushbuck and tiny dik-dik that used to pick a way with sharp, slender hooves across a trace to nibble at the sweet green grasses of an open *vlei*.

The sons of the Dorobo are now employed as forest pruners and guards; one drives a truck, another tends an engine; in the once silent valleys thriving villages shelter thousands of Kikuyu families who extract from soils enriched by the accumulated fertility of millennia their generous crops. The skeletons of unwanted trees end up in sacks of charcoal, to perform their last service to the human race.

Once you step across the old footbridge you are in a plantation of queer little trees covered with bristles, like vegetable porcupines, whose straight branches poke out at awkward angles; they bring to mind monkey puzzles in suburban gardens, and must dismay the local birds. These are *Pinus radiata,* or Monterey pine, a native of California. To compensate for their lack of charm, they embody solid commercial values and grow with remarkable speed. After only seven years they start to bring in revenue from thinnings; you thin again twice more and harvest your mature crop in thirty, or at most thirty-five, years—a nineteen-inch bole four feet three inches from the ground is the aim. In forestry this counts as lightning speed. Native cedars take four to five times as long to reach maturity.

"Junipers and *Podocarpus,*" said a forester somewhat disapprovingly, "are a primitive form of pine." What goes to make a tree primitive? "A rudimentary form of cone and methods of seeding: a *radiata* pine cone is much more sophisticated." Even the trees must give up being primitive, but cannot be educated, so must go.

Forest Squatters

I have often wondered whether trees mould a man's character, or whether a certain type of man is attracted by trees; a bit of both, I dare say; in any case, foresters are something of a race apart, and I never remember meeting a nasty one. They seem, in general, to be happy men. They live in magnificent surroundings, often in solitude, thinking of the future; and are seldom, if ever, well paid. To balance that, they are creators, destroying one world and making another. Like God, they say: "Let there be forests," and forests there will be, provided that Satan, who has established his headquarters in the Treasury, doesn't nip in with a smart piece of sabotage. Thinking in centuries must impart a sense of proportion denied to those of us whose lives are ruled by pips, chimes and minute hands.

As with animals, you select and breed from the best trees. Foresters mark them, and in due course collect and germinate their seeds. At a forest station above Elburgon, in the crisp air of nearly nine thousand feet, boxes of seedlings were going out in trucks to be planted, for heavy rain had brought a burst of activity. These sturdy little trees were about fifteen months old and of three kinds: the Monterey pine I have mentioned; another pine, called *patula;* and a cypress, *Cupressus lusitanica,* the latter both natives of Mexico.

The foresters of Kenya have evolved a way of starting new plantations which is, so far as they know, unique, and must be the cheapest in the world. Two factors make it feasible. First, the richness of these mountain soils. In most countries only land too poor for any other purpose is normally allocated to trees. My guides led me to a pit excavated to show the root system of a pine. The roots had penetrated thirty feet, and every inch was rich, red, fertile loam. This had staggered a party of Australians, who'd said their trees were lucky if they got half a foot of decent soil.

The second local factor is the land hunger of the Kikuyu. From a marriage of these two the forest squatter system was born. Into each block of native cedar and olive, as its turn for demolition comes, move the squatter families—they *need* not be Kikuyu, but they always are—who fell and burn the trees, grub up the stumps, clear the bush, dig it and plant their crop. In spite of every warning, they insist on maize, which often fails at this altitude; potatoes, however, save them. They take a crop for three years and, with sidelines like charcoal and sheep, do very nicely. There is great competition to become a forest squatter, even though they must move on after every three or four years to clear a new chunk of forest. The work is hard, but the Kikuyu are hard workers. While the women do most of the shamba work, each man is guaranteed paid employment for nine months of the year. And after fifteen years he gets a gratuity which is by local standards munificent—£300 ($840). This is supposedly in lieu of pension, but few squatters retire.

"Most of them invest the money in a second wife, and then of course they have a second family. Next thing, there's school fees to pay and they're back asking to be taken on again." The forest village schools are packed with little ones.

After the first year's crop is off, in go the young trees. They need continual attention. We watched pruners trimming pines about eighteen years old. The men stood on flimsy ladders and sawed branches as if they were cutting rind off cheese. This was piecework; they finished their stint by ten thirty or eleven, and then went off to their own shambas.

In their bustling villages are schools and radios, reading rooms and football fields, dispensaries and shops. An Asian trader was buying potatoes humped by the women on to his scales. A full sack weighs one hundred and eighty pounds, and plenty of women carried full sacks, walking with bent knees and that curious shuffle they use when doubled under heavy loads. No man will carry one. A few—very few—nowadays use donkeys. The Masai always do.

Here, in the forest, the older women still adorn themselves in the old way: beads strung on loops of wire are suspended from earlobes which have been stretched to hang down to their shoulders, and coils of copper wire sheathe their forearms and shins. They shave their heads bare as billiard balls, and wear a patient, timeless air of wisdom which evokes an admiration for their fortitude. Any trace of pity would be out of place. Far from resenting a life which to others must seem hard and brutish, they take pride in their strength and industry, and in the customs and traditions they preserve.

The Cause of Trees

In the school African rangers in green jerseys were receiving instruction in the rudiments of scientific forestry. These

are practical men who look after the plantations and have not hitherto needed to know the theoretical basis of their trade. But now they must man the rank above them, that of forester, to replace departing Europeans. So a "crash course" is attempting to fit the pick of them for work they will find difficult, since they lack the educational groundwork. They are literate, but none got beyond a primary school and the instruction they were receiving was in Swahili, not in English. All are keen, efficient rangers, but more at home with pruning knives than departmental estimates.

One of the departing white foresters took us round: a young man, Kenya-born and -raised, devoted to his native land (for which he plays Rugby football), his forests and his job. He hates the prospect of leaving, and no one wants him to go, least of all the Africans, either at a ministerial level or among the villagers, who when he left his last district on transfer to this one spontaneously clubbed together to buy him a dinner service.

As he is not being thrown out and has no wish to go, why his departure? He is married, with a family, young enough to make a new start elsewhere, and his "lumpers" are generous. Even if he stays on for the present, he will have to go in four or five years' time, when Africans now in training are equipped to fill the places rightfully theirs. In four or five years his chances of a new start will be poorer and the time left to him to climb a new promotional ladder will be less.

So, sadly and reluctantly, he must emigrate, leaving his heart among these forest ridges and taking a skill his country needs. The ranger who will replace him, however excellent a man, cannot by the nature of things acquire his expertise; that ranger's son may do so, but this is the stopgap generation. Like the end of the cedars, these things are tragic and inevitable.

Above the rank of forester come the forest officers, with university degrees. These, too, are leaving. Another kind of crash course, for boys with School Certificates, has started at Egerton College, to train replacements in two years. Twelve young men have just started this course. One solitary African studying for a forestry degree in Nigeria is due back next year, and there are five to come (if all succeed) the year after. A meagre bag. "Educated Africans aren't interested in forestry. I don't blame them, there's no gold in these hills." The forester added bluntly: "If you've only just come down from the trees, why should you want to go back again?"

Meanwhile what will happen to the forest services? "Non-British officers will have to come in on contract from the F.A.O. or under A.I.D. That is, if they can be found. It will cost a lot more, and they won't know the local conditions or the people, but . . ."

But there you are. *Uhuru* must not only be done, but must be seen to be done. If there has to be a white face it mustn't, at least immediately, be British. Common sense sneaks out of the window when politics bound in by the door.

Trees, like wildlife or cruel sports or nuclear disarmament, constitute a Cause, and perhaps the last service the departing expatriates have rendered has been to convert some of their new masters. "Until they saw what we were doing on the spot, the Ministers and Parliamentary Secretaries hadn't much clue. But after a day bumping all over the plantations and sticking in the mud and talking to rangers and squatters, one of them stood up in the Land-Rover and threw out his arms and cried: 'We must have more trees, we must cover all the hills of Kenya with trees, and we must punish severely all who destroy them. . . .' Now he's a real ball of fire." (Though he still has to reckon with Satan in the Treasury.)

So pines and cypresses advance in ranks over the mountains, devouring the cedars and olives, but adding to the country's resources and protecting its soil. On the other face of the Mau, in Masai country, the cedars and olives are going almost as quickly, but no new trees are replacing them. Foresters shake their heads gloomily. "We posted a man down there who did nothing else but go round trying to persuade the Masai to stop the rot. They wouldn't listen. 'It's our country,' they said. 'It's our business how we treat it, not yours.' If things go on like this, soon they won't have any country left to treat."

Bonfires

Plumes of bonfire smoke curl above a long ridge sloping on one side towards the river and the forest, on the other towards the Rift; they dispense an aromatic tang of smouldering vegetation, now and again shot through with whiffs of jasmine and honeysuckle. Everywhere people are at work with hoes, or hauling weeds and the grey foliage of pyrethrum to fires that burn night and day.

All exude cheerfulness, and one or two small gangs sing as they hoe together. The ground is hard and lies in red lumps. Pyrethrum roots and weed stalks crackle as they are piled on top of bonfires.

Settlement schemes are in the air, and this one, wholly unofficial, is Tilly's. Over the years her acres have dwindled but her labour force has not. Old men stay on, their sons and grandsons find employment hard to get or keep, and some have drifted back, glad even of part-time employment at the agricultural wage. No small farm can be run indefinitely as a charity for the unemployed or unemployable. And the time has come, in Tilly's case, for at least a partial retirement.

In theory, all are retiring together: Tilly to her garden,

her Kikuyu retainers to the shambas into which she is dividing her farm. Muchoka, the headman, has been going round with sticks which he thrusts into the pyrethrum and the old maize field and the paddocks and every bit of available land, marking it all out into bits and pieces. The only rule is that no one may cut down a tree.

Muchoka himself is going. He has been here for nearly forty years and headman for the last thirty, and is the only non-Kikuyu; he is a M'Kamba. Although there has been little love lost between Kamba and Kikuyu in the past, they have close affinities in language and custom, and Muchoka, after all these years, must be almost a Kikuyu himself. Yet he hasn't lost touch with his native land. Of his three wives, one stayed behind to cultivate his inherited plot and tend his goats and cattle. An annual visit provided her with children and kept family affairs in order.

He is a smallish, light-skinned man with charming manners, whose appearance gives no hint of his age. Slanting eyes, a wispy moustache whose ends hang down and a little line of beard encircling his jaw give him an oddly Chinese look. He has a mass of children and, in Ukambani, a large herd of cattle in which he has invested every cent derived both from his wages and from the sale of surplus maize grown here by his two Kikuyu wives in residence. Back in his own country he will be a rich man.

It is interesting to see the pattern of Kikuyu land ownership repeated on this small scale, and without the structure of clan, land elder and family to bolster it. Despite all official propaganda devoted in the last ten years to persuading the Kikuyu to consolidate their holdings—each man his plot, all in one place and one piece—in their hearts they, or at any rate these, prefer the traditional system, by which each man has one fragment here, another over there and a third a mile off in the opposite direction. So although Tilly's plots are very small—between one acre and four—most are split into two, or even more, fragments.

Old Karanja the herd, for instance, has one acre of the old pyrethrum shamba, one behind the store, and half an acre by the top road. Wamwea has one acre of the old pyrethrum, half by the top road and half by the bottom road. Kangethe has only an acre, but in two bits. (He oughtn't really to have any, as Tilly took him over from a neighbour only a few years ago and he is notoriously idle; she found him, once, curled up fast asleep in one of the trays in which pyrethrum is dried, under cover; it was raining, and all the pyrethrum he was supposed to be looking after was outside.) Mbugwa has the largest plot, four acres, but then, in addition to his lazy wife, his household includes two mothers. "The mother of the belly" is dead, but these are widows of his father, and have become his responsibility. One is employed in the garden.

Tilly's garden flourishes because she is not only green-fingered but has ingenious ideas. Many of these centre, as so much does in Africa, on making better use of water. To this end she took to planting out her seedlings in polythene bags. Now she has the top foot or so of ground dug out, a polythene lining inserted and the soil replaced. In dry times a very little water satisfies her plants, and if there are theoretical objections the plants ignore them. Nowhere in the world can you find crisper, fatter, juicier and tastier vegetables, and in greater variety.

The flower garden sings with colour all the year round. Whenever a local flower show is held, there is a burst of activity as Tilly, with the aid of Nanga the old gardener and, of course, Mbugwa, prepares exhibits. Unless thwarted by *force majeure*—a hailstorm, miscalculation by the roses—she always enters something, partly because she believes in supporting flower shows and partly because the urge to compete, always strong in her blood, is by no means extinguished. Tilly loves a battle of skill or wits as dearly as in the days when only those with stout hearts and strong fingernails dared to challenge her at racing demon and her prowess at mixed hockey was renowned. In Uganda, I met a man who still recalled bruised shins and her participation in a bicycle race in Nakuru in the late twenties. "She didn't win it," he added, "but she got the most cheers; she pedalled twice as fast as anyone else, but had a dwarf bicycle."

"It was a child's," Tilly explained when I repeated this. "I thought that smaller wheels would go round faster. But I was wrong."

Retirement

As part of the retirement programme Karanja wa Kinoko, the cook, is going from the kitchen, though not from the farm. He wears a chef's cap all day, keeps his separate kitchen at the back in terrible disorder, is overfond of beer and can turn out a complicated dish with Gallic perfection or, through lack of interest, a simple one with contemptuous clumsiness. But he will always rise to an occasion, has perfect manners and speaks English with an Oxford accent of remarkable purity; this we overhear when he answers the telephone. He talks Swahili normally to us, but in the early mornings the musical Italianate cadences of his native tongue are often poured into the instrument as he conducts complicated trading deals. On final retirement he means to join a syndicate which trades in charcoal.

Kariuki the handyman, who really *has* retired, came the other day in his rags and tatters—surely the oldest, most bat-

tered and grubbiest in existence—to construct a plywood recess off the dining room and install a little sink, some shelves
and small cooker. Here, in future, Tilly means to fend for
herself. Always a skilled and adventurous cook, now she has
assembled a collection of fascinating recipes no one else has
heard of, and invents dishes of her own, mainly of vegetables
in unusual combinations, which are either excellent or (much
more rarely) total failures. On one of her infrequent visits to
England she spent six weeks at the Good Housekeeping Institute in London taking the Brides' Course, which she passed
with honours.

Seven dogs render it unsafe to put anything down almost
anywhere except on the top shelf; too often she has been
called away at a crucial moment and returned to find a tasty
morsel gone and a dachshund licking its lips. A great devotee
of gadgets, she has taken to inventing some of her own; for
example, a device to heat a single plate economically without
turning on the grill or oven. "I found a stewpan with a loose
lid, dug out some scraps of coffee-tray wire from the store,
and Kariuki made a sort of cake stand to fit into the pan; a
bit of rubber tubing cut off an old enema makes a handle to
lift the whole thing out with; it works like a charm. . . ."

The only trouble is, Karanja the cook hasn't actually gone
—not, at least, off the payroll, because he has several children
still at school. "He's sunk so much money in them already it
would be so wasteful to stop halfway. They all think that in
a few years' time they'll be headmasters or Cabinet Ministers;
young Kibochi is quite useless, and has been turfed out of
two schools, but Karanja wants to give him one more chance,
and after all these years . . ."

Mbugwa brings tea before the first light creeps into the
valley under Menengai and touches a starlit sky above the
Aberdares; then we have the dawn chorus, the fluting and

whistling, bubbling and cooing from shrikes and barbets, coucals and doves, the robin chat; suddenly the stars are there no longer, the eastern sky is apricot and lavender, the hills are black; long, wispy ghost-grey clouds lie along the valley and conceal the lake. The tabletops of the umbrella thorns are dark and sharp across the sky.

The sun floods up and gilds their crinkled boles as if with searchlights; every leaf is clear against a fresh and tender blue; dew silvers the lawn; bees are busy in the honeysuckle, smoke rises, voices call, the clang of metal against metal summons to work those who have not yet quite retired—including Tilly, who, in a babble of dogs, goes out to weigh freshly gathered vegetables. Later these will travel to Nakuru in sacks and baskets roped to the roof of her dilapidated Peugeot, its back seat piled with rabbits in cages for the butcher, and Kachinga the night watchman, alert after his refreshing sleep, squeezed in beside.

Uhuru comes, empires go; weather and crops, rain and sunshine, drought and flood, death and childbirth, these remain.

UGANDA'S BEASTS

By the Nile

A land of content. Climate, vegetation, soft warm air—everything is drowsy, placid and generous. Grass grows eight feet tall, cotton blooms in rows like single open roses, fat cobs weigh down the stalks of maize. Heat and humidity, bananas everywhere, vermilion *Erythrina*, tall forest trees—a lotus-eating land.

The largest woman I have ever seen entered the dining room of the Crested Crane Hotel, at Jinja, like a sailing ship with all her masts crowded, her canvas billowing—sails of saffron yellow, orange red, petunia purple, apple green, of umber, ochre, sienna, puce, all mixed and blaring. On top of her enormous bulk she was heavily pregnant. She swept in with a sublime self-assurance and two well-dressed male escorts, African executives (probably) from the big Owen Falls hydroelectric plant, and ordered cold drinks. Everything here seems fruitful, bright and bold, life-size and over, free of haste and strain.

In the Murchison National Park we sat on the veranda of our little detached villa overlooking the Nile, which in its time has seen more violence, pain, cruelty and disaster than most rivers. On its banks battles have raged, civilizations arisen and decayed; tormented slaves died in legions; people

281

have been drowned in its rapids, lost in its swamps, massacred on its verges; it teems with diseases like bilharzia and malaria, vicious crocodiles and savage carp, is infested by mosquitoes and leeches. Yet there it flowed, placid as silk, quiet as sleep, mild as a marrow, between gentle, spongy banks offering their bounty to mammals, reptiles and incredible quantities of birds.

A party of hippos below us gently stirred silvery waters as they broke the surface with deep contented grunts, a cross between a hog's snort and the bray of a donkey, their stubby little ears and flat, knobbled faces just awash. Their rubbery hides have a pinkish iridescence. Two grey turacos with yellow beaks and long tails dozed in the branches of a tree, waking now and then to exchange caresses. Spread-eagled on the wall behind us was a lizard with a vivid orange head and tail and deep delphinium-blue body. Now and again he gently nodded his head. Outside, sunshine was absolute, the moist air like a tepid bath. The earth and its creatures dreamed and dozed.

In every other game park I know, the world wakes at sunrise and the best time to find the animals is before breakfast, in the cool of the day. Not so at the Paraa lodge. "Nothing much to see before eight o'clock," said the warden.

People are his problem, not beasts. Arriving, for the most part, in packaged and tightly scheduled tours, they scurry hither and thither and yon in coaches, cars and launches; the lodge is packed with bevies coming and going, the individuals mostly clad in the briefest of shorts and making the briefest of visits, sometimes lasting only twelve hours.

A tour from Frankfurt had just arrived at four, completed the launch trip on the river by seven, and were scheduled to be off by five next morning to catch an aircraft from Entebbe so as to lunch in Nairobi, see the Serengeti in the afternoon and sleep that night at the Victoria Falls, on the Zambesi.

Park rules forbid anyone to leave Paraa before eight o'clock because it's not considered safe for vehicles to travel in the dark among elephants and buffalo; anyway, the staff doesn't come on duty until then. Heated arguments took place in several languages. Schedules couldn't be rearranged at the last moment, but park rules couldn't be broken. The warden won.

Birds of the River

The launch trip to the Murchison Falls and back is a journey through abundance. Possibly the birds are even more wonderful than the animals.

The goliath heron is the most spectacular, a six-footer clad in slate grey with a rich rufous chest and stomach and a six-foot wing spread. He broods on the verge with his spearlike beak poised for the pounce. Between herons and fish eagles an armed neutrality prevails which now and again breaks out into open conflict when the eagle tries to snatch an especially tempting fish the heron has just impaled. Dropping the fish, the heron will strike back with his beak: a battle between the swift and the static. Such struggles have been observed to continue to the death of both contestants.

Proud and imperial with their pure white heads and black wings, the fish eagles perch on branches, often in pairs—they mate for life, and keep year after year to the same nest. It is a fine sight to see one of these eagles swoop over the water, half fold back its wings and whisk off with its claws a fish that has exposed a flash of silver to those unresting eyes. The eagles are said to spot the movement of a fish nearly half a mile way.

A flat, shady litle beach was shared by several dozen croco-

diles, knobbled and motionless as limpet-encrusted rocks, and a flock of brown-and-white African skimmers, or razorbill terns, with bright orange beaks, which they seemed to keep open when at rest, like the crocodiles—though scarcely for the same reason, which in the crocodile's case is commonly said to be to allow the small grey-and-white Egyptian plover to pick leeches from its jaws. But no reliable living naturalist has actually seen this occur. Herodotus first told the story; and recently a famous American film company is said to have dyed some young white Leghorns the right colour, propped open the jaws of a dead crocodile, scattered maize among its molars and recorded the scene.

Pied kingfishers are everywhere, the shape of hammers—an exception to the general rule that tropical birds are brighter in plumage than those of temperate zones. These are neat birds, but dull compared with their English cousins. We passed a sandbank honeycombed with holes, a nesting place of green bee-eaters. These superb birds, whose backs and wings are emerald green and breasts carmine, darted in and out of holes, some with bees in their curved, slender beaks. As our launch approached, they retreated to some bushes overhanging their sandbank, put out at the disturb-

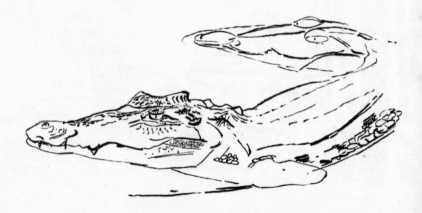

ance, and sat there swaying, red and sparkling, waiting to plunge back into their holes.

But smartest of all are the little lily-trotters, with brilliant chestnut backs and wings, white heads marked with black and spidery legs, so brisk and delicate as they lightly tread the floating leaves and marsh grasses. One shared a swampy promontory with an elephant. The young bull stood by the river's edge and scooped the grass with a sideways, scimitar-like sweep of his trunk, while the lily-trotter, equally intent on a meal, kept just out of reach, entirely fearless of this monster. Happy-go-lucky little waders, Jackson contemptuously described their nest, "if a leaf or two of wet green weeds or a few blades of grass can be considered as such, placed on a bed of floating weeds or water lettuce or a tiny islet of floating mud, rocked by every movement of the water," and remarked that their eggs often came to grief.

Parties of hippos lay half submerged on banks, or totally submerged in water, save for the tips of their compact little ears and their eyes on stalks, which act as periscopes. The advent of our launch sent those on or near the shore plopping heavily into the water with a series of snorts, babies skilfully balanced on their mothers' broad, shining backs. Every hippo looks enormously fat, sleek and prosperous, like a rich Baganda woman, or the archetypical alderman gorged on turtle soup and oysters. Their lives must surely be freer of care than most creatures'; their only predator is man, who eats their flesh and makes their hide into thongs. (He used to turn it also into instruments of torture for use on his fellows; the East African version of the sjambok was the *kiboko,* the Swahili word for hippo.)

Cropping Hippos

Here they are protected, and with the usual result: they are increasing to a point where they threaten their food supplies.

In Uganda's other main game park, the Queen Elizabeth, numbers mounted to the point where the countryside was stripped of its vegetation and the rules against killing in sanctuaries had to be suspended. The hippos there are being "cropped" to the tune of about eight hundred a year, which has stabilized their numbers. Hippos are not nearly so difficult to crop as elephants. They seldom turn savage when shot, and are easily accessible. On cropping days butchers arrive with trucks, and within a few hours the carcasses have been dismembered and removed. Sale of the meat helps to pay the costs of cropping, which also forms the basis of a scientific inquiry into the biology of hippos, their habits of eating and breeding, their health and disease, their parasites and digestions and "population dynamics"—everything about them, carried out by a team from the Cambridge Unit of Tropical Animal Ecology, under Dr. F. Laws and Dr. Hugh Cott.

In the Murchison Park elephants are building up in numbers towards a danger point just as hippos have done in the Queen Elizabeth. It is the Tsavo story over again, with one big difference—the Murchison area enjoys between forty and sixty inches of rain annually, so its vegetation is lush, rich, thick and green instead of bare, spiky and easily discouraged.

Even here in the Murchison Park population pressure is changing the landscape. It used to be thickly wooded. In places, forests of a tree called *Terminalia* (of the *Combretaceae* family) grew. Elephants have ring-barked the *Terminalia* trees and left a devastated landscape of toppled ash-grey corpses or leafless skeletons dead on their feet, soon to join their prone companions. We drove through depressing stretches of these dead *Terminalia* forests. No one knows just why the elephants strip off the bark; one theory is a search for some substance lethal to internal parasites, another is the need for a calcium.

Pressure is not only converting much of the Park from forest to grassland, but is converting elephants from tree feeders to grass eaters. An American student of their habits, Dr. Buss, believes that most of them have adapted themselves almost completely to a grassy diet. They seem to have little choice. Scientists speculate as to whether they can extract from grass alone all the elements they need, especially minerals. Here is one more of the many fields waiting for research, which in turn waits for money.

The Murchison Falls

As you approach the falls, the current strengthens and turns back your launch below a pool creamed with foam into which the waters of the Nile, emptying from the Lake Victoria basin, cascade through a rocky funnel less than three yards wide. It is an exciting spectacle, this vast bulk of spray tearing, gushing and spurting through the narrow jet into a churning pool below covered with apparent soapsuds. The scene can have changed little since Sir Samuel Baker "discovered" the falls in 1864—quotation marks are needed because, as Africans rightly point out, they had known about these natural features for centuries; the use of the word is very genocentric—and, getting his measurements wrong, described them thus:

> Upon rounding the corner, a magnificent sight burst suddenly upon us. On either side the river were beautifully wooded

cliffs rising abruptly to a height of about three hundred feet; rocks were jutting out from the intensely green foliage; and rushing through a gap that cleft the rock exactly before us, the river, contracted from a grand stream, was pent up in a narrow gorge of scarcely fifty yards in width; roaring furiously through the rock-bound pass, it plunged in one leap of about 120 feet perpendicular into a dark abyss below.

The fall of water was snow-white, which had a superb effect as it contrasted with the dark cliffs that walled the river, while the graceful palms and wild plantains perfected the beauty of the view. This was the greatest waterfall of the Nile, and, in honour of the distinguished President of the Royal Geographical Society, I named it the Murchison Falls. [From *The Albert Nyanza*, 1866.]

For centuries these falls have acted as a plug. The whole of the water system embracing the great central African lakes—Victoria, Albert, Edward, George (how unimaginative and royalist the British were about names!) and Kioga—once shared a common piscine fauna. Roughly, perhaps, twenty or thirty thousand years ago, a drought of an intensity we can scarcely imagine dried up every one.

Life shrivelled, but somehow enough creatures must have survived in pools and mud to recolonize the lakes and rivers when they filled up again in the last pluvial period, corresponding to the European ice age, about fifteen thousand years ago.

Ever since, the water fauna above and below the Murchison Falls has been quite different. In Lake Albert, and in the Nile below the falls, lives the giant Nile perch, which may be six feet long and weigh two hundredweight; the tiger fish; and various other fishes unknown in Lake Victoria. During all these centuries they have failed to find a way up the falls. Equally, Lake Victoria contains fish not found below the plug—mostly smaller ones, which have flourished in the absence of the larger predators, and include a kind of cichlid which hatches its young in its mouth.

Below the falls the Nile spreads out, as if grateful to be freed of its wasp waist, into a wide, placid river no more than twelve feet deep in normal times. But these times are not normal: since the floods of 1961 the river has risen by eight feet. Not only that, it has at long last rebelled against its compression and forced for itself a second channel at the falls, bursting a way through rock to leave an island between two arms of water. So now there are two Murchison Falls.

When I asked the chief warden, Mr. Roger Wheater, whether elephants swam the Nile, he replied that they certainly crossed it, possibly by swimming, but they might also "bounce along the bottom." They could not bounce now.

White Rhinos and Black Buffalo

That afternoon we saw a pair of white rhinos: relics. It is a sad story.

Once they were fairly common. (They are not, of course, white; the name is a corruption of an Afrikaans word meaning wide, and referring to their upper lip; the more correct name is square-lipped.) Slaughter reduced their numbers until they survived only in a few isolated, inaccessible spots, of which the principal was a stretch of the Nile's western bank, partly in Uganda and partly in Sudan. Here, until quite lately, they existed in respectable numbers—several hundred, anyway. In the last few years poaching has reduced the total to between forty-five and fifty individuals. The point has been passed where the extermination of the species is inevitable unless such drastic action as removal of the survivors to a place of genuine safety can be taken in time.

The game authorities decided to move ten to the Murchison Park, where they could at least enjoy closer protection. This was before the technique of darting had passed an experimental stage. So animal catchers were called in to lasso the rhinos, and three died from injuries. The remaining seven are now at large in the Park. They are much more shy and nervous than their smaller black brothers, and would not allow us to approach close enough for photographs.

About ten thousand buffalo—roughly the same number as the elephants—are believed to dwell in the Park. As a rule, these creatures are wily, elusive and wholly bush- or forest-dwelling; they are hard, and sometimes dangerous, to approach, and take refuge from Land-Rovers in thickets and gullies. Not so these Murchison herds. They graze like the most placid of beef cattle on the open downs. We might have been driving across parts of Sussex, past herds of, say, Galloways, strung out in long lines. They don't even lift their heads as you go by.

We saw a single herd estimated to contain eight hundred buffalo, and altogether, in two hours' drive. Mr. Wheater estimated, about fourteen hundred head, all in the open. It takes the sting out of the opinion I have heard expressed by many hunters, that of all big game the buffalo is the craftiest, most dangerous and unpredictable. These buffalo would have been dull if it had not been for the very fact that their tameness was so surprising. It only needed a lot of flags, stands, pavilions and a band to turn the whole place into an agricultural showground.

A Hippo Wallow and a Dung Beetle

We inspected a concentration of hippos in a swamp composed of the Nile cabbage (*Pistia stratiotes*), an incredibly prolific plant that floats down the river and, if not kept in check, colonizes every bay and calm stretch, forms a mat and kills aquatic life beneath by sealing off the air. Here the cabbage has colonized the pool. Packed together shoulder to shoulder, fat haunch to obese stomach, were hundreds of hippos, their backs glistening like aluminum blisters, or like silvery pustules on the flesh of some stricken mammoth—a revolting sight. The slime must be foul with their excreta, but in it they lie and sleep, and now and then wallow in lethargic content. This contentment conquers everything in Uganda.

The most attractive creatures are the oribi, fawn-coloured antelope about two feet high or less, with the neat movements, flickering tails and limpid eyes always so appealing among small buck. They go about in family parties and are as skittish as kittens. Sometimes they jump into the air with all four legs straight and stiff and appear to bounce, as if on springs. At other times they lie in clumps of grass and are as invisible as hares until you get right up to them.

On these open downs the vegetation is mainly the poor but long and coarse grass of the genus *Hyparrhenia*, and queer little dwarf *Borassus* palms which stick up like green fans, no more than two feet high. A *Borassus* palm is normally a largish tree. Why do these fail to develop? Probably because fire stunts their growth, but possibly some element in the soil is lacking. Mr. Wheater echoed the remark I've heard from almost every wildlife authority: "There's so much we haven't found out, so much to be done. . . ."

There is a game biologist at work, mainly on elephants, but he is busy in a new park recently scheduled in the north, the Kidepo Valley, in the still primitive, largely roadless province of Karamoja. The first problem here is to find out what animals survive there and what do not, so little is it known, and so devastated has the area been by poachers who raid across the borders of Sudan in organized gangs of several hundred armed men. These gangs snare or slaughter everything that moves and return with tons of dried meat to a rendezvous with trucks. So bad is the poaching in this region that although it has been scheduled as a park the public cannot yet be admitted, and little wildlife, in the opinion of experts to whom I talked, is thought to survive. The hope is that if poachers can be kept out animals will be able to build up their numbers. The "if" is a big one.

By Lake Albert's shore, on a level stretch of brilliant green, against blue waters and distant purple mountains of the Congo, a frieze of elephants, each with a white egret perched on its back. . . . By the roadside two pale brown Uganda kob fighting, their wide horns locked. . . . A guinea hen scurrying with her fluffy, speckled chicks across the sandy track, red-gold in evening light. . . . A *batailleur* eagle with crimson beak and legs and black plumage, pitiless and imperial, perched heraldically on a bare branch above the open rolling grassland, and below the gold-rimmed cloud banks darkening as night falls. . . . Evening scenes.

On the way home we paused to watch a dung beetle push her ball of nutriment patiently, persistently, along the track. The ball, four or five times the beetle's length in diameter, kept slipping back despite all the efforts of the insect, who was obliged each time to pedal harder than ever with her back legs against the perfectly rounded, smooth ball of dung— she pushes in reverse.

She was coal black, this beetle, dull to look at, but incredibly tenacious and strong—a kind of scarab, related to the Egyptian branch. She pats her ball into shape, rolls it to some spot she considers suitable and buries it in a scooped-out chamber. There she earths herself up and proceeds to eat the whole ball before emerging, taking wing, and gathering up the wherewithal to make another ball.

This is the ploy of males as well as females, but when the time comes to lay her eggs the female makes a larger chamber for her ball, buries it and lays a single egg in the moist dung. Then she closes the chamber and goes off to repeat the process elsewhere. The grub hatches into the midst of a delicious food supply, which it consumes; it then pupates, and in due course emerges as an adult beetle, to fly off, in its turn, in search of dung.

Attached firmly to the ball we watched there was a second beetle, clinging to the surface, rolling over and over with the ball and making no attempt whatever to help to propel it. Obviously the male, going along for the ride, the female pushing. This was Africa.

Bunyoro and the Lord Mayor

After lunch we flocked out of the lounge of the game lodge to photograph a bull elephant standing on the terrace, nibbling the hedge. He paid no attention whatever, but went on quietly flicking off twigs with his trunk. Some of us retreated backwards—not out of respect for the elephant, but to get a bit more of him into the picture, he was so close.

This was Bunyoro, a successor to the Lord Mayor of Paraa, who was sacrificed to the folly of humans. Tourists took to feeding him from their cars. Then they put bananas on the seats, in order to photograph the Lord Mayor reaching for the fruit with his trunk through a window. Naturally, the elephant came to regard every motorcar as a kind of fruit-bearing tree. When he found a tree that yielded no fruit he behaved as he did in the bush—picked it up and shook it. He did this to several cars, and eventually to one that had people in it. So, harmless as he was, he had to be shot.

Wardens put up notices everywhere to explain that these elephants are wild and should be respected, but the visitors pay scant attention. One day someone will go too far with Bunyoro and he, too, will have to be sacrificed—like the dolphin who, just about two thousand years ago, gave the boys of Hippo a ride on his back; so many people flocked into this North Africa seaside resort to see the dolphin that the city fathers rewarded the creature's friendliness by having it destroyed, in order to get rid of tourists, who were evidently not cherished then as they are now.

If you hear a rumbling sound at night, heavy footsteps, a thumping on the roof, or see a grey object writhing through a window, this will be Bunyoro's friend Dustbin Nellie on her rounds.

When we drove south towards Masindi, several hundred elephants were strung out over the shadeless, downlike hillsides, just like flocks of browsing sheep. Twice we had to pull up to wait for two or three to move aside and allow us to pass. It is hard, after pushing a passage through these sheep elephants, to believe in a latent ferocity or get back into a frame of mind to take seriously, let alone enjoy, those hairy-chested tales of past elephant hunters. Neumann, Sutherland, Karamoja Bell, Henry Tarlton, Samaki Salmon, Alan Black —all dead now as the innumerable pachyderms they slaughtered. It must have been somewhere in this region that Karamoja Bell records shooting nineteen elephants with as many bullets in as many minutes; a feat, certainly, but the puzzled elephants were standing still.

When Bell first reached Karamoja, all the killing was done by tribesmen with snares, pits and traps, but it was not long before demand for ivory outran supply and prices rose to a point where it paid the Arab traders to equip their own armed expeditions and make alliances with sections of the tribesmen, whom they supplied with rifles in return for ivory. Thus the first footsteps of civilization trod this part of Africa. In *The Wanderings of an Elephant Hunter,* Bell dryly records:

> Complete and magnificent success attended the first raiding venture and the whole country changed magically. The hitherto more or less peaceful-looking camps gave place to huge armed *bomas* surrounded by high thorn fences. Everyone—trader or native—went about armed to the teeth. Footsore or sick travellers from caravans disappeared entirely, or their remains were found by the wayside. Native women and cattle were heavily guarded, for no man trusted a stranger.

Bell collected eight Snider rifles and some porters and crossed the Turkwell River into Karamoja to shoot his own ivory. After a slow start his success was such that he was complaining: "Although I had the herd well in hand by about 2 p.m. the total bag for the day was but fifteen bulls." In other ways times have changed little. An elderly African who walked six hundred miles with a packet of letters (mostly bills) to find Bell's camp somewhere near the Nile handed over some six-month-old newspapers, which "produced an extraordinary feeling of uneasiness and disquietude. It had rather the effect of a sudden chill to read of strikes, famines, railway accidents, unemployment, lawsuits. . . ." Bell needed several more dead elephants, and resorted to his favourite bush reading, *Pickwick Papers* and "the dear old *Field*," to restore his morale.

Wildlife Exploitation

Yet hunting goes on, now with the financial help of the Uganda Government, which sees in it an economic asset. The tourist industry ranks next to coffee (first) and cotton (second) in the country's economy.

The Uganda Development Corporation is an ambitious, go-ahead body, formed to support, with public funds but under business and not bureaucratic management, enterprises whose future appears to be sound and promising but may be too remote, experimental or political to attract commercial investment. A chain of excellent modern hotels for tourists; factories turning out cement and flour, enamelware and cotton goods and dried fish; copper mines; banking; steel mills; tea growing, fertilizers and ranching; these are among the corporation's babies. Now it is backing the Uganda Wildlife Corporation, whose aim is, frankly, to exploit the human wish to slaughter wild animals. Only, the corporation's sponsors believe, if wildlife is considered in this unsentimental fashion, and seen by the people of Uganda to yield solid profits, will there be any wildlife left at all within a decade.

"Nowhere in the *world* will there be a single wild animal or game bird or fish left alive if the local people don't see a profit in it. This may be unpleasant, but it's true. People don't want to preserve wildlife for its own sake. They do it for gain."

That is the hardheaded opinion of one of the joint managers and moving spirits of the Wildlife Corporation, Mr. E. G. Juer. A multilingual cosmopolitan with a British passport and headquarters in Madrid, he travels widely and ropes in customers, whilst in Kampala a former head of the Game Department, Mr. John Blower, organizes their safaris. The number of Americans who hunt, it seems, doubles year by year, and the wildlife of North America is now being so managed as to keep up with, and even to outstrip, these demands for its blood. The same can happen in Africa—but only if the African people see its advantages.

"There's only one way to get wildlife preservation across to Africans and that is by enabling them to handle a cash profit." Already the Wildlife Corporation is paying into the treasuries of five of Uganda's local governments—Ankole, Bunyoro, Toro, Karamoja and Madi—about £20,000 ($56,000) a year among them, and this should rise quickly. These local bodies get the visitors' fees, roughly £10 ($28) a rifle, various other payments and a bonus on all tusks over a certain size.

"A demand is coming now from the people themselves to be brought in. That means we schedule their country as a controlled area. Properly managed, hunting is a form of light cropping which strengthens the species by removing old males. The secret is control."

In each controlled area a local committee suggests the number of each species that, in their opinion, can be safely shot without danger to survival. A central committee reviews and revises these estimates and fixes the district totals for each species, and then the number of rifles to be allowed in can be settled. Last year each of the corporation's clients averaged a bag of eight and a half animals. As a rule, this includes an elephant, a lion and a buffalo. This is how the scheme works in theory, and perhaps in practice, too; all schemes have their critics. The criticism here is mainly that despite these precautions the game is being shot out.

Safari shooting, as all know, is a sport for millionaires. Sums spent by patrons of those hunting firms which cater to the rich are sometimes fabulous. The avowed aim of the Wildlife Corporation is "to bring hunting safaris within the reach of the middle classes"—the middle-income classes, that is.

The term middle class here seems optimistic, for your safari isn't going to be cheap. But it will cost one third of the average sum hitherto paid by the rich. Economies are made by streamlining everything. Several clients share a white hunter, transport is pooled, buying and catering are centralized; and safari parties, instead of following where the game may lead, are based on a few fixed camps.

Game within reach of these camps inevitably comes under heavy pressure. Is this "light cropping"? The critics say no. They say also that the temptation to exceed official quotas in order to satisfy frustrated clients can be too strong for some of the white hunters in the corporation's employ. After all, it's their living and they are hunters, not conservationists.

To this the retort is that certain Nairobi safari firms, piqued because this government-financed concern is (as they think) unfairly poaching their business, have started a whispering campaign to traduce the Uganda Corporation. An angry war of words and allegations sputters between Nairobi and Kampala.

The more idealistic conservationists don't like the scheme. "A butchers' club for rich Mexicans," I heard one describe it. He added that too much had been spent on permanent camps which would become useless because the game would go, and that the scheme had grave financial weaknesses. And: "Should governments back the slaughter of animals? Isn't it hypocrisy to stop Africans with poisoned arrows and then bring in rich foreigners with guns?"

Meanwhile business is booming and safaris are booked up for two years ahead. African enthusiasm is said to be growing—even among the Acholi, a people of the north, famous for organized tribal hunts carried out on a massive scale with nets, fires and gatherings of thousands of spearmen on the grassy, rolling plains.

These hunts can result in a holocaust of animals, many of whom are burned alive or escape with fatal injuries. Nearly

a century ago Sir Samuel Baker took part in one, and thus
described it:

> The men carried their nets and spears: the boys were also
> armed with lighter weapons, and the very little fellows carried
> tiny lances, all of which had been sharpened for the expected
> game. The women were in great numbers, and upon that day
> the villages were quite deserted. . . .

At the rendezvous:

> A line of about a mile and a half was protected by netting,
> and the natives were already in position.
>
> Each man had lashed his net to that of his neighbour and
> supported it with bamboos, which were secured with ropes
> fastened to twisted grass. The entire net resembled a fence, that
> would be invisible to the game in the high grass until, when
> driven, they should burst suddenly upon it.
>
> The grass was dry as straw, and several thousand acres would
> be fired to windward, which would compel the animals to run
> before the flames until they reached the netting. . . . Before
> each section of net, a man was concealed both within and with-
> out, behind a screen, simply formed of the long grass bound
> together at the top.
>
> The rule of sport decided that the proprietor of each section
> of netting of twelve yards length would be entitled to all game
> that should be killed within these limits; but that the owners
> of the manors which formed the hunt upon that day should
> receive a hind leg from every animal captured. . . .
>
> A shrill whistle disturbed the stillness. This signal was re-
> peated at intervals to windward. In a few minutes after the
> signal, a long line of separate thin pillars of smoke ascended
> into the blue sky, forming a band extending over about two
> miles of the horizon. The thin pillars rapidly thickened, and
> became dense volumes, until at length they united and formed
> a long black cloud of smoke. . . .
>
> The wind was brisk, and fire travelled at about four miles
> an hour. We could soon hear the distant roar, as the great vol-
> ume of flame shot high through the centre of the smoke.

Some of the beautiful *leucotis* antelope now appeared and cantered towards me, but halted when they approached the stream, and listened. The game understood the hunting as well as the natives . . . a herd of hartebeest dashed past. . . .

The natives killed many antelope, but a rhinoceros had gone through their nets like a cobweb. Several buffaloes had been seen, but they had broken out in a different direction. . . . Most of the women were heavy laden with meat; the nets were quickly gathered up and, with whistles blowing as a rejoicing, the natives turned homewards. [From *Ismailia*, 1874.]

These hunts continue to take place and continue to be cruel, but Mr. Juer, who watched one, considered the methods to be so inefficient that most of the animals broke back through the nets and evaded flying spears; the total bag he estimated at some two hundred oribi and one hartebeest. Between three and four thousand spearmen in war paint gathered from their scattered homesteads, and for days women converged upon the meeting place with loads of beer and food. It was, said Mr. Juer, a wonderful party; the slaughter was on a scale so much smaller than he had anticipated, and the hunt retained so much of the drama, colour and *élan* of a vanishing and not ignoble tradition, that he would regret its passing. If, for the sake of gain to their local treasury, the Acholi's country does become a controlled area, they will have to give up their tribal hunts.

Official Slaughter

If the organized slaughter of Uganda's wild beasts by the Acholi and other tribesmen has lacked efficiency, that conducted by the Government has not. With its right hand the Government has supported the Wildlife Corporation with its built-in, if subsidiary, aim of preservation, and set up national parks; with the other it has destroyed wildlife in abundance in pursuit of an outmoded policy.

During and after World War II several species of tsetse fly which carry a disease—trypanosomiasis—lethal to cattle appeared to be spreading at such a dangerous rate that in 1947 a department was set up to arrest and drive back these bush-dwelling insects. Tsetse flies live on the blood of animals, including most kinds of game. Buffalo, rhinos, antelope, pigs, giraffes, all these were blamed for acting as hosts and thus enabling the flies to thrive and spread.

So the Tsetse Control Department started to clear bush—a very slow and costly operation—and to shoot out the wild animals. Their self-imposed task was to clear from about eight thousand square miles virtually every living wild creature. In this they followed the example of Rhodesia, where at least half a million animals were destroyed before this policy was abandoned as a failure.

Uganda stuck to it for longer. Admittedly the task was, and is, formidable in size and complexity. There is only one way to defeat tsetse flies for good and that is to clear the bush and keep it cleared by means of close human settlement. But, as an official report stated, "In Uganda there is no shortage of land and the people are reluctant to move into new areas." So gains were not consolidated, and cattle died in droves.

At first fly fighters met with success, and in 1952 announced, not without a touch of *hubris,* that "advances by tsetse flies which had overrun almost three quarters of the country's land surface have been halted. Active reclamation measures have recovered some 4½ million acres. . . . The task of controlling tsetses—putting them in their place—is approaching completion."

Famous last words. . . . "By the end of 1957, more than seven thousand square miles of country invaded by *Glossina morsitans* and *G. pallidipes* in central and northern Uganda had been fully reclaimed from these savannah tsetses, chiefly by the game elimination method. Work was continued on the final phase. . . ." But then an uneasy note was sounded.

"The outcome of a very careful re-appraisal of the problem was a decision reached in March, 1958, that the demands of the immediate situation could only be met by resorting as quickly as possible to the method of game elimination. . . . Hunting started in north-east Ankole on July 1st, 1958. . . ." At the same time bush-spraying trials were carried out, and biologists explored an ingenious device of releasing sterile male tsetses to undermine the reproduction rate.

By the middle of 1959 it had become "quite clear that the levels of tsetse density were still appreciably higher than they had been a year or even two years earlier. . . . This area of north Karamoja was the scene of the most pronounced of the widespread and quite unexpected rises of numbers in the latter part of 1958. . . ." The tsetse counterattack was on.

It was the game that suffered. Scores of African hunters were armed, and everything on four legs that moved condemned. An intensified campaign was waged for three years.

These comments are quoted from official reports. Unofficially I was told:

"On the borders of Ankole and Toro they have shot out a thousand square miles, including the Katonga Valley, which was a game paradise full of eland, topi, impala, buffalo and rhinos. You can still see piles of bones in the bush. They said they'd clear it of every wild animal in two years, and they've been shooting for five. The average was five cartridges per animal shot—you can imagine how many were wounded and left to die.

"In Bunyoro they shot fifteen thousand head of game and cleared the area. The game went, but not the tsetse. You can't eliminate every creature—snakes, lizards, pigs, even birds. Some smaller antelope, like bushbuck and duiker, seem to step up their breeding rate to compensate, so their numbers may become stabilized.

"Now the tsetse are back. Suppose the Government had developed it as a hunting area, or even as another game park, think what they'd have made of it for Uganda! They've destroyed priceless assets to no avail."

Only in the last few years has it been found that each of the main species of game animal differs in the attractiveness of its blood to tsetse flies. These insects will prefer the blood of warthogs even when vastly greater numbers of elephants, buffalo, eland and waterbuck are available. Antelope are easy to destroy and can be wiped out, although the great majority are harmless; a number of warthogs, who retire into holes, certainly escape.

The only way to make amends would be to reverse the policy, restock some of the denuded areas with game and exploit them for tourists. There's a long way yet to go before enough Ugandans are really convinced there's enough money in the business to persuade them to encourage animals that by tradition, instinct and inclination they like killing and want to kill, and whose living space they will increasingly need for their multiplying cattle.

Minister of Tourism

If anyone could persuade them, it would be the Minister of Information and Tourism, Mr. Adoko Nekyon, a half brother of Mr. Milton Obote, the Prime Minister. He looks strong and tough and *is* strong and tough: dictatorial timber. What he says goes; self-assured, decisive, outspoken, intelligent, fearless of public opinion, and still not much over thirty, he is a man to be reckoned with.

It is no accident, I think, that the Prime Minister belongs to one of the smaller, non-Bantu tribes aloof from the jealousies and internecine struggles native to the people of the five Bahima-ruled kingdoms. A Baganda national Prime Minister would excite fear and resentment among citizens of the other, less powerful kingdoms—Toro, Bunyoro, Ankole and Busoga; and the Baganda would not willingly accept as their political leader a man from any one of these four rival and distrusted neighbour states.

The people of these five kingdoms are of interrelated, mainly Bantu, stock, with some admixture of the blood of the Bahima, a taller, paler race of Galla origin who brought long-horned cattle and a more efficient form of government from the north, and conquered the softer cultivators of the lake basin. The ruling families and attendant aristocracies of all five kingdoms derive from this conquering race.

The people to whom Mr. Nekyon and his half brother belong, the Lango, are not Bantu, but Nilotic. Their racial affinities lie with the cattle-owning Shilluk of the Sudan and the warriorlike Acholi, who share with them a language group called Gang, worship a god called Jok, formed anciently the queer habit of standing on one leg with the other foot cocked against the knee, preserved a contempt for bodily clothing and, by comparison with the Bahima-dominated Bantu, accorded their womenfolk more freedom, governed themselves more democratically (they had no hereditary rulers) and set more store by the manly pursuits of fighting and hunting than by the more sophisticated ones of legal argument and political intrigue. While education has changed them, some of these racial attributes remain.

When I entered Mr. Nekyon's office, he was on the telephone. "Good morning, your Highness." A king on the line. ". . . Then tell the Busoga to listen to the radio instead of drinking all the time."

He has great visions for Uganda, big ideas. "We must industrialize or perish. We shan't perish. . . . We're going to build a welfare state in Uganda. Neither capitalism nor Marxism suits us: on the one hand, we've little capital; on the other, no large working class; differences between rich and poor aren't wide enough to give Marxism its bite. We shall build a system of our own—equality, opportunities for all, government investment. . . ." African socialism. For five years Mr. Nekyon studied political economy in India.

Opportunities for all? What about the Asians, harshly squeezed between Africanization on the one hand and a sporadic, sometimes vicious trade boycott on the other? Mr. Nekyon has little sympathy for Asians and doesn't mind saying so. "What does Uganda owe them? They've grown rich from exploiting Africans. They can have shops, no one's stopping them. If they don't like that, they can work as labourers." Land? A settlement scheme? "My people in the north wouldn't agree to that. Asians have been sending their money out of Uganda. Let them keep it here and put it into local industries."

The opposition? Their future's in their own hands. They can never win an election. They must decide whether to go on as they are or to join the Government. Traditionalists have had their day—finished. "The mystique of the ruler can be a powerful force, but economic laws can never be overridden by individual human beings." Economic law is carrying Uganda forward into industrialization and the welfare state. And that will be the end of tradition.

Equality for all—what about women? Ah, women—they exploit the men. "In the north, among my people, if a man

307

has four or five acres of cotton, his wife will have two acres of it and keep the money for herself. But the husband has to provide for the children, pay their fees and buy their clothes.

"Take my own case. My wife works at the hospital. I don't even know how much she earns; she has her own bank account. Then she asks for money for a dress! Aren't I exploited?" Mr. Nekyon grinned engagingly, and added: "Money! I never have any for myself. Sometimes I go to bed without a shilling in the world. Yes, Ministers get three or four thousand pounds [$8,400–$11,200] a year, but what the income tax doesn't take I give away. Equality—that's an African tradition we shall keep. You know there's a proverb: 'A true friend shares even a white ant.' I'm supporting six younger brothers, all at school. There's nothing left for me, but I don't worry. I don't care."

This vigorous Minister of Information is determined to gain for Uganda a worldwide reputation as the most attractive tourist centre in Africa. A passionate nationalist, he considers that his country isn't being justly treated by her partners, that Kenya hogs an unfair share of the trade. Nairobi's proximity to an international airport rankles. Uganda, like its males, is suffering from exploitation—a favourite word.

Although the animals are not directly under Mr. Nekyon, but belong to another Ministry, in so far as they are the prop of tourism they are his affair. So long as he is convinced that they are not exploiting anyone, they could have no more powerful, energetic ally.

UGANDA'S LABYRINTH

Asian Crunch

If the day of the traditionalist is over, so is the day of the *duka*. That was the opinion of an Asian businessman of wealth and repute, who added gloomily: "The Asians face a jobless future."

The *duka* is as ingrained a part of East African life as elephants, corrugated iron, dust, goats, red ochre, Land-Rovers, bush, smudgy little newspapers, displays of Kamba carvings, political meetings, half-starved cattle, rustling maize stalks, argument, vultures, biting ants and the cooing of pigeons. Those poky, grubby little one-room shops with everything from tiny packets of tea to coloured blankets, shirts to spices, laxatives to snuff, displayed together in the front, and an enormous Asian family packed into the back; the *duka* with its rusty roof and stale smell and narrow veranda where a tattered African (always male) plies a treadle sewing machine —the *duka* is everywhere. You can't imagine life without it.

And of course it's not the *duka* whose day is said to be done, but that of its Asian owner. Like the civil service, like the cotton trade, like the railways and post offices and the clerical grades of industry and commerce, they must quickly be Africanized. The big squeeze is on and the Asians are caught in its grip.

Some have made fortunes here out of trade, out of big sugar plantations round Jinja, out of buying, processing and selling the cotton crop, and in other ways. Some possess rich houses, large cars and fat bank accounts. But the great majority rear their copious offspring at a level little, if any, above that of most Africans and work a great deal harder. By and large they are industrious, provident, sober, law-abiding citizens. Rather than expect everything to be done for them by the Government, they have seen to the education of their own young, and seen to it well. They are, it is true, evasive taxpayers, but are not alone in that. They have carried retail trading into remote areas, where the *duka* has been, with the *boma* where government resides, the sole point of contact with an outside world. With their skills and industry they have filled that vital medial layer with station-masters, post office clerks, accountants, carpenters, dispensers, masons, storekeepers, bus owners, bootmakers, lawyers.

Inevitably, Africans now want their jobs, envy their success and resent their racial and religious cohesion. The civil service has been closed to them, cotton ginneries are being taken over by co-operatives, trade schools are turning out African artisans, industry and commerce are Africanizing as hard as they can.

What are the Asians to do? "Nine out of ten of us have been born here and have no roots in India or Pakistan. We can't go, we are Ugandans, we belong here. Over half our whole community are under nineteen. The Government must realize that their future has already become a major problem."

This was a rich Indian talking, who'd been delayed in his appointment by a telephone call to London about spot prices. He himself would be all right, but he was worried. "The trouble is, we have no leadership. We are experiencing a revolution, but few of our community will face this. We must accept the facts, make adaptations. . . ."

Such as? "Only ten per cent of Uganda's land is being properly used. I believe that is unique in Africa.¹ There's still no population pressure. We Asians came from the land originally, and we can go back to it. The Government should launch a major Asian settlement scheme."

Would Africans tolerate alien ownership of land? "Not ownership, leaseholds. There's land leased to Asians already in Buganda and Busoga, and there's no resentment. Cultivation helps the country, it brings employment and revenue. It needs to be organized. Do you know the average yield of cotton here is only three hundred and fifty pounds an acre? Without any great changes, merely by planting at the right time, using better seed, weeding properly—by harder work— it's easy to get yields of a thousand pounds an acre. We could double the output of Uganda—sugar, cotton, coffee, tea, anything will grow, we have fertility, rainfall, climate. Markets? There'd be co-operatives and boards, centralized control. . . .

"Yes, I know we've become an urban people. Our young men and women will have to change, or face unemployment. It comes back to leadership. In Israel they've taken people from the cities and turned them into farmers, made the desert bloom. We could do the same if we had the inspiration.

"Every African country has increased its output in the last few years except Uganda, which relies too much on peasant cultivation.² Uganda needs more output, we Asians need

¹ The facts: out of an estimated thirty-five million acres of potential arable land, about five and a quarter million acres are under cultivation at any given time. Total land area, about fifty-two million acres.

² More facts: between 1947 and 1955 Uganda's economy boomed; exports of coffee, for instance, rose fourfold by volume, thirteen times by value. Between 1955 and 1962 production within the money economy (i.e., excluding subsistence) rose by only 1.1 per cent, population by over 2 per cent, p.a. (Report by I.B.R.D.—World Bank, 1962).

employment—and more than that, a future, grounds for hope.
The time has come for a round-table conference to work out
a scheme to join the two."

To these suggestions African Ministers, politicians and
professional men are chilly. Africans, they say, won't lease
land to Asians. "Why should we do anything for them?
They've done nothing for us except exploit us and take their
money out of the country. Now they must look after themselves."

Yet there is talent going to waste, lives that could enrich
the country, skills Uganda badly needs.

"Discrimination?" said a Minister. "Perhaps it is. I stick
to my position. I'm a nationalist."

A few respected Asians occupy high positions. One is in the
Government as a Deputy Minister; another, Mr. Patel, was
Kampala's Mayor at the time of my visit: an elderly, desiccated, kindly man, who sat in his parlour beside french windows opening on a garden full of hibiscus bloom and
twittering birds, worrying about the city's finances and how
to educate its children, who hatch like locusts and need more
and more schools, while rates have reached their ceiling. In
another part of City Hall an association of African traders
was in session to work out ways of getting easier credit, and
so equip themselves the better to drive Asians out of the
duka trade. The Government was offering a fund of two million pounds ($5,600,000) to help the African traders.

The Minister of Community Development, who opened
the conference, looked into the Mayor's parlour for a friendly
chat. He is one of the new men: enthusiastic, fluent, smooth,
impeccably dressed, a graduate of Makerere topped up by
study overseas, under thirty-five, comfortably mounted on
the pig's back with his ministerial salary, house, car and
heshima. Youth and age, confidence and experience, hope

and doubt, a beckoning future and a long past: they greet each other, one coming in and one going out.

Boycott

The Asian boycott was ugly while it lasted and, in an underground fashion, it rumbles on still.

The last person you would suspect of organizing anything so unkind is Mr. Eridadi Muliro, a soft-spoken, polished, mild and charming Muganda gentleman, whose wife is chairman of the Uganda Council of Women, his eldest son a prosperous coffee broker. They entertained me at tea and introduced me to a cross section of Kampala's social and intellectual elite—Establishment figures, every one, not boycott organizers; but the violence and intimidation which accompanied the boycott, Mr. Muliro said, had never been intended.

It all arose, he explained, from a constitutional matter: a British proposal to water down the pure milk of universal suffrage by reserving seats in parliament for Europeans and Asians. All the parties then contending for leadership united to oppose this design. They wanted straightforward universal suffrage, with no strings attached, and invited the Asians to support their protest. The Asians refused. Very well then, said the African leaders, you refuse to renounce your privileged position; we shall refuse to trade with you.

All went well at first, but then the boycotters became overzealous: Asians were threatened, abused, beaten up; the Government asked the leaders of the Uganda National Movement to call off the boycott. This they refused to do.

Mr. Muliro owned, and owns, a newspaper; according to his own account, he urged nonviolence; according to the Government's (then, of course, colonialist), he fanned the flames. He and several colleagues were arrested and rusticated

313

at Gulu, the capital of the Acholi's province, a quiet and pleasant spot. This, according to Mr. Muliro, exacerbated matters; violence grew; people refused to sell their coffee to Asian traders; coffee piled up, farmers grew short of cash, violence was intensified. Youth wings enjoyed themselves with homemade bombs. "This was never intended," Mr. Muliro said. "It all got out of hand. But it was Sir Frederick Crawford's government that brought it on." (Sir Frederick was the Governor.)

The official version is rather different, naturally. "A crowd of thugs and hoodlums went round extorting money from Asian traders for protection, and beating them up," said a member of the C.I.D. "The Asians had a very thin time. Africans denied them milk and water, meat and vegetables. Their *dukas* were picketed and they sat on their verandas for months, with very little to eat and nothing to do. It went on for two years, and we had over a thousand cases of violence and intimidation *reported*—many more probably weren't. Very ugly at times.

"And we haven't had a break in violence ever since," this policeman added. "Under the surface it simmers on. Last year Uganda had nine hundred murders and attempted murders, in a population of under seven millions, compared with a hundred and thirty in the U.K. with fifty millions. And they complain over there! In 1932 we had sixty-one. The difference isn't all due to failure to report offences in those days.

"Then we had the Bukedi riots, the worst we've ever had, in 1960—a minor civil war. Nearly fifteen hundred cases of murder, arson, riot, malicious damage and assault reported; attacks on chiefs, crop slashing, almost every county and sub-county headquarters razed to the ground." Contentment is evidently only skin deep sometimes.

"Yes, on the surface everybody's friendly and smiling. We

get some pretty brutal murders, though. One family of six was wiped out with pangas and horribly mutilated—a gang of young men with no apparent object, all for a haul of a few shillings. They were caught and hanged. The officer responsible for tracing them has gone now, Africanized. In this work there's no substitute for experience. A trickle of educated young men only started to flow into the force in the last year or two. We've got one youngster from Makerere, that's all. Now the force is being filleted—its expatriate backbone removed. I suppose it'll be all right in the end. Meanwhile . . ."

The Inspector General was less gloomy. The quality of his African replacements, he considers, is high; within two years he hopes to have the force, himself included, wholly Africanized. As for corruption, of eight officers prosecuted last year, three were Europeans, three were Asians and two were Africans.

Night Life

The troubles ended only when a law was passed enabling the Government to declare boycotts illegal. Now there's a "no give" campaign—don't give your custom to Asians. I met one of its instigators at the White Nile, or it may have been the Top Life—one of Kampala's several packed, noisy, cheerful, uninhibited but well-behaved night clubs, where, to the music of a Congo band, everyone twists with dash, drinks with relish, talks with fervour, sweats with profusion and enjoys life with gusto and *élan*. A youngish, thick-lipped, excitable man, he makes Sunday speeches by the Tree of Liberty, near the bus stop, "in an atmosphere of rebellion." Now there's no colonialism, what does he rebel against? Anything—last Sunday it was Kenya milk. There shouldn't be any Kenya milk in Kampala, it should all be Ugandan.

315

"I am a house painter," he said. "Like Hitler. He had the Jews, here we have the Asians. . . ." His English was clotted. "This is Mr. So-and-so, he is the son of a Bishop." We shook hands. The Bishop's son said: "The future of Uganda is bright, but we must stop the agitators and trade unions who want to spoil our government." Was he in politics? No, business—he travelled in tobacco in Ghana and Nigeria.

We got on to the subject of women, the wonderful fat market women of Accra and Kumasi, their countrywide trading in mammy wagons, the female business tycoons of Port Harcourt who deal in thousands, tens of thousands of pounds: independent, forceful, rich and free. And, by contrast, Baganda women, physically splendid but trodden down socially and economically. Shouldn't Baganda males change their ways? The Bishop's son looked grave.

"Ghana . . . President Nkrumah is a great man, but that doesn't mean we must adopt all their customs. Women traders . . . Out by six in the morning and back late at night, their husbands and their children neglected. What becomes of home life then? No, that wouldn't suit us Baganda."

Night life pulsates with gaiety, good nature and human warmth, oiled by beer, cheap whisky and gin. The tarts look well fed, neatly dressed, contented—no standing about on street corners or waiting by the telephone, but comfy seats in crowded cafés, convivial company, a sweet syrupy drink always at hand. The chic ones have their hair dekinked and do it in a sort of helmet, like a coal scuttle clamped on upside down.

Our evening started at a restaurant where whites, browns and blacks got along together famously. A pink-faced, gangling young British technician cuddled a shiny chocolate tart; a squat and broken-nosed Asian stood a group of the sisterhood Seven-Ups; two intellectual English girls in glasses with

very tight black skirts and cropped hair—unquestionably from Makerere—put the world to rights with a couple of lean and serious young African lecturers. A thickset, nattily dressed African at the bar told us he'd come from Nairobi to sell cars on commission. Across a doorway leading into a recess, like a box at the opera, a net lace curtain was drawn; within, a little den of assignation held, I'm sure, a potted plant or two and pink frills. *Fanny by Gaslight* all over again. We didn't get our meal until ten thirty: a mammoth four-inch steak, surmounted by a vast omelete.

On then to Jolly Joe's. A short, fat, broad-faced man in spectacles, Jolly Joe himself, exuded goodwill and proclaimed: "I'm a Communist!" I asked why. "I'm friendly to *all* people, including Communists." The Communists had stood him a trip to Peking and given him a printing press, but this had fallen by the wayside; Jolly Joe is not a type to whom the world's goods cling as he bounces on his way.

A former leader of the Uganda National Congress, Jolly Joe has boldly opposed the Kabaka's Government of Buganda and the feudal system it perpetuates. To challenge this determined, crafty, dug-in set of men can be dangerous; once he was beaten up and left for dead, but a passing policeman saw an arm sticking up out of a swamp and fished him out just in time. On another occasion the Buganda courts sentenced him to fifteen years for attempting to assassinate the Kabaka, but he got off on appeal to the protectorate authorities.[3]

Jolly Joe has also been an active boycotter of Asians, but when I asked his present views I found his mind preoccupied.

---

[3] Party politics in Buganda is no game for milksops. A war between the Democratic Party and the Buganda traditionalists' party, the Kabaka Yekka, centred on the general election of 1962, resulted in nearly 800 prosecutions, including 336 for threatening violence, 134 for assault, 79 for crop slashing, 67 for arson, 46 for robbery and theft and 40 for malicious damage.

"Twenty-nine to avoid the follow-on at close of play. What a different picture from this morning—ninety-three for eight! Amazing! If it hadn't been for Lock and Titmus' splendid stand. . . ." "Were you a cricketer yourself?" I inquired. "I captained Uganda!" he replied. He is a Budo boy.

King's College, Budo, was founded by the Church Missionary Society about half a century ago for chiefs' sons, and since then everyone who's anyone has sent his sons to be shaped into true Uganda gentlemen by its first-rate academic discipline—only the best masters, intellectually and morally, have taught there—and its muscular Christianity in the Dr. Arnold tradition. Now Uganda's Establishment is almost solidly Old Budonian. (The Prime Minister is not, and some say this has placed a chip on his shoulder.) Nothing like the Budo influence is to be found elsewhere in modern Africa. It's like being ruled not merely by Old Etonians but by members of their debating society; they're all prosperous, bland and charming, with manners that would make most Old Etonians appear sadly farouche.

Jolly Joe was not the only Old Budonian at the White Nile and the Top Life. Among them someone pointed out a man who's in insurance and is building himself a house for fourteen thousand pounds ($39,200). Another was a barrister earning, I was told (perhaps erroneously), ten thousand ($28,000) a year. He paid no income tax before independence, since the protectorate government exempted Africans; now he's liable; *uhuru* has its harsher side. No wives were present—they look after home life.

The Top Life is said to have the largest dance floor in Africa. Congolese bandsmen in red shorts manipulating electric guitars were singing in a tongue called Lingala, composed of mixed Swahili and Congolese dialects. We recognized old friends: the Makerere lecturers twisting rather primly, the

Kenya salesman propping up the bar, the Bishop's son with an elegant coal-scuttle-headed partner in a black-and-gold-spangled dress. No one was even holding hands, let alone taking other liberties: no teenage thugs or layabouts. At the Top Life such fry would soon be seen off by Top People.

"This is the editor of the *Uganda Nation*. . . ." He told us he had just received a strange missive posted in a mining town deep in the Mountains of the Moon. Amid the haunts of chimpanzees, gorillas and birds of brilliant plumage, a fanatic called Isaya Mukirane wishes, with his followers, to secede from the Kingdom of Toro and start a little nation of his own. (Toro is ruled by a Mukama called King George: a huge, hearty mountain of a man with appetites to match his lusty size, who impressed an English hostess by doing justice not only to her salad, but to her flower decoration in the middle of the table as well.) Isaya is partly a pygmy, and his fiery nationalism is centred on his tribe, the Bakonjo, who he thinks have been pushed around insultingly by King George's ruling-race colonialists, the Batoro. His proclamation ran:

"God, King of Ruwenzori, is sending down the heavenly spirits with sharp swords which will slash down those who are invading the innocent country. Poll tax is now being collected by the Ruwenzurumu Government chiefs. The Government will welcome friendly relations with other governments." Isaya had taken to the mountains on the Congo border, leaving behind him a disturbed, explosive situation and easily evading the less nimble-footed police.

Lost Counties

The Kabaka of Buganda, Sir Frederick Mutesa II, a slight, light-skinned, headstrong and attractive young man generally known as King Freddy, is an accessible monarch, but was away hunting—rumour had it, even bigger game than elephants. Every day cars carrying his Ministers on mysterious errands sped to and from his seat of government on Mengo Hill and a hunting lodge in the farthest part of his domains, in one of the notorious "lost counties"—a very hot political potato indeed.

These were lost to Buganda by the neighbouring kingdom of Bunyoro under the agreement of 1900 establishing the British protectorate which was wound up in 1962. Ever since, Bunyorans have been trying to get these counties back. At the time of independence they secured an undertaking that the two counties—Buyaga and Bugangazi—should be administered by the central government until a plebiscite could be held to decide their future.

The counties have not yet been handed over, nor the plebiscite held. Bunyorans are hopping-mad, and the Kabaka had taken with him on his hunting trip three thousand of his loyal Baganda subjects, most of them ex-soldiers, not to drive the elephants but to participate in a "settlement scheme." Each settler is to take up a plot of land and become a sturdy and industrious peasant, strengthening the country's economy and, no doubt, casting his vote when the plebiscite can no longer be postponed.

Bunyorans, understandably, are furious; they have manned roadblocks with spearmen, beaten drums and have had to be dispersed by the police. They, too, have a parliament and King, the Omukama, who traces his lineage back to the fifteenth century. The lost-counties issue has been simmering on for sixty years—neither Bunyorans nor Bagandans are ones to forgive and forget—and now bedevils the relations, always strained, between the Kingdom of Baganda and the central government.

Uganda's politics form a labyrinth through whose secret chambers few outsiders can hope to find a way. The thread is the resolve of the Baganda people to keep their separate identity, not to merge into that conglomeration of races, tribes, kingdoms, savages, pygmies and nomads known as Uganda; and the equally fierce resolve of Buganda's ancient monarchy—King Freddy is the thirty-fifth Kabaka—to cling to its feudal traditions in a modern world.

Supporters of the Kabaka, who enshrines the spirit and *mystique* of the Baganda people, and of his government, which gives this spirit practical expression, are therefore known as the traditionalists, and in the kingdom certainly command majority support. But there is a growing body of anti-traditionalists, mostly younger men who chafe against the authoritarian rule of the Kabaka's government, accuse its Ministers of corruption and intrigue and believe that the Baganda should scrap their ancient but outmoded institutions in favour of unconstrained democracy and join with their non-Baganda fellow citizens to build a new, egalitarian, forward-looking world. Some of these dissidents have formed an active body called the Bawejjere (meaning common man) Association.

Once again here is the dichotomy, the Janus head of modern Africa—a pride in African tradition at odds with an urge to join, as full members, the modern technological world. Even the most fervent anti-traditionalist is proud of his country and feels loyalty to his King. It is the King's Ministers and feudal institutions he repudiates. The Kabaka is young and some of his Ministers are able, but others are old, inflexible and crusty men, nurtured in a creed outworn, who draw the wraps of power round them and turn their faces from the rising sun.

Where does King Freddy stand? A reed who bends before

the tide or a barrier who resists it? He is a wily monarch—
he would not be a true Muganda if he weren't wily—and
seldom brings his views into the open. He is always polite.
But he can be judged by his actions, or perhaps by his lack
of them. Hitherto he has shown little inclination to bend before the oncoming forces. His Katikiro—the Prime Minister—
is an elderly archtraditionalist at odds with reformers, and
the Kabaka has hitherto resisted pressure to replace him
with a less uncompromising man. On the subject of the "lost
counties" the Kabaka has evaded rather than opposed the
legitimate claims of the central government.

The Court of the Kabaka

Kampala plays a double role. The handsome new buildings
of the National Assembly, complete with clock tower, mark its
status as a national capital; a mile or two away, on Namirembe Hill, stands the Bulange, seat of the Kabaka's government. Here, in a pleasantly designed modern building, is
another parliament, another Prime Minister, another cluster
of Ministries, another police force, prison, Chief Justice with
his separate laws, another treasury and set of taxes, everything. On the adjacent hill of Mengo—Kampala has about
twenty of these small protuberances—stands the Lubiri, the
Kabaka's palace. An ugly brick wall now encloses it. Formerly there was a high fence of yellow reeds neatly plaited in
designs no one was allowed to imitate. A fire burns day and
night by the main gate and is extinguished only when a
Kabaka dies, to be relit as soon as his successor is proclaimed.

Many changes have come since the days of its glory—a
cruel, barbaric glory certainly, but glory nonetheless. A century ago the explorer Speke wrote that the whole hillside was
covered with gigantic huts thatched with reed "as neatly as

so many heads dressed by a London barber," and fenced into courtyards and compounds like an enormous house of cards. It was here that "most of Mutesa's three or four hundred women" were kept, the remainder being attached to his mother's household.

His innumerable courtiers wore neat bark cloths resembling the best yellow corduroy cloth, crimp and well set, as if stiffened with starch, and over that, as upper cloaks, a patchwork of small antelope skins, sewn together as well as any English glover could have pieced them; whilst their head-dresses, generally, were abrus turbans, set off with highly polished boar-tusks, stick-charms, seeds, beads or shells. . . .

Men, women, bulls, dogs and goats were led about by strings; cocks and hens were carried in men's arms; and little pages, with rope-turbans, rushed about conveying messages as if their lives depended on their swiftness, everyone holding his skin-cloak tightly round him lest his naked legs might by accident be shown.

If this should happen in the royal presence, the punishment was either to be thrown to the sacred crocodiles or to have lips and nose cut off, a common penalty. In the King's presence even the best dressed of his subjects had to grovel in the dust, and ran the risk of instant death if he gave the least offence. A rigidly disciplined chain of chiefs and sub-chiefs, and a highly centralized system of land tenure and taxes, kept the whole kingdom under the thumb of the Kabaka. This was a real tyranny in the Greek sense, conducted according to certain formulated rules but allowing to the tyrant unrestricted powers of personal, and sometimes whimsical, rule. The same applied to the other Bahima kingdoms, whose fortunes fluctuated with their rulers' abilities and characters.

Although it is no longer necessary to rub your face in the earth in the Kabaka's presence, all loyal Baganda kneel and clap their hands, and many still fling themselves flat on their faces, like a fish on the bank, as of old. An expatriate who took office under the new Government started a controversy by prostrating himself at a reception, taking the line that as a Uganda citizen he ought to accord to its royal personages the same measure of respect as a native citizen would show —just as he would expect a Ugandan in Britain to stand for "God Save the Queen."

It was the Kabaka's determination not to be shunted on to a siding as a constitutional monarch that led to his deportation by the protectorate government in 1953, when negotiations were proceeding to revise the Buganda Agreement as a step towards Uganda's independence. The Kabaka stood firm both for his own traditional powers and for his kingdom's autonomy, and demanded for Buganda immediate independence as a separate state.

An Impetuous Governor

The Governor of the day was Sir Andrew Cohen, a sport among Governors about as far removed as you could get from the popular image of the prudent, stuffed-shirted civil servant arrayed on state occasions in a white uniform with medals and feathers. A brilliant, impatient, unconventional and outspoken man, Sir Andrew was known to be actively sympathetic towards African nationalism; liberal-minded, a socialist and resolved to liquidate colonialism as quickly as possible; a friend of Fabians, the darling of the British left. (There is a story that when in Malta, in his early days, he prosecuted a firm of bakers for selling short-weight bread; so absorbed did he become in his own cogent arguments that he began to break and munch pieces of the exhibits, the delinquent loaves; by the time he had completed the case for the prosecution, the exhibits were no more.) When it came to a clash of wills between Governor and Kabaka, it was the Kabaka who went—literally; Sir Andrew deported him summarily in the good, or bad, old-fashioned colonialist way. He was exiled to London on a tax-free British allowance of £8,000 ($22,400) a year.

It was in the interests of democracy that Sir Andrew Cohen acted; he was on the anti-traditionalist side. But his action appeared high-handed, and, as one would expect, by infuriating the Baganda it made them more intractable. In two years' time the Kabaka was back, welcomed at the airport by Sir Andrew, dressed up in his sword and feathers; and in due course a new agreement was signed. In the British and the non-Baganda view this did, at last, turn the Kabaka into a constitutional monarch obliged to act on the advice of his Katikiro and the Lukiko, his parliament, on Mengo Hill. In the Kabaka's view it evidently did not—or, if it did, the advice of the Lukiko and the Kabaka's inclinations always seemed to coincide.

After the Kabaka's return relations between the kingdom and the protectorate (as it then was) grew more and more strained. The various ways in which this strain was manifest were complex in the extreme, but the basic cause never changed. Uganda had to get its independence as soon as possible: the British, the Baganda and all the other peoples of this motley nation agreed on that. (While the Buganda form the largest single group, they constitute only about one fifth of the total population; a tremendous diversity of peoples makes up the remainder, ranging from pygmies and camel-trekking spear-blooders to coffee barons and university lecturers; Uganda has six major languages, the Gospels are printed in twelve, there are ten tribal groups with more than

327

two hundred thousand people in each and about thirty separate tribes.)

Uganda had to get its independence quickly, and the only
basis for that independence in a modern world was one-man,
one-vote democracy—universal suffrage, free elections, political parties, a representative parliament, a ministerial system,
the lot. And a strong, viable central government: the unitary
state.

This was the point where the aims of the Baganda on the
one hand and of the British and the non-Baganda on the
other sharply diverged. The Kabaka, speaking for his people,
shunned a strong unitary state. Buganda was willing to federate, but not to merge. This was, in his view, the basis of
the agreement of 1900, revised and restated—not abrogated—
in 1960. Nor did he favour undiluted democracy. One man,
one vote and full representative government would bring
the whole traditional Baganda system toppling down. Neither
the Kabaka nor—he claims—his people want to see it topple.
It has, after all, served them for about four centuries, and
is their own.

The retort of the central government was simple: the
wishes of the majority must prevail. And a majority of the
people enclosed in Uganda's arbitrary borders, or at least
their representatives, favoured a unitary state.

In its essence, this is a situation to be found in all parts of
the changing world. The new order is a juggernaut crushing
the old orders, with their colour and tradition and their cry-
stallized responses to human needs, and leaving behind a
throng of people much the same: boiler-suited toilers, parrot-
trained children, traffic jams and assembly lines and rocket
stations: a crowded, monotonous and perhaps directionless
new world. But, as we know, old orders must corrupt and
mummify; plants die when they have dropped their seed,

new buildings arise from rubble, nothing is final. The unitary state has won, even though many of the Baganda shut their eyes to this reality. Whether they will retain the trappings of a constitutional monarchy is perhaps irrelevant. More relevant is the question of whether Uganda, like its neighbour Tanganyika, is proceeding from the unitary towards the single-party state.

UGANDA'S MEN

Prime Minister

Mr. Milton Obote's first and major task is to create Uganda. It is there on paper, but not in people's hearts.

"Everyone must learn to look to the centre and to be proud of belonging to our country. They must pass beyond their tribal loyalties which divide and weaken us. Tribalism looks backwards, it disrupts and weakens. I hate to hear of what the Lukiko is saying, of all the regional and tribal bodies pulling things apart." There was an edge to his voice when he spoke of regional and tribal bodies. He had touched the core of his belief.

We talked in the sitting room of a mansion built for the Resident, who in colonial times formed the link between Buganda and the British administration. It was much as the last Resident had left it: a plain room, stiffly encircled by empty chairs, equipped with an ugly red carpet and furniture as serviceable as it was graceless. Books stood at attention in their case, dusted but redundant: nondescript reproductions adorned the walls, empty ashtrays lay on occasional tables; it was like a tidied-up and anchored *Marie Celeste*. A silent servant in a long white *kanzu* brought tea.

As politicians go these days, Mr. Obote, at rising forty, is a ripe man. Slim, energetic, alert, abstemious, hard-working and full of charm, he's said to keep himself going on little else but frequent cups of tea.

As a child he herded goats on the shores of Lake Kioga, where his father was a headman charged with the special duty of keeping down wasps, and was twelve before he went to school. That was a false start; the relatives he was sent to lodge with kept him as a drudge, beat him for helping himself to mangoes and drove him out when he rebelled. A second attempt led him to a secondary school, through the portals of School Certificate and so to Makerere.

His first adult task was to start a trade union on a sugar estate in Kenya, and then, in Nairobi, when Mau Mau was being organized, in the words of an official biography, to "establish what were called social clubs; they were in fact political clubs. As a blind, prominent Europeans like Blundell and Grogan were invited to give talks on social problems, but at other times Africans were called in and expressed what Mr. Obote describes as 'violent political views.' "

It was not until 1959 that Mr. Obote impinged on the politics of his native land by forming the Uganda Peoples' Congress, which he now leads. The first general election, held in 1961, he lost to the rival Democratic Party, now in opposition.

The skein of Uganda's politics is too tangled for any but an expert to unravel, but the upshot was that Milton Obote led his country into independence in October, 1962, as head of a party which, while it had come out on top in the elections, had not won an overall majority. Here is another irony: his party, the most radical and in the old colonial parlance "extremist," took office only by means of a coalition with Buganda's archtraditionalists. These had formed themselves into a party called the Kabaka Yekka, whose representatives were elected to the National Assembly not directly by the voters, but indirectly by the Lukiko, the Kabaka's men.

This was the result of a compromise. The Kabaka's government, resolved to have no part in any unitary state, boycotted the first general election in 1961, and the advance towards independence would have become hopelessly bogged down in Buganda's demands for autonomy had not Mr. Obote managed, by a brilliant stroke of diplomacy, to strike a bargain with the Kabaka's government. Buganda would take part in another general election; the Baganda would form their own party, which Mr. Obote's Uganda Peoples' Congress would not oppose, and which would subsequently support Mr. Obote; in return, the Uganda Peoples' Congress, when in office, would do nothing to impair or diminish Buganda's autonomy.

If ever there was an uneasy partnership, this is it. A constant tug of war goes on between, in the last analysis, the Kabaka and the Prime Minister. The Kabaka Yekka Party is the rope. It's not surprising that in places it has frayed. There is talk of defection to the Uganda Peoples' Congress, and rumours and counterrumours fly about the capital like its innumerable bats.

Mr. Obote entertains no doubts as to his ultimate success. Constitutionally Buganda is a Region, although a special one. "The Regions are nothing," he said. "They will weaken and fade away."

How to Unify

How can Uganda, that colonialist invention, genuinely unify? First, Mr. Obote said, through political parties. "They are for the whole country. They draw people together." Then through education. "We have made it clear that all schools will accept pupils from any part of Uganda. In the secondary schools English is the language, and will remain so. Now we are reorganizing our system of technical education. Instead of a lot of little trade schools in the districts, we are to build five big colleges, each to concentrate on one main subject. This will unite our young people instead of dividing them. They will become Ugandans, not tribalists."

On the future of the opposition Mr. Obote's views were at once robust and cautious. "I don't mind an opposition, I should find it dull speaking only to members of my own party. A little opposition is stimulating, like sharpening a knife."

A little, possibly, but not a lot. I am sure that it never enters Mr. Obote's head, or the head of any other leader on this continent who holds the steering wheel, that he might voluntarily yield his place to another driver. To do so would seem an act of lunacy. You don't strive for the possession of a vehicle and then give it away to someone you distrust and probably dislike and who'd be certain, in your belief, to smash it to bits on the nearest tree.

"I was in opposition and I know the temptations," the Prime Minister added. "Say the Government does something you think is right and would do yourself if you were in power. The temptation is to oppose it and stir up the people. This tears down the country's unity and undermines the people's faith in their leaders. Then you have plots, violence, rioting.

"The essence of leadership," he added, "is to keep right out ahead, but never out of sight of the people."

Mr. Obote's most serious worry is Uganda's economy. It is too stagnant, depends too much on peasant agriculture and is starved for capital. He believes that large companies are needed to develop the land with machinery and irrigation—co-operatives, state-backed corporations, kibbutzim, the form of organization doesn't matter so long as money and skill come in. There is nothing doctrinaire about any of these leaders, except presumably the Communists, and (unless you count Jolly Joe) I haven't met any. Capital from "the Outside," expatriates on contract, industrialization—needs are the same everywhere.

"Right now we are in real trouble," Mr. Obote added, and ticked his troubles off on his fingers. The lost counties, a running sore; revolt in Toro headed by its mad messiah, which has led to a state of emergency; slashing of coffee trees and burning of houses in Bugisu, moves in a war between two co-operative societies; in remote Karamoja, cattle raids in which only last week nearly eighty people were killed. "All this must stop."

Both Milton Obote and his half brother, Mr. Nekyon, are men of quick intelligence and strong personality. Mr. Obote started with all the attributes of the "agitator," and might have won his prison graduate's cap had he blossomed a few years earlier, when colonial governments were still trying to slow down the nationalist surge to power and look for "moderates" to treat with. By the time he entered politics, they were trying to disengage as quickly as they could and welcomed with relief a leader of sufficient weight and stature to glue together several squabbling splinter parties, command the loyalty of most Ugandans, cope with the Kabaka and his Ministers and accept from an outgoing power the staff of office. It needed a brave man as well as an able one to do all this, and Mr. Obote's stature has grown with his responsibilities. If he has not yet united Uganda, he has more or less united its Government, which is a fine start.

Now and again some of the old Milton peeps through. He returned from the conference of independent African states in Addis Ababa once more breathing fire and fury against colonialists, this time at a remove—colonialists a long way south, but still abhorred; and offered Uganda as a training ground for half a million freedom fighters who would march down to free Mozambique, Rhodesia and South Africa from white rule. Lately he has severed all relations, and boycotted all trade, with Dr. Verwoerd's republic. The crusader's spirit may slumber sometimes, but it's far from dead.

Opposition

I met the leader of the opposition in less immaculate surroundings, above an Asian general store off one of Kampala's side streets. An air of squalor hangs around such buildings with their long, dirty corridors, off which office doors open like prison cells to afford glimpses of people lounging on benches in barely furnished rooms with dirty and uncurtained windows; there's a smell of stale urine, suspicious-looking pools, a littered courtyard below where washing flaps on lines and grubby children squat in the dust.

A mountainous woman bulging from a purple dress too tight for her, with a mop of frizzy hair, was very slowly filling in a form in an outer office, where half a dozen men were studying newssheets at a bare trestle table. This was the headquarters of the Democratic Party. Mr. Benedicto Kiwanuka sat in a small inside office with a smart young male secretary and a telephone. He looked quite old for a modern politician, although little over forty.

A smallish, compact man with a moustache, he displayed an air of reserve, even severity, unusual among the suave Baganda, to whose ruling class he belongs; certainly he'd have been a Budo boy if he had not been a Roman Catholic. Perhaps his wartime service as a sergeant major has stiffened him, or the bitterness of loss of office. When as an African politician you are in, the world is at your feet, and all the red carpets; when you are out, you are right out on a limb, where there are no carpets, sometimes not even floors.

The Democratic Party, led by Mr. Kiwanuka, started as a Roman Catholic pressure group in Buganda and is still predominantly Catholic. Mention of this annoyed its leader. "Who told you that? Did they tell you the U.P.C. was Protestant? In my government we had several non-Catholic Ministers, in the U.P.C.'s there are Catholics. Our parties are not based on religious differences."

During the short interlude of "internal self-government" that under the procedure for the transfer of power evolved by the British normally precedes full independence, Mr. Kiwanuka became Uganda's first Prime Minister; but his time of glory lasted only thirteen months. It was because the Kabaka ordered the boycott of the elections of 1961 that his party came to power. Only three per cent of the qualified electors of Buganda registered in defiance of the ban. They voted for the Democratic Party, who thus captured all but one of Buganda's twenty-one seats in the National Assembly.

This gave Mr. Kiwanuka's men a majority over Mr. Obote's party, who polled considerably more votes, and so Mr. Kiwanuka and his Democrats took office. Now he blames the British for his defeat in the election held just over a year later. "They agreed at Lancaster House not to have direct elections in Buganda, but to let the Lukiko say who was to represent Buganda in the National Assembly. That betrayed democracy." It also ousted Mr. Kiwanuka, who lost his seat.

Kid Gloves

So the Democratic Party's leader cannot lead his party in parliament. This office is performed by a rather young barrister totally unlike the kind of politician who normally comes to the top in lands where a salty tide of nationalism runs with vigour. Mr. Basil Bataringaya springs from the ruling class of Ankole and has the fine bones, cream-and-coffee colour, deerlike eyes and subtle intelligence typical of Bahima aristocrats. He is gentle, soft-spoken, mild in manner, thoughtful, engaging; you would place him in the senior common room of a university rather than in the bar of a National Assembly, still less at the Tree of Liberty, bus stops, clock towers and community halls, where African politics, like Rice Krispies, pop and crackle. He, too, is a perfect Budo type, but a Roman Catholic.

His views are as measured and restrained as his manner. "The future of the opposition? It rests largely in our own hands. This is not the time to tear Uganda apart. We must give the Government a chance. It is trying to do what we should do ourselves. I believe that given a government that's fair, we will hold our own because we have a well-organized party in the country. Outside Buganda we won forty-five per cent of the votes cast. Yes, it's true that two of our members have defected to the U.P.C., but they were from Toro, from the counties that want to secede.

"I think Uganda needs a parliamentary opposition, I don't follow Julius Nyerere in that. Party activity should strengthen, and not weaken, the state. We must be constructive. The difference between opposition and obstruction should be clearly drawn and laid down within the party ranks. The Government can't always be wrong."

In his conduct in the National Assembly, Mr. Bataringaya

337

has been as good as his word. There has been very little acri-
monious or ill-founded criticism of Mr. Obote's policies and
actions. Some of the more robust parliamentarians think
there has been too little; criticism that isn't voiced inside the
chamber may fester outside it.

On the one hand, by his restraint Mr. Bataringaya may be
keeping alive the principle of opposition and staving off the
single-party state; on the other, if his leadership becomes too
mild and co-operative, dissidents may seek more outspoken
champions. No doubt this is part of the dilemma of all states-
men. Mr. Bataringaya leads in the manner suggested to him
by his temperament and nature. Everyone likes him. In a
world that's pretty red in tooth and claw, he wears kid gloves.

DOCTORS, ARTISTS AND A POLITICAL PRISONER

The Hill of Early Start

The Buganda names of all Kampala's hills have a meaning. Kampala itself means "the place of the kob antelope"; Mengo is the word for millstones; Namirembe, for the servant of peace.

The name Makerere is said to have originated in the eighteenth century, when the Kabaka of the day rose at dawn to surprise a girl who lived there, and to mean "early start." Now it is the site of the University College, whose start, if not so early as all that, at any rate preceded the birth of its sister colleges in Nairobi and Dar es Salaam. A technical school opened there in 1921 and pupated into a University College just before World War II.

It was a surprise to see so many white faces above the smart red gowns the students wear for dinner in the hall, and even more to see underneath them, instead of the usual neat dark suits, several striped football jerseys. The jerseys and faces belonged to young American volunteers for the Teachers for East Africa scheme, who if they have no teaching qualification take a Makerere diploma before their two years in local schools. The professors, whether white or black, disapproved strongly of the striped jerseys. Makerere already has entrenched, respectable traditions.

The campus is an architectural jumble without, it would appear, a central plan. Through the years buildings have been added as money could be found; while a few are interesting or pleasant in themselves, they don't match or even complement one another. But the situation makes up for this: the wonderfully green lawns and graceful trees, the flowering shrubs and creepers, glimpses over treetops of other hills, the sunlight and storm. Most of the staff live on the hill, and their gardens are full of birds.

As in Nairobi, there's a dreamlike quality about the laments of the Faculty that so many places here are unfilled. Makerere could take a thousand students, and has about seven hundred and fifty. More and more potential graduates are being enticed overseas to universities already overcrowded. And Africans cannot be found to teach the students. Nine out of ten of Makerere's teachers have white faces. "The Africans are being offered three or four times the pay as Ministers or Permanent Secretaries."

Although Makerere lies in the heart of Buganda, the biggest racial group here is Kikuyu. The Baganda come next, then two more Kenya tribes (Luo and Abaluhya) and then the Chagga, from the slopes of Mount Kilimanjaro. Sixty tribes are represented here. There is a single Karamajong.

Is tribalism fading out among these intellectual leaders and future rulers? Slowly, said the Principal. (Sir Bernard de Bunsen has just become the first Vice-Chancellor of the University of East Africa; as Vice-Principal a zoologist of distinction, Dr. Peter Wasawo, of Kisumu—an authority on swamp worms—has been appointed.) The notice board used to be plastered with announcements about meetings of tribal groups—Luo Union, Kikuyu Association and so on. Now most of the notices concern meetings of political parties or of students' societies. "The Baganda are the slowest to change; their pride is too strong."

It is among students that you look for growing points of future causes. For years these young men have been passionately preoccupied with the cause of freedom; Makerere was a spawning ground for "agitators"; most of the present nationalist leaders were students here. Now that the agitators have become Cabinet Ministers, what next? There's still Portugal and South Africa to be dealt with; but after that? Pan-Africanism?

"Lately a certain cynicism and disillusionment with politics has become apparent. The golden dream has faded, and nothing much seems to have taken its place."

It was a refreshing change to meet people interested in topics other than politics: a Kikuyu doctor who centred his considerable abilities on anatomy, and seemed scarcely to have heard of KANU; a zoologist from Toro who spoke of his specialty, nematode worms, of books of travel and the question whether life on other planets could be sustained by elements other than oxygen; one of his students, a Muluhya fresh from Durham University who displayed with pride his specimens of fruit bats odorously pickled in formalin. Upwards of half a million of these big bats, he said, inhabit an avenue of eucalyptus trees in Kampala and fly up to ten or eleven miles every night to feast on pawpaws, the ubiquitous green bananas and on wild figs.

Poor teaching facilities in schools have combined with the magnetic pull of politics to incline the great majority of students into the Faculties of Economics, English, Sociology and Education. Getting rid of colonialism has absorbed so much of the energies of the elite—if that's the right word; perhaps Toynbee's "creative minority" is better—that the tree of intellect has become distorted. Perhaps this will now throw out more branches on the scientific side to give it balance.

Doctors and Nurses

Makerere turns out doctors for all East Africa—full-blown ones qualified to practice in Britain if they so wish. On the adjacent hill of Mulago a magnificent teaching hospital, built at the cost to British taxpayers of nearly two and a half million pounds (seven million dollars), recently opened. One of the best equipped in Africa—and, I would suppose, in the world—it is to most British hospitals as a jet aircraft is to a biplane preserved in a museum.

The seed was sown just fifty-five years earlier by one of Uganda's true heroes, Dr. Albert Cook, who reached Kampala as a medical missionary in 1897 and started a primitive dispensary in a hut on Namirembe Hill, using cow dung to cement the floor, storing his mixtures in bottles that had held Communion wine and operating on a camp bedstead with instruments kept in vegetable dishes. Western medicine caught on instantly. An entry in the doctor's diary three weeks after he started work reads: "Saw fifty patients in the morning and did five operations in the afternoon." Cowrie shells were then used as currency, and Albert Cook records in his *Uganda Memories* that seven men were needed to carry five pounds' worth.

After a while Dr. Cook and Miss Timpson, the nursing sister whom he subsequently married, opened a hospital with two wards, containing six homemade bedsteads in each, mattresses of dried banana fronds and bark-cloth curtains. "A monotonous series of bullet and spear wounds" had to be dealt with; no one knew that malaria was carried by mosquitoes, and syphilis was rampant—and, of course, sleeping sickness, then incurable. So far did Dr. Cook's fame spread that an old and blind Somali walked two thousand miles from Berbera to seek a miracle, and found it; Dr. Cook operated for double cataract, and the old man's sight was restored.

Albert Cook was an earlier and less publicized Albert Schweitzer, minus the musical talent; he lived beloved, and died full of years and fame in Kampala. It was a pity that he and his equally devoted wife did not live to see the splendid fruit on Mulago Hill of the seed he had planted on Namirembe, and to rejoice in the high quality of the doctors trained there, even though their numbers cannot begin to match a continent-wide need.

Now Mulago trains nursing sisters and midwives as well, but they have lately been in trouble; an entire intake of trainees had to be evicted by the police because they refused to accept their dismissal by the Government. They were sacked because they refused to wear badges, and they were ordered to wear badges because of the need to identify those accused by disgusted patients of cavalier treatment, neglect and refusal to bring glasses of water or to empty bedpans without bribes.

Artists

Of all the peoples of these parts, the most artistically inclined appear to be the Baganda. In basketwork, in clothing and in ornament especially, their talent for design and neatness of execution impressed itself on every visitor to their kingdom in pre-colonial days, as it must today on every visitor to the Kampala museum. The beauty and intricacy of their beadwork are especially remarkable.

The Baganda appear to have invented the art of making a

light, crisp, attractive kind of cloth from the bark of a tree. This was peeled off, scraped and repeatedly beaten with heavy wooden mallets into thin sheets, which were then tailored into cloaks, breeches or aprons. So skilled were the Baganda as tailors and furriers, Samuel Baker remarked, and so anxious to obtain the best tools, that they would trade a healthy girl for thirteen steel needles.

Baker also remarked upon the passion for music demonstrated by many of the peoples he encountered on his explorations, and suggested that "the safest way to travel through these wild countries would be to play the cornet, if possible without ceasing." An organ-grinder, he added, could march unscathed through Central Africa, followed by an admiring and enthusiastic crowd. Listing the qualities he considered most desirable in Europeans who might enter these regions, then ravaged by a cruel slave trade centred at Khartoum, he put an ability to play the bagpipes second only to prowess with a rifle; a kilted Highlander, he remarked, who could play a lively air on the bagpipes, would be listened to when an Archbishop by his side would be totally disregarded. Yet in other branches of art, such as sculpture, painting and dancing, people of Uganda demonstrated little or no native skill.

Makerere's School of Fine Arts, started by Mrs. Margaret Trowell single-handed, with practically no money, in a borrowed room, now hums with activity. Its teaching staff, under Professor Cecil Todd, includes Gregory Maloba, the first East African sculptor to make his mark outside his own country—or inside it for that matter—and Mr. Jonathan Kingdon, a young man born in Tanganyika, as an instructor in painting.

There is nothing like a Makerere, or indeed an African, "school." The students paint and sculpt as the spirit moves them, and the wide range of their responses to the world visible or invisible fascinates by its unfamiliarity and a sense of breaking new ground. These students start with no tradition, no preconceived ideas—above all, without feeling that they must strain after originality of technique to express ideas and responses that were old in the days of Mabuse and Giotto. Some have never before handled a pencil or brush. These are the students most interesting to develop, but nowadays more and more have been taught in schools, like European children, to put lines on paper representing in two dimensions the three-dimensional world.

To start with, most of the students want to draw and paint scenes from their own lives—villages, cattle, landscapes; after a while they discover patterns, colours and designs. The abstract, however, has little appeal, and we are (for the moment) spared action painting; creating works of art with bicycles, watering cans and besoms perhaps appears to most of them too clumsy, even though no tradition ties them to crayon and brush.

There are talent and originality, but so far there is no genius—for that it is very early. Several ex-Makerere art students have already made names for themselves. One such is Elimo Njau, a Tanganyikan, now working at the Scorsbie Galleries, in Nairobi, best known for his murals on the Crucifixion theme depicted in African terms, to be seen in the little open-sided memorial chapel at Fort Hall, in Kikuyu country, put up to Christians martyred in the Mau Mau civil war. He has been preoccupied, it seems, with religious themes; at Makerere, I saw an interesting series inspired by Christ's temptations; in sombre, stormy browns and purples their queer, tortured elongated figures, the disturbing shapes of rocks, recall El Greco, with here and there a hint of Hieronymus Bosch.

Mr. Njau interpreted the core of Christ's temptation (so

the owner of the paintings believed) not as power to sway the multitude and possess the kingdoms of the world, but as doubt of the ultimate support and succour of the Father—*why hast thou forsaken me?* Mr. Sam Ntiro, now High Commissioner for East Africa in London, is another Tanganyikan ex-Makerere artist who has made his name and held exhibitions in New York and London.

The difficulty of these artists is, of course, the old one everywhere—how to make a living out of art or, if you make it out of something else, how to be a Sunday painter and yet not an amateur. Many fail to overcome it: their talent spurts, flares and dies. In this there is nothing specifically African. I admired a powerfully conceived and brilliantly executed carving of a woman and child by a Kikuyu girl, and learned that she had since married a railway guard and given up art. To train designers of textiles, on the other hand, has been from the start one of the school's major tasks, and now quite a number of Makerere-trained designers are fruitfully employed in the industry. Here there is scope to marry to the needs of modern commerce the traditions, skills and imaginations of Africa.

Political Prisoner

About thirty miles from Kampala lies Entebbe, the ex-colonial capital: a lotus land of green lawns, yellow-candled cassias, eye-assaulting bougainvillaeas and flame-bright cannas with their feet in runnels of water. Now that the headquarters of government have shifted to Kampala, it has become a sort of flowery ghost town, standing forsaken by the moist and sleepy borders of the lake.

Here, in a gilded bower, dwelt, at the time, East Africa's foremost political prisoner. Outwardly no jail could be more like paradise. Entebbe's is the nicest of the various Government Houses bequeathed by the colonial regime—like a big, white, rambling English country house immersed in sunshine and serviced by a whole tribe of tall, handsome, soft-footed butlers clad in the long white *kanzu* traditional to the country, worn with a red sash or with a scarlet waistcoat embroidered in gold. From a wide, shady first-floor balcony you can see the lapis lazuli waters of the lake, the green shores, the shadow-casting trees with sunlit sweeps beyond them; it was like the setting for some light comedy by Noël Coward. At any minute in would come a lovely girl in a bikini, to encounter an attractive, white-flannelled, middle-aged man. "Didn't we meet in India, darling?" "Africa, surely, sweet." "Very hot, Africa. . . ."

In this sybaritic setting was confined a hard-working, plain-living, anti-lotus-eating Lowland Scot, who by ability, industry and character had worked his way from the bottom rung of the ladder as a District Officer, through a turbulent commissionership among the Kikuyu, whose language he was one of the few Europeans to have mastered and where he was once besieged by mobs of women, pricked on by agitators, to repudiate soil-erosion works; then by way of administering the island of St. Vincent, directing Kenya's education, introducing the electoral system into Zanzibar and captaining Kenya's administration to his high but empty office in Entebbe. He was the Governor-General, Sir Walter Coutts. At barely fifty Sir Walter was a reluctant figurehead, and the real world beckoned from beyond Entebbe's lawns and flowerbeds.

In Kampala a British High Commissioner handles everything political. While everyone agreed that a Ugandan should replace Sir Walter, no one had then been able to agree on who that Ugandan should be.

The Baganda would accept no overlord but the Kabaka; the Kabaka was not acceptable to the other kingdoms; the anti-traditionalists wouldn't countenance a king at all. So every time Sir Walter tried to resign, his better nature was appealed to by politicians who dreaded the major crisis this would precipitate. "All I can do is to open cotton ginneries," he said gloomily. Eventually he was given a bridge as a change. Release came when, on the first anniversary of Uganda's independence, the Kabaka accepted the office of the country's first President. Now he, like Mr. Obote, must strive to unify Uganda, and to end the tug of war between traditionalists and democrats. But cats will give up mousing before the Baganda will relinquish politics.

So back to Kampala through the evening shadows, along a red road crowded with bicycles and bordered by innumerable banana trees. Beyond, green hills atwinkle with corrugated iron roofs; closer at hand, the vivid yellow candles of acacia blooms.

On speed the bicycles; deep-prowed women sail along in their *busutis,* those splendid dresses with their full bodices, flowing skirts and hint of the bustle, introduced by missionaries, who have left so deep a mark upon Uganda, deeper perhaps than anywhere else in Africa. (And there clings to these *busutis,* like cigar smoke to velvet curtains, that faint aroma of the Victorian era emanating still from Christian households, where on the parlour walls gaze the stern but faded visages of bearded Baganda patriarchs stiffly seated in upright chairs and surrounded by a numerous progeny; where girls in tight pigtails address their elders with respect and grace is said before meat.) Red earth, green banana fronds, the flaring, riotous, clashing hues of the *busutis,* as if the sunset had exploded and littered the road with fragments of

348

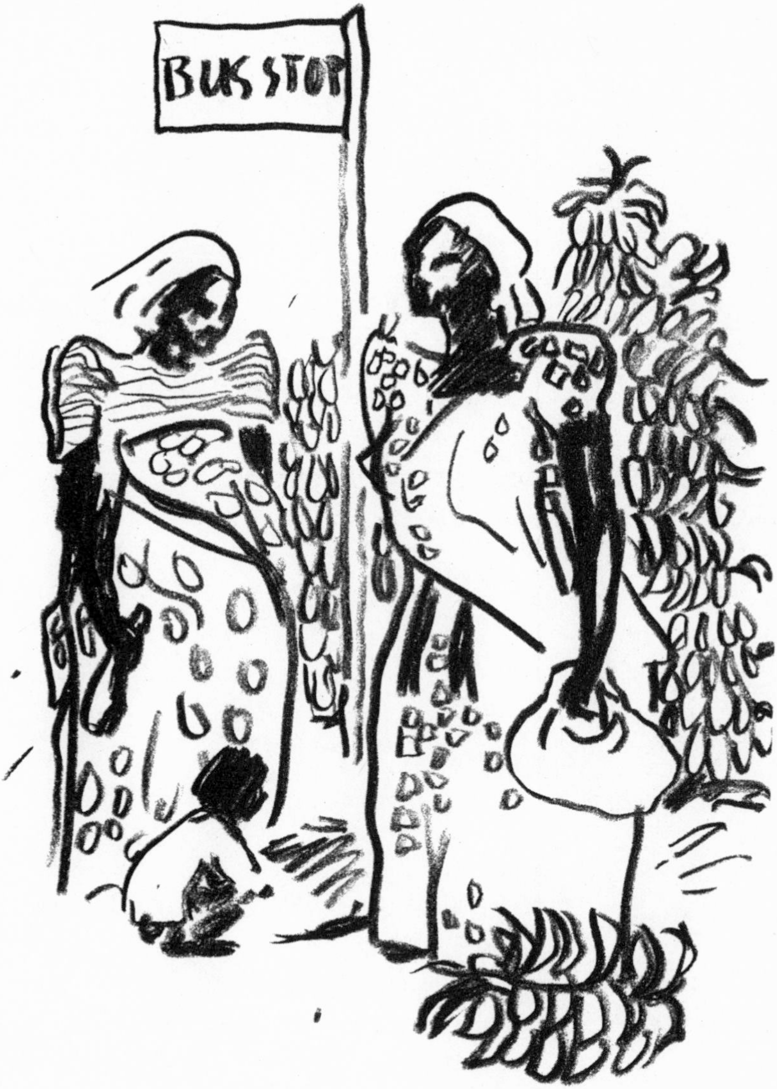
BUS STOP

coloured cloud; "opal and ashes-of-roses, cinnamon, amber and dun."

Back to Kampala with its dreamy bustle, its sallow anxious Asians, its mosques and churches, bird-rich gardens, wealthy Indians' mansions with fountains and swimming pools; its bars and night clubs, bicycles and crowded buses; its boycotts, breweries and intrigues, its legal banana beer, the universal *pombe,* and its illegal and even more universal *warigi,* the Nubian gin.

The lights of the tall Mulago hospital shine from the hill-top opposite Makerere like those of a towering vessel dressed for some splendid celebration, at anchor on a black velvet sea. Below it, from a long avenue of eucalyptus trees, the silent armies of the fruit bats set forth to forage in the countryside. No one tries to stop them. In Uganda's generous bosom there is plenty for all.

THE TWO FACES OF NATIONALISM

A Day of Consolation

"This has been a day of consolation," Wilfrid Scawen Blunt wrote in his diary on the fall of Khartoum, "and I could not help singing all the way down in the train." (He was going to his place in Sussex to hunt, and next day "had a capital run of six miles quite straight over the Downs.") For General Gordon, and for the many thousands massacred, raped, tortured, and enslaved on that November day on the Nile, consolation must have been more elusive.

Blunt was the archetype of the English liberal prepared to go any lengths in sacrificing himself and others—he was imprisoned in Ireland—to right wrongs. He was fortunate enough to have no doubts as to which side was in the right and which in the wrong. Those in the right, who were never English, were endowed with every virtue. Egyptians were sublime, the Mahdi—actually a voluptuous fanatic as cruel as Tamerlane—a wise and noble gentleman anxious for peace, and certain to make it if only a debased British Government would send Blunt himself as envoy to the Sudan.

The Mahdi's ferocious followers, who enslaved such prisoners as they did not disembowel, were "men with the memory of a thousand years of freedom, with chivalry inherited from the Saracens, the noblest of ancestors, with a creed the purest the world ever knew, worshipping God and serving him in arms like the heroes of the ancient world they are." Against them went "mere murderers"—that is the British soldiery—"a mongrel scum of thieves from Whitechapel and Seven Dials."

> I confess I would rather see them all at perdition than that a single Arab more should die. I desire in my heart to see the Arab Blood avenged and every man of Stewart's butchering host butchered in their turn and sent to hell.[1]

Although such frankness is now out of fashion, Blunt has many spiritual heirs who, in their hearts, would rather see every white man in Africa butchered than that a single African should be denied the vote. True colonialists believe, if they have the cast of mind that needs a moral basis for action, in their own superior virtues and qualities, and in the general inferiority, even if this should prove only temporary, of the "subject peoples." Wholehearted believers in anti-colonialism turn this upside down and endow the "subject peoples" with virtues and qualities superior to their own.

The wickedness that warps humanity in other lands, and especially in their own (they consider), has passed the darker brethren by: somehow these are purer, simpler, deeper, better men than Europeans steeped in mean, self-seeking, self-destructive vices. Somewhere, if no longer in our own behaviour, the golden rule can be realized; somewhere, if never in our own country, the golden age can dawn. Rousseau's fantasies, in short, go marching on. "The world apprehends," suggested Laurens van der Post, "that Africa may hold the secret of its own lost and hidden being."

For Blunt, the Arabs held this secret, and the path to virtue lay through Islam: until, when he was nearing sixty, he

---

[1] *Gordon at Khartoum,* by W. S. Blunt, 1911.

undertook a pilgrimage to a Senussi monastery in the oasis of Siwah. Here a band of ugly tribesmen set upon him, and nothing saved him but the British nationality he had so often felt to be a badge of shame. "My experience has convinced me that there is *no* hope to be found anywhere in Islam," he concluded. "I had made myself a romance about these reformers, but I see that it has no substantial basis."

The City of God

There have been many other days of consolation following retreats from many cities since Khartoum—and no going back thirteen years later. Union Jacks have come down like washing off the line with a storm breaking. The nationalists, like the liberals, have won their battles and, except in South Africa, Mozambique, Angola, and possibly Rhodesia, colonialism has given up. Must there be other cruel awakenings at the hands of the Senussi's heirs?

Colonialism imposed law, order and a set of Western values on people who never asked for them and in a manner they resented. But out of the decay of strength, liberals believe, shall come forth sweetness: after some experience of these things, wrongfully imposed yet in themselves in the main desirable, those at the receiving end will self-impose them in a sensible manner.

So steeped is Europe now in crime and folly, even her culture running out into the sands of technology, that it really does not any longer seem possible to build the City of God among its semi-detached council houses and ant-heap spindrier apartments. Yet there must be *some* good building site, somewhere, waiting for this gleaming city. And where but in Africa, the green belt of hope—still, in the recesses of the Western mind, a strange, mysterious, semi-magical land sheltering fabulous beasts and men with heads underneath their arms? And so, like many other institutions, Utopia has been Africanized.

But do Africans, on their side, want to be Utopianized? Do they want the New Jerusalem to arise in their tawny and eroded land? Some evidently do. Western universities are full of eager students preparing to return with the principles of democracy, trade unions, superannuation, logical positivism and nitrogenous fertilizers packed into their briefcases and, with any luck, a junior ministership awaiting them at the other end. They are the agents of the new, the cultural colonialism, which liberals are as anxious to propagate as ever nineteenth-century Tories were to spread their brand of conquest and profits. ("A despotism tempered with gymkhanas," as Shane Leslie described it.)

Freedom is like Tweedledum and Tweedledee. There is Freedom From and Freedom For. Freedom From has won his victory, except in a few, though formidable, pockets of resistance. But Freedom For—what is he after, what does he intend? When asked, it appears that he wants to liberate a spirit, trapped like Ariel in a tree. This spirit lacks a more precise name than the African personality.

Liberals are of course on the side of liberating spirits, especially one called the African personality. But what if it should turn out to have nasty, spiteful, undemocratic habits? To bite the hand that liberates it? Caliban, not Ariel? One must hope not, and the spirit has still to struggle clear of its imprisoning tree. In its painful effort to break free it is bound to writhe and snarl. Once liberated, it will settle down to a display of tolerance, common sense, energy and goodwill. To those who have helped it out of the tree it will come to show gratitude.

Users of the expression "African personality" have never,

355

so far as I know, defined it. A definition is badly needed, and only Africans can make a true one. But we are all concerned. There are now thirty-four independent African nations where ten years ago there were three. Soon that personality will impinge upon us all, so we are bound to grope towards some understanding of it.

The sort of society Africans have actually evolved over the centuries must surely give some pointers to the sort of society they are likely to re-create after colonialism. Of course there will be great differences. Two streams of culture and tradition have joined, two systems of morality and government, two divergent approaches to life. By glancing back towards one of these two sources, can we draw conclusions as to general trends? I shall try—pure guesswork—without expecting anyone else to agree.

The Tribal Umbrella

All races and peoples started with tribes of one kind or another, and in Africa tribes remain the basic unit of society: close-knit, persistent, exclusive, all-pervading. The tribe is simply the family writ large, the great umbrella under which everyone shelters. A man is nothing without his tribe. Exile is truly worse than death, for the tribe is a community of the dead and the unborn as well as of the living. Past, present and future huddle together under the umbrella. The libation is not an empty gesture, it is an actual sharing of the meal. The dead do not lose their place in the community, they communicate in dreams and often return in other guises to give warnings or advice.

Readers of Camara Laye's *The Dark Child* will remember the little black snake that came to visit his father. "That snake," the father said, "is the guiding spirit of our race.

He has always been with us; he has always made himself
known to one of us. In our time, it is to me that he has made
himself known." He came first in a dream, and gave the precise time and place when he would appear in reality. Then he
took to making regular visits. The father would stroke the
snake, who quivered in response to his hand.

> You can see for yourself that I am not more gifted than other
> men. . . . Nevertheless, I am better known than other men,
> and my name is on everyone's tongue, and it is I who have
> authority over all the blacksmiths of the five cantons. If these
> things are so, it is by virtue of this snake alone, who is the
> guiding spirit of our race. It is to this snake that I owe every-
> thing, and it is he likewise who gives me warning of all that is
> to happen. Thus I am never surprised, when I awake, to see
> this or that person waiting for me outside my workshop; I
> know already that he or she will be there. No more am I sur-
> prised when this or that motor bicycle breaks down, or when
> an accident happens to a clock; because I had foreknowledge
> of what was to come tó pass. Everything is transmitted to me
> in the course of the night, together with an account of all the
> work I shall have to perform, so that from the start, without
> having to cast about in my mind, I know how to repair what-
> ever is brought to me; and it is these things that have estab-
> lished my renown as a craftsman. But all this—let it never be
> forgotten—I owe to the snake, I owe to the guiding spirit of our
> race.

Along certain forest roads in eastern Nigeria you pass many
fascinating statues of the departed, some primly seated, hat
on lap, in best suits and painted in bright colours. Attached
to reed screens behind them are offerings for the spirit who
is presumed to visit the shrine. On the other side of the continent, near Lake Victoria, a campaign to register individual
titles to small holdings ran into trouble because many house-
holders had buried their fathers under the floor of the hut.
While people might exchange fields, to exchange ancestral

bones would be impossible, if only because of spiritual fury. Everything that goes wrong—a leg broken by a falling tree, a sick calf, a miscarriage, an attack of flu—can be traced to an offended spirit. In the identification and then appeasement of offended spirits the witch doctors find their principal employment and their main source of power.

Sylvan Equality

In Tanganyika there is a belt of vegetation known as the Itigi Forest. It is less forest than bush, made up of small mixed trees and creating an effect of suffocating monotony. The top is as level as a mown lawn. A desperate struggle for existence on poor soil with low rainfall has obliterated variety. Merely to survive is enough, and bare survival allows no frills; as in the human world, the individual can excel only where there is privilege. The spreading oak needs space around it, light and air.

This Itigi Forest is a sort of ideal egalitarian sylvan state, the climax of vegetable tribalism. While the human tribe never approaches this degree of monotony, the tendency to inflate, magnify and glorify the individual rarely operates; society's pressure is exerted to cut down any sport that tries to rise too high above his fellows. And the obligation to share wealth turns each family into a miniature welfare state. No relation, however distant, can be refused hospitality for as long as he pleases, nor money to help educate his children, nor a cow towards the bride price needed on behalf of a son. To contribute is not an act of goodwill, it is an obligation at least as inescapable as that of Westerners to pay taxes— which, after all, help to educate children who are not even related to the taxpayers.

Although in Africa the principle has not been carried so far as in Fiji, where a custom called *kerekere* obliges every man to give any relative anything he asks for, great or small, very few individuals are prepared to challenge both public opinion and their own beliefs by rejecting such claims. So the relatively well-to-do civil servant or teacher pays up, gets into debt and succumbs to bribes to fill the gap; and the corruption of which the outgoing British so sadly complain deepens and widens.

Can this Itigi complex, this continual cutting down to size, have exerted, over the centuries, a genetic effect upon African tribes? The geniuses, misfits and innovators of the West, while often reviled, have sometimes been respected, and generally allowed to breed. As growing points in a competitive society, they have been valued; a static society does not need growing points. And so in Africa, for century after century, most of them have been pinched out.

The mechanisms for enforcing this conformity relied heavily on jealousy, with its attendant suspicion. Jealousy and suspicion are of course ingredients of the peasant's life all the world over, but the African reliance on magic gave them tremendous scope. Jealousy aroused suspicion, suspicion called in magic, and in no time the man with qualities to lift him out of the rut at best found his cattle poisoned and his granaries burned, at the worst was himself secretly poisoned or openly executed. A man or woman had only to be accused of sorcery for the whole community to close in like a pack of wild dogs round an antelope.

Witch doctors, scattered throughout the continent in even more profusion than Buddhist monks in Asia, formed a vast college of cardinals far more obscurantist than the worst the Roman Church ever achieved. On every day of the year, in some bush-enveloped village, some potential Galileo found himself poisoned, burned, or impaled. And so for centuries

Africans have been breeding only from conformers. Perhaps the genes of rebellion and inquiry, if there are such things, still await their chance. But all this persistent suppression of the nonconformer must have had some effect: if not genetic, then social. It created an environment resolutely hostile to innovation.

The chief was an exception to this rule of conformity. He stood out from the rut: not as an individual, but as a link between the spiritual and mundane worlds. Only where things had run to seed was he wantonly despotic; his responsibilities were greater than his rewards, and the rules governing his succession, duties and powers were generally rigid and closely defined.

Should he exceed the limits of his power, the spirit world, acting as usual through witch doctors, would intervene to curb or destroy him. (As with the Yoruba, where if a chief went too far his council might present him with a parrot's egg, he was then obliged to retreat into the bush and commit suicide—the life of the god-descended could not be taken but could be demanded, for rulers must serve the people, not their own ambition.) Chiefs seldom made important decisions without consulting their people, normally through elders qualified to speak for them by age and status. Those who voiced opinions did so by reason of their position in a hierarchy stretching from the newly circumcised youth to the departed spirit of the greatest ancestor.

Respect for elders was fundamental: the older you got, the closer to the spirit world. The Western system by which the judgment of an untried youth without responsibility or experience carries equal weight with that of a man bearing family and public cares seems to tribal Africans not merely ridiculous, but a threat to the basis of a society sustained by the observance of degree, priority and place. The whole of

Ulysses' speech in *Troilus and Cressida*—"Take but degree away, untune that string, And, hark, what discord follows!"— might have been spoken by almost any tribal elder confronted for the first time by the Western fetish of one man, one vote.

Prospero and Caliban

This time-honoured reliance on the chief, an image of the dominant father, appears to have embedded in the tribal mind that feeling of dependence on which O. Mannoni lays such stress in his study of colonialist psychology, *Prospero and Caliban*.[2] Mannoni gave a Malagasy some quinine tablets. A few days later the young man asked him for a pair of old tennis shoes, and then for various other gifts which Mannoni perceived him to regard as a right and not a favour. From this, and from other comparable situations, Mannoni concluded that the original gift of quinine had established between himself and the young man, in the latter's mind, a relationship of protector and protégé which fitted into the pattern of Malagasy life.

Repeated many thousand times all over the continent, this was the colonial situation—the white men had unwittingly stepped into the protector's position. A Congolese says to a doctor: "Your herbs cured me. You are now my white man. Please give me a knife. I shall always come to beg of you."

The Malagasy was cured not so much because quinine is an excellent remedy for malaria as because a Malagasy who has a protector he can count on need fear no danger; what means his protector may employ to safeguard him is of little interest.

If the Malagasy and the Congolese needed a protector, so

2 *Prospero and Caliban: A Study in the Psychology of Colonization*, by O. Mannoni, 1956.

did the European need a protégé. Mannoni goes on to suggest that many Europeans who chose a colonial career did so because of a psychological failure in their own competitive society to complete their adaptation to an adult world. They had succumbed to what he calls "the lure of a world without men" because they could not come to terms with men as they are. To compensate for this failure, they felt an urge to dominate easily satisfied among people ready to hitch their need to be dependent to a new star. The two states of mind "nicked."

In *The Dark Eye in Africa,* Laurens van der Post remarked upon the "enormous hush" that fell when white men arrived on the scene.

> In the African heart there was a calm and tense air of expectation and growing wonders to come, and as a result there was also the most moving and wonderful readiness of the African to serve, to imitate and to follow the European, and finally an unqualified preparedness to love and be loved.

Then two changes came. Tribal society began to crack, and the white man began to fail in his duty to shelter and protect.

In this he was seldom a free agent: the liberals who had won the day at home controlled his actions. Equating the colonial situation with a feudalism they traditionally abhorred, the liberals set out to humble the white colonial and to teach the tribesman to stand on his own feet.

In so doing they inflicted a profound psychological shock. Once his comforting bonds of dependence were loosened, the tribesman began to feel insecure, and then abandoned. This desperate feeling of abandonment, experienced subconsciously, underlies race hatred, according to this theory. The cheated tribesman turns in anger on the protector who has failed him. You loved me once, Caliban cries to Prospero:

Thou strok'dst me and mad'st much of me,
wouldst give me
Water with berries in't . . .
and then I lov'd thee.

But now things have changed.

. . . you sty me
In this hard rock, whiles you do keep from me
The rest o' th' island.

Resentment is born and hatred follows.

You taught me language; and my profit on't
Is, I know how to curse. The red plague rid you
For learning me your language!

Here lies the root of nationalist bitterness. It is not that independence was once taken away, but that Europeans have insisted on abruptly restoring it.

A Golden Past

It is hardly necessary to make the point that Africans, even if they retained a need for dependence, were very far from being the children they were often said to be by patronizing Europeans. They may even have reached the opposite pole. Far from standing in pristine innocence upon the brink of enlightenment, African society may well be like the soil on which it lives, immeasurably old. Leakey has suggested that our species started on its strange journey in the region of Lake Victoria. Climate and white ants have destroyed most traces of the many cultures that have risen and declined, but archaeologists have found enough to demolish the theory that Africans hung back from the march of material progress because they were isolated, jungle-bound and debilitated by disease. They did not, it now seems, hang back at all; they pioneered.

The great Egyptian monuments have always been there to prove it, and now we can add the achievements of Meroe and Kush, and the Nok cultures of the Niger and Benue valleys, dating back beyond 2000 B.C. Axum flourished before Rome; later, but still in the van, came the empires of Mali, Songhay, and Ghana, now giving their names to countries linked to them only by racial pride. Later still arose such kingdoms as Benin and Ife and, in the east, the more legendary Zanj (or Zinj). And there is Zimbabwe, now generally held to be the ruin of a medieval Bantu palace in the kingdom of Monomotopa, whose people worked in metal and gold.

All these have disappeared, if not without trace at least without much impact. Artistically and materially African creativeness seems to lie in the past. Even the celebrated bronze workers of Ife and Benin have lost their skill, and no one now builds dry-stone walls like Zimbabwe's. Is African culture decadent rather than nascent? At any rate, it has proved itself remarkably resistant to alien influences. In the shadow of honey-coloured forts built four hundred years ago by the Portuguese, modern Giriama women come in their neat palm-frond skirts to barter cotton, and return to huts of mud and mangrove pole with three stones for a kitchen; to head-borne earthenware water pots filled at the spring, to plantain-leaf plates and calabash drinking vessels.

Simple, sensible, adapted to the climate: wise Giriama, whom only agents of the export drive would itch to change. Why build thick stone walls to last a thousand years if a cool round hut will answer, and crumble when no longer wanted? Why toil to make a glazed pottery when it is just as clean and much less trouble to eat from a leaf? Why spin and weave cotton when palm-frond skirts do just as well? Arabs have been settled on the Azanian coast for over a millennium, and the tribes whose land abuts their ancient cities continue in a way of life almost wholly unchanged. They have not even been converted to Islam. They have seen, but have been unimpressed, and continued to prefer their own way of expressing their personality.

What *is* this African personality? All an outsider can do is to attempt a personal impression. Rooted in tribe and family, it is inward-looking, defensive and sustained by intricate patterns of kinship and age-grade stratification which afford protection against a world always hostile and dangerous. "The individual"—Mannoni again—"is held together by his collective shell, his social mask, much more than by his moral skeleton." So he evades the kind of responsibility schoolmasters try to put upon prefects, the army upon officers, industry upon managers: the grappling of loyalties to an institution or an idea. Loyalties belong to people, mainly of one's own flesh and blood.

It is a personality at once sustained and ruled by spirits who practice no apartheid between ghosts and men. Causality arises not from logic but from natural mysteries and from human malignancy. People are judged not by their fruits but by their flowers: not by what they do, but by what they are. If accepted, they are to be followed with uncritical devotion; if rejected, they may be spurned and tortured with a frank delight in others' pain. Human life counts (and then it counts enormously) only if it enlarges your own family and clan; in itself it has no more value than that of a rat or an elephant. God is aloof, and has never troubled to redeem mankind. So it is sensible to live the moment with enjoyment, song and dance; for time is a servant, not a master; it runs on without divisions, as the years without changes in the length of days.

It is also proud, this personality, and passionate. It has expressed itself in chiefs adangle with gold ornaments, attended by courtiers and concubines in profusion and honoured by the sacrifice of a thousand slaves. It likes colour and panache, and a leader who looks and behaves like one. It respects wealth. The ascetic has never appealed. Everyone would admire Solomon, but John the Baptist would seem an idiot. The puritan ideal is not only absent, it is not understood. While moderation may be sensible, self-denial is absurd. The moral code seldom condemns sensuality, greed, lust, cruelty, pride and slavery; it does condemn disloyalty, inhospitality, bad manners, sorcery, treachery, the disregard of obligations and indiscipline. It respects old age and children, and despises and exploits women, who are everywhere considered inferior to men. It is hierarchical and often merciless, never squeamish, fond of argument and debate.

The African climate is extreme and sharp, and either fine or stormy; it lacks those indeterminate halfway northern days, neither one thing nor the other. So in the climate of personality there is little room for compromise and postponement, for everyone giving way a bit, for keeping an open mind. Like the weather, it swings from one extreme to the other; since it has for so long created little that is permanent, there now seems nothing that cannot be quickly and easily achieved.

It is a personality that puts manners above principle, family above self, race above humanity. Responsive to nuances of relationship, it is often blind to the consequences of acts. There is at the heart of it a profound cynicism, derived partly from a religion based on fear of the supernatural rather than on a trust in the divine, and partly, perhaps, on the multiplicity of termites. The soil of Africa is permeated and seething with white ants which have gnawed to nothing all that man has tried to build. The cloud-capped towers, the gorgeous palaces, have been eaten down. So what is the use of trying? Only the powers of magic could defeat them and raise up new towers. Insects have eroded African history and left a sort of white-antism in the soul.

Education and Tribalism

Graduates and "been-to's" say that tribalism is as archaic as Morris dancing among factory workers in Coventry. Education—that is, literacy, the greatest revolution since the smelting of iron—is sweeping the tribe into limbo. The African personality is being transformed; even time is out of date. In this rocket age it is silly to expect nations to grow from their roots by adding rings like trees: they must be fused in a kind of cyclotron like atoms. And it is happening. To question it is to show that you are so buttoned into a colonial mentality as to be unable to tell the famous wind of change from a gin and tonic.

It is happening, but of course different things are happening in different places. In the common rooms of Oxford, Cambridge and the red brick colleges, tribalism is an old love turned to hatred; in the Congo it has been on the rampage; in Kenya it has put on the garb of political parties. There is a simple test. Can a man of, say, the Luo tribe readily acquire a plot of land among the Kikuyu; a Gogo among the Chagga, a Yoruba among the Ibo, Tiv among Ibibio, Mashona among Ngoni?—almost any two unrelated tribes would do. If not, then the tribal spirit lives.

In claiming that education kills it, nationalists are on shaky ground. Education often seems to quicken rather than to soften a xenophobic pride in the race or nation that grows out of the tribe. Education has revived the Erse, not buried it. Singhalese has replaced English in the government and law courts of Ceylon, Swahili has become Tanganyika's official tongue. There are other examples. A chief does not cease to be a chief because he has exchanged ostrich plumes for a collar and tie and is labelled a stooge. It is no more a sign of savagery to boast of Zulu blood, Yoruba tradition or Ashanti custom than of French culture, Russian achievement or British nationality.

Pride in her clan and in her Xhosa people, rediscovered after years of Western conditioning, is a theme of Noni Jabavu's *Drawn in Colour*. It was the tribal approach to the death of her brother, not Western philosophy, that healed the wound. When Xhosa met Baganda at the graduate-to-graduate level, tribal differences were what stood out, especially differences in sexual custom. Noni Jabavu's sister had married a Kampala lawyer, and the Baganda attitude to women shocked the sophisticated visitor, who arranged meetings to face the difficulties.

At another of these marriage councils, something else had been raised: about some part of my sister's anatomy. "Not having been pulled," as according to their ideas it should have been. She and I were puzzled. . . .

The family spokesman then painstakingly explained their tradition of concubinage, for example. The knowledge seemed terrible for me and my sister. Here a modern man, even if a dignitary of the Church of England and therefore presumably striving after different ideals, often had a "ring wife" along with "other wives" and concubines. He would also have "other ladies" to whom he could, if I may put it scripturally, "go in unto" at any time the mood seized him. And it seemed to us southerners that . . . such moods tended to seize a man at any time. . . .

Later Noni Jabavu came across an explanation of the custom whose practice by the Baganda had puzzled her.

I read how at nights the Lovedu women and nubile girls sit in their "special houses" and carry out a tribal custom of pulling one another's clitoris to ensure that it should grow long and hang down, a special attraction to the male partner in sexual intercourse. . . . I saw what a gulf there was between our backgrounds. I thought I saw the root of that feminine distrust, contempt, resentment going hand-in-hand with conditioned acceptance of subjugation. Women humbly sank down and knelt, yet inwardly despised "these men" in the very act of humouring them. The difference I saw was that in the south, even before Western philosophy was introduced, our ethics regarding the personality of the individual were not of this order. . . .

What as a rule kills tribalism is not enlightenment but conquest. Someone gains the upper hand and squashes it. The colonial conquest held it down, and now, if tribalism is to go, there will have to be a new internal fusion. Within a year of the British withdrawal from Ghana, Dr. Nkrumah had destroyed the safeguards entrenched in the Constitution to protect minorities, and had cracked down smartly and effectively on the largest of them, the Ashanti. In Africa minorities have to be suppressed, not protected, lest they challenge the central authority and disrupt the state.

The Habit of Colonialism

The habit of colonialism dies almost as hard as that of tribalism. It is the habit of knowing what is good for others and seeing that they get it. In this, liberals are archcolonialists and have God on their side. ("If we were not humble enough to see ourselves as instruments of *le bon Dieu*," wrote Colonel David Sterling, founder of the Capricorn Society, "we could not have the arrogance to do what we are trying to do in Africa.")

369

What is good for others, of course, is what is good for our-selves: freedom, peace, democracy and the rule of law, to-gether with derivatives like free speech and assembly, minority rights, trade unions, pensions, local government, co-opera-tives, a middle class, children's clinics, women's suffrage and many other of the more creditable aspects of Western life. These are the things that are to replace tribalism and remould the African personality into one less like Chaka's or the Mahdi's and more like that of David Livingstone, Lord Attlee or Keir Hardie.

For the last thirty years Britain has employed a hand-picked, high-powered, well-paid force of missionaries in the shape of the colonial civil service, to spread in benighted places the doctrine of democracy. This force has put the Christians in the shade. Scarcely a waste of bush or tangle of forest now lacks its council or committee formed to supervise schools, direct community development, market eggs or regulate the grazing of cattle. From this humble level an ambitious man may rise to be a member of parliament or even a £4,000-a-year ($11,200) Minister with house, car and the command of patronage. The prizes of democracy are almost fabulously rich, and are available in this world, not the next. The cost seems to be nil. No wonder it has caught on.

To get, as it were, baptized into the faith, all you need do is to register for a vote. This vote is first of all a kind of dignity, and then a kind of promise. A promise of more wealth, less interference; more land, fewer taxes; more rights, fewer duties.

In the fly-heavy village among humped cattle and naked children, and women trudging off to gather firewood and the men playing *bao* in the shade, political theories lack urgency; you are more concerned with your father-in-law's demand for another goat, or talk of making a new dam. If you vote, you vote for a man. A fellow tribesman if possible, an orator and the possessor of a quality hard to define: the winning streak, perhaps, the instinct for success, the quality that armies respond to in commanders and that the Greeks saw as the protection gods afford to certain heroes. It has nothing to do with brains, experience, honesty, reliability or common sense, although of course its possessor can have any of these qualities, or none: the point is irrelevant.

If it should prove that the freedom of the individual to secure justice without reprisal and to speak his mind without fear rose to its peak under colonialism and sank again once liberty was won, the point would still be that no one asked for this kind of freedom. Europeans conferred it *de haut en bas* as a boon, like vaccination, quinine and elections. To liberals, the freedom of the individual is an absolute good, desirable for all men at all times. They may be right, but in their acts, that is to say in their own social achievements, Africans have never affirmed it. To transplant its cult was still a piece of moral and cultural colonialism. Now that Africans are regaining racial freedom they are free to repudiate individual freedom.

The Scent of Battle

It is the same with peace. After two recent bouts of world carnage, and with a pretty plain idea of what will happen in the third, few Westerners retain much active belligerence. But the traumatic experience of those two wars and imaginations weaned on science have missed out Africa, where most people over forty grew up to handle a spear. Old men still show their scars and talk about St. Crispin's days, when they repulsed tribal enemies or raided cattle. At this moment, in

371

several parts of Africa, men may be hunting other men with bows and arrows and blooding spears.

It is no good expecting young men to repudiate fighting where scientists have not made it into calculated mass extermination. Of course people can have too much of it, just as there can be too much drink or even sex. Among the decapitated bodies, burned villages and homeless children, there were doubtless martial hangovers, but they did not prevent another raid at the next moon. Fighting and the expectation of it gave the warriors their status, their sexual pride, their sense of purpose: it is this of which they have been deprived, and it is this deprivation which, mainly at the subconscious level, they hold against colonialism. (And of course they have noticed the hypocrisy of banning other people's spears and cattle raids while letting all hell loose with guns and blockbusters twice in thirty years.) Enforced peace has emasculated their pride. A Kikuyu proverb says: "A young man is a piece of God." A red-limbed warrior in plumes and rattles might almost make you think so; a tattered engine cleaner, even a bespectacled office clerk with his briefcase, could not.

But have we not all had to go through it? Redcoats no longer advance with fife and drum and a skirl of bugles; kilted Highlanders have ceased to brandish claymores behind the fiery cross. Transmute and sublimate! Football, athletics, the Olympic Games; climb mountains, outrace sound, win the Duke of Edinburgh's awards, join Outward Bound.[3] . . . At the end of the journey we are all embarked upon together beckons the affluent family in its own four-bedroom house, everything fully automatic: not only with two cars in the garage but with its constant visits to art galleries, its interest

---

[3] A semi-official educational program in leadership for teen-age boys and girls.

in archaeology and music, its holidays in Mexico and Greece. We must all stop being primitive and like it, Africans as well as everyone else.

Yes, but . . . Africans are being asked so suddenly, and by someone else. *They* did not invent nuclear fission, even gunpowder; they were perfectly happy with spears. They did not invent aircraft which abolish distance, radio which abolishes privacy, vaccines which abolish the balance of nature, and all the other things that make it impossible for them to go on living as they used to and necessary to live in a way invented by Europeans. They did not even ask for peace. They may not be more aggressive than others but they are almost certainly more bored, and they have plenty of excuses, some of a nature that have caused wars throughout history. The end of colonialism is like the end of a frost; it reveals all the burst pipes and leaking valves. This end is a beginning of upheaval and realignment of boundaries, alliances, nuclei of power. Freedom must include the freedom to unscramble the map of Africa.

After the splintering comes regrouping on new lines. This can be done either by conquest or by treaty, and no doubt we shall see both. Conquest depends on the existence of an ambitious, astute and ruthless leader. The departure of the white overlord has left a field wide open to a struggle for personal ascendancy that seems likely to occupy the sixties with a pageant of Florentine intrigue. Guelphs and Ghibellines may again be locked in picturesque combat, offering a spectacle of plot, counterplot, coup, alliance and assassination a great deal more entertaining than the Empire Day parades, afforestation drives and cleaner-village competitions that formed the usual diversions of colonialism.

Beneath the conflict of politics lies a deeper conflict of the mind. Broadly speaking, and oversimplified, it is a question of whether the African personality struggling to emerge is to accept and build mainly upon Western values or whether—leaving aside Western techniques, which it will certainly borrow—it is to follow a specifically African path of its own—nonalignment, as its leaders say. To quote Mannoni once more: "It may be said that they [the Africans] accept everything in detail but refuse our civilisation as a whole." He wrote that in 1947. Is it still true today?

In 1947 the Malagasies rebelled, and in Kenya the seeds were sown of the Mau Mau revolt, whose essence was as he described—a rejection of Western civilization. With an almost textbook completeness it illustrated the second of the two faces of nationalism, the backward-turning face gazing nostalgically at the vanished simplicities of tribalism. But there is also the February face, which you can see especially in the schools; in the expressions of the multitudinous, bright-eyed, spellbound children gazing at blackboards as if at the face of God. And you can see it in many other places: peering through a microscope, masked at the operating table, patiently explaining how to cure tobacco, pluck tea, or stop soil erosion, driving locomotives, giving Holy Communion, doggedly soaking in facts at public libraries. (In Kitwe, I saw a young miner who was reading right through the Encyclopaedia Britannica, from start to finish; he had reached CROCODILE.)

All this is remarkable and moving: here is a people that has seen salvation on the march towards the light. It engenders hope that once the torrent of youth has poured from these proliferating schools through the new colleges and training centres and universities and out into the current of African life, the changes that have to come will come quickly and with far less muddle; that once their destiny is back in their own hands, Africans will gain the confidence to run their countries sensibly, without the need to prove their mastery by shouting at everyone else. Here is the positive pull, through literacy and Western values, to carry Africans away from their old shrines and into the main stream, such as it is, of nuclear-age life.

Both pulls are strong and agonizing, and the most likely outcome seems to be that neither will achieve total victory. If the African personality does not resume the wizard's mask, neither will it assume the noble mien of the Western liberal. For a time it will very likely continue to look both ways. However many rockets hit the moon, their inventors go on touching wood, catching fish, supplicating saints, giving and taking in marriage and loving and hating one another just as if they lived in Chaucer's age.

The revolution that is simultaneously shaking off colonialism and letting in Western values with a rush is not yet spent, but must already meet a counterrevolution; not to re-establish colonialism (this could come only at the hands of Russia or China) but to "refuse our civilisation as a whole" while accepting its technical details. After years of being made to feel inferior, Africans are beginning to think that, after all, they had something of value.

They want to revive it: that is their meaning when they speak of the African personality. They want to escape the suffocating cultural weight of the West, as they have escaped from its political grasp. The hope is that their escape will bring about a new growth of their own culture, a new way of seeing things—a renaissance; the danger, that the revolution, like a flash of lightning, could split the aging tree of African life.

AFRICAN DREAMS

The Federal Paradox

Yet another irony: the federation of Kenya, Tanganyika, Uganda and Zanzibar, to which East African political heads are now committed, had as one of its exponents the leader of Kenya's white settlers, the late Lord Delamere, and was for some forty years bitterly, at times fanatically, opposed by all indigenous leaders in the four territories. So explosive was this African fear of federation that a casual reference to its economic merits by a Colonial Secretary at a London dinner party in 1953 was enough to put Uganda in a ferment and so deepen the Kabaka's suspicions of British good faith that he demanded autonomy for his kingdom, and his deportation followed.

Yet, ten years later, an East African Federation was accepted as the territories' first aim just as soon as their independence became a fact. The explanation is simple. From the moment when, in 1925, Lord Delamere began to urge the political association of the three mainland countries, and convened a conference to prepare the ground at Tukuyu, in southern Tanganyika, until colonial rule was abrogated, Africans regarded federation and white domination as Siamese twins.

To the citizens of Uganda and Tanganyika, federation

equalled domination by Kenya, which in turn equalled settler rule. (This feeling rumbles on today; when Kampala
politicians inveigh against Kenya milk under the Tree of
Liberty they are still hating Kenya settlers.) Only when the
bogey of settler rule was seen and believed to be well and
truly dead was it possible for Africans even to think about
the matter calmly, much less to turn round and cheer federation on.

They do not always think about it calmly now, for it remains a symbol, but of the exact opposite to settler rule: a
symbol of resurgent Africa's triumphal march towards the
golden gates of continental unity. And that political unity is
itself a symbol of something even greater and more splendid:
of the realization of the African vision of a sense of community, of oneness, of belonging, cherished in the hearts of men
and women with black skins who at long last have trodden
down centuries of indignity to build their own kingdom in
their own land. Federation is a step towards Pan-Africa, and
Pan-Africa is the great African dream. "African nationalism
is meaningless," President Nyerere has written, "it is an anach-
ronism, it is dangerous if it is not at the same time Pan-Africanism." (A pity some less awkward word can't be found.)

Négritude

Pan-Africanism is the political expression of the idea of
négritude, and the origins of *négritude* go back a long way—
at least as far as an address given in 1881 to the Liberia College by Dr. Edward Blyden, a West Indian of Togo blood
who made his way to Liberia, became a professor, a Cabinet
Minister and then Liberian Minister in London, and died in
1912. While in this address, quoted by Mr. Colin Legum in

his illuminating book on the topic,[1] Blyden did not actually use the expression Pan-Africanism, he outlined its motive force and inspiration:

> We must show that we are able to go alone, to carve out our own way. We must not be satisfied that, in this nation, European influence shapes our policy, makes our laws, rules our tribunals and impregnates our social atmosphere. We must not suppose that Anglo-Saxon methods are final, that there is nothing for us to find out for our own guidance, and that we have nothing to teach to the world. We must study our brethren in the interior who know better than we do the laws of growth for the race. . . . We look too much to foreigners and are dazzled almost to blindness by their exploits, so as to fancy that they have exhausted the possibilities of humanity. . . . The special road which has led to success and elevation of the Anglo-Saxon is not that which would lead to the success and elevation of the Negro.

The founding fathers of Pan-Africanism—John Edward Bruce, Edward Blyden, Marcus Garvey, Dr. W. E. Du Bois—were Americans or West Indians, not continental Africans. This was not fortuitous. Pan-Africanism, as Colin Legum has perceptively pointed out, has the same root as Zionism. It is a movement, an emotion, generated in the diaspora to seek a racial home and a spiritual centre: to return from exile.

The exile of the American Negroes and West Indians was physical; they were transported, stateless, recently enslaved people who wanted to go home to their lost origins. Even when the movement spread to Africans in Africa, they were still stateless, they had the same need for spiritual and cultural roots. They still had to put an end to the condition of being dominated by an alien culture, often despised as sub-humans of inferior mentality and barbarous habits, converted to foreign religions, removed from their homes by a

[1] *Pan-Africanism,* by Colin Legum. Pall Mall, 1962.

repugnant economic system and generally being pushed around. They had to show themselves as well as others that they were not, in the words of the American sociologist Dr. Harold Isaacs, savages and cannibals "at the tail end of the human race."

Négritude, Pan-Africanism, the search for the African personality—all these are related aspects of the one essential need: the restoration of dignity. If talk of dignity may seem pompous, it does not so appear to Africans, to whom, in their own societies, dignity is cardinal, and from whose loss they have so painfully suffered.

Dignity, equality and an end of being pushed around— these are the ultimate aims of Pan-Africa. *Négritude,* its spirit, has been many times defined: most briefly, perhaps, by Sartre—through its poetry it exists "to make manifest the black soul."

Négritude was hatched by a group of African poets and intellectuals, deeply imbued with French culture, living in Paris in the thirties—exiles again, even if voluntary ones. It was a young man from Martinique, Aimé Césaire, who made the first major impact on the Paris scene with an often quoted poem, *Cahier d'un Retour au Pays Natal,* which, after some acid strictures on the white world:

> *how their protest is broken under the rigid stars,*
> *how their steel-blue speed is paralyzed in the*
> *mystery of the flesh.*
> *Listen how their defeats sound from their victories.*
> *Listen to the lamentable stumbling in the*
> *great alibis. . . .*

proceeds to extol those human qualities, despised by the conquerors but now rediscovered with pride:

> *hurray for those who never invented anything,*
> *hurray for those who never explored anything,*

> *hurray for those who never conquered anything*
> *hurray for joy*
> *hurray for love*
> *hurray for the pain of incarnate tears.*

Césaire inspired these expatriate French-speaking Africans whose home, both spiritual and mainly physical, was Paris, and whose outlet was the journal *Présence Africaine*. In the tradition of Goethe he combined the writing of poetry with affairs of state, and so did his colleague and successor as the leading poet of *négritude*, Léopold Senghor, who carried it even further by becoming, as he still remains, President of the Republic of Senegal.

"Our God Is Black"

The essence of the matter is that the stone which the builders rejected—the stone of blackness—has become the head of the corner: that Africans, no longer prepared to take themselves at a white valuation, now glory in their blackness and all that this implies, especially in those human qualities they believe that they possess and the white races lack. "Our God is black," writes the Togo poet Dr. Raphael Armattoe, "Black of eternal blackness, with large voluptuous lips"; and M. Senghor extols the black woman:

> *Clad in your colour which is life,*
> *Your beauty strikes me to the heart,*
> *As lightning strikes the eagle.*

Sometimes the politicians, if not the poets, overdo things, as when the Ghanaian authorities issued a set of postcards depicting black man "discovering" almost every aspect of civilization, from Socratic argument to electricity, from family life to printing, from the art of writing to the practice of surgery.

The main theme of this fresh, vigorous African poetry, written in a foreign tongue, is the search for Africa as a meaning, a concept, and then its exploration. As Europeans once "discovered" (in their own terms) the sources of its rivers, so do the new, Westernized Africans now attempt to rediscover the sources of their own origins and of the meaning of blackness. It would be a miracle if they did not sometimes find the waters bitter or tend to overdramatize. The French-born Senegalese David Diop (killed in an air disaster in 1960) wrote:

The white man killed my father
My father was proud
The white man seduced my mother
My mother was beautiful
The white man burnt my brother
*   beneath the noonday sun*
My brother was strong.
His hands red with black blood
The white man turned to me
And in the Conqueror's voice said:
"Hey, boy! A chair, a napkin, a drink!"

This bitterness is branded into folk memories, but a mellower tone, a blend of kindliness and realism, seems discernible now that African freedom is a fact over most of the continent. There is, for instance, the charming end to Abioseh Nicol's saga of the "been-to" student who tired

of the cold Northern sun,
Of white anxious ghost-like faces
Of crouching over heatless fires
In my lonely bedroom,

and returned to his native Sierra Leone (where Dr. Nicol is now Principal of Fourah Bay College) to write:

I have gained the little longings
Of my hands, my loins, my heart,

And the soul following in my shadow.
I know now that is what you are, Africa.
Happiness, contentment and fulfilment.
And a small bird singing on a mango tree.

The English version of *négritude* is the search for the African personality, to which I have already alluded. On this the last word in these pages should certainly be said by Africans. M. Senghor picks out as its three essentials "the sense of communion, the gift of mythmaking and the gift of rhythm," and defines the genius of the continent as "our need to love."

Family Love

This is carried forward by Dunduzu Chisiza in a study published in the *Journal of Modern African Studies,* in Dar es Salaam. (Posthumously, alas; he was killed in a motor smash in 1962.)

Unlike Easterners, he writes, who are given to meditation, or Westerners, driven by curiosity, Africans are (by and large) observers: "penetrating observers, relying more on intuition than on the process of reasoning." Rejecting mysticism on the one hand, science and technology on the other, they have concentrated on human relations: in particular, on living together in groups, first in the family—that great, complex, formalized, subtle and mutually sustaining "extended family" which is the basic unit of society from one end of the continent to the other—and then in the larger community of clan, tribe or nation.

Westerners, Mr. Chisiza believed, live to work; Africans work to live. That is why, in Western estimation, they are so often idle, why they put so high a value on leisure. In their view the idle rich are sensible, not reprehensible, in being idle; Bertie Wooster would seem a much wiser man than

Samuel Smiles. "With us, life has always meant the pursuit of happiness rather than the pursuit of beauty or truth."

In this pursuit (in which, seemingly, truth and beauty may be red herrings) they reject individualism, isolation, privacy and striving with heart and soul after some personal goal, whether material, intellectual or spiritual (no indigenous African saints or recluses). They live at an easier tempo in the present, accepting life and not questioning it, considering the lilies of the field and the sparrows who do not gather into barns. In this the climate is with them. If you live in a cold climate and don't gather into barns you starve next winter, and the lilies of the field retreat underground.

Another quality common, Mr. Chisiza thought, to most Africans is a love of change. Impelled by this, they will chop and change their religious faiths lightheartedly; sometimes they are converted and then reconverted, to the dismay of the original converters. Sometimes they linger undecided between several faiths, while at others they just marvel at all the panaceas offered by the various dogmas.

But the strength of the family is the supreme African quality. Love, Mr. Chisiza says, begins at home, in the family circle. "By loving our parents, our brothers, our sisters, cousins, aunts, nephews and nieces, we cultivate the habit of loving lavishly, of exuding human warmth, of compassion, and of giving and helping. But I believe that, once so conditioned, one behaves in this way not only to one's family but also to the clan, the tribe, the nation, and to humanity as a whole." How can you love a Chinese peasant, Mr. Chisiza asks, if you balk at your brother? "The unification of mankind ultimately depends on the cultivation of family love. It would seem, therefore, that in this respect we in Africa have started towards that noble goal from the right end."

His thesis is, I am afraid, arguable. The welter of intertribal warfare into which Africa was formerly plunged scarcely suggests universal brotherly love. Chaka was not a prince of peace exactly, nor did the affection of a Masai warrior for his cousins prevent him from plunging his spear with the greatest of eagerness and enjoyment into almost every non-Masai he encountered. (Or even into other Masai; one clan, the Purko, totally wiped out a rival one, the Laikipia.)

Family love got stuck, alas, within the family circle. There is a tendency now to picture pre-colonial Africa as an Eden where peace and harmony prevailed until pale-skinned serpents crept in to set man against man, brother against brother. This, I fear, is an example of the gift of mythmaking singled out by M. Senghor as an African characteristic. History suggests that Africans were in this respect, as no doubt in others, neither more or less virtuous than the average bloodthirsty man.

But at living together in families, and in the exchange of human courtesies, they did, and do, excel. Any Westerner wishing to glimpse the inner workings of that most complex and sophisticated system built up through the centuries to smooth the irritating wrinkles and remove the prickles from human intercourse could do no better than to read the account of life in an educated, bourgeois Xhosa family given by Noni Jabavu in *The Ochre People*. There he may learn how a situation that in all ages and among all peoples has been fraught with danger and explosiveness—the resentment felt by the children of a happy marriage towards a new step-parent—is dealt with by those elements within the family considered best fitted to do so, with infinite tact and patience; of how the sting is slowly, softly drawn, the poison fang milked of its venom. The very structure of the language seems to have been designed for such purposes.

So in Xhosa society, if all works well (presumably it doesn't always), there is no explosion, no tragedy. The plot of *Hamlet* couldn't arise. Instead of a ghost on the battlements, there would be a family council (presided over, undoubtedly, by Polonius) and days of talk—humorous, good-natured and elliptical, full of metaphors and similes; at the end Hamlet and his stepfather would have been reconciled and suspicion drowned in tankards of ale. Perhaps that is why there has never been an African *Hamlet?* No plot, no play. The mirrored nature has a different mould of form.

Balkanization

This talent for living together in communities has fused with the passion to renew the glories of a proud, creative black Africa—"black as the deep and productive earth, strong and black"—to shape the dream of Pan-Africa. It is a dream at once political, cultural and spiritual. Only though unity can Africans assert their blackness and their powers, and win from other nations the recognition and respect to which they are entitled. "We must not be assimilated," M. Senghor has said, "we must assimilate." Only thus can the swineherd become an emperor. Their greatest danger is the "balkanization" of the continent—its disintegration into small, and therefore weak, political units. This they believe to be the nefarious aim of the neocolonialists.

More ironies: it was the colonialists who imposed upon rival kingdoms and tribal regions a measure of unity, and who laid the foundations on which the Pan-African structure will, if it ever comes about, be built. What are now fourteen independent states were linked into two large blocs by the French. When the French departed, these two political units fell apart and the efforts of African leaders to reunite three of them (Mali, Sudan and Senegal) quickly foundered. (The

Federation of Mali, a union between Senegal and Sudan, was born in April, 1959, and died in August, 1960—a life of sixteen months.) The United Arab Republic also collapsed. The former Belgian Congo would have disintegrated into its component tribal regions had not the United Nations been forced to intervene and preserved a nominal unity by the skin of their teeth. (An unstable unity, at that.) The little statelets of Ruanda and Urundi, administered in one unit by the Belgians, have parted company. The Central African Federation forced upon Northern Rhodesia and Nyasaland has been shattered. The much-publicized union between Ghana and Guinea was stillborn.

It is true that in West Africa several rather loose regroupings have emerged. Of these the weightiest is the Union Africaine et Malgache, an association of twelve French-speaking states which have maintained and even strengthened economic links with France, set up an organization to co-ordinate their trade and financial policies and pursued a course regarded by the West as "moderate." In opposition is a less coherent group led by Morocco, Guinea and Mali to which Ghana adheres: more revolutionary in outlook, suspected of Communist leanings and dedicated to the more uncompromising, xenophobic aspects of Pan-Africanism.

Neither of these groups, nor any other, amounts even to the shadow of a true federation. There has been no surrender of sovereignty. In fact, since independence, and despite a spate of conferences, the Pan-African dream has not merely failed to materialize, in practical terms it has receded—everywhere except, perhaps, here in East Africa.

For years President Nyerere has been resolved at all costs to unite the three mainland countries. To him it is a vital need: not for the sound economic reasons that underpin it, but for symbolic ones; he sees in it the seed of that great tree of continental unity under whose branches all Africans will find their refuge and their fulfilment.

Mr. Kenyatta's open commitment to the same cause goes back to the Pan-African Conference held in Manchester in 1944. But, by another irony, such regional progress as has been made towards the continental ideal is due in the main to a generation's work and effort by colonialists. Had they not managed to fashion in East Africa a pretty solid edifice of co-operation between colonial governments, their successors would have inherited no foundations on which to build.

Origins of Federation

It would be tedious to trace in any detail the history of the federal idea. It goes back, as I have mentioned, to a campaign launched by the late Lord Delamere to "open up" (in colonialist terms) the undeveloped regions of eastern Africa to white settlement and at the same time to strengthen the British hold on Tanganyika, later administered as a trusteeship territory under the United Nations. It started, therefore, as a movement to expand and fortify colonialism. The African leaders spotted this without any fumbling and implacably opposed it. The British Government kept their customary seat on the fence.

A long series of commissions, committees and inquiries set out the economic advantages, listed and relisted the political objections and postponed a decision; interterritorial jealousies thrived; nothing happened; the separate countries of East Africa continued to operate two sets of railways and communications, but did achieve a common currency, co-operate over such matters as defence and research and uneasily maintain a joint tariff agreement.

World War II changed all this, as wars do; various services

were kneaded together by military necessity, and when the fighting ended it seemed a pity to unravel what had been wound together into strands which obviously strengthened the economy but did not seem to chafe political skins. Sir Philip Mitchell, Governor of Kenya from 1944 to 1952, was a powerful protagonist; pro-federal vested interests appeared; the eyes of Africans, while wary and watchful still, were drawn away by the sudden dawn of hopes of freedom; the foundations stayed. On them was erected the East Africa High Commission, with headquarters in Nairobi, a small central civil service and a Central Legislative Assembly, the nucleus—though with limited and delegated powers—of a future federal parliament.

The East Africa High Commission consisted, then, of the three colonial Governors who met at stated intervals, took it in turns to act as Chairman and thrashed out a common policy on major issues; but there was still no surrender of sovereignty. In the political sphere each country developed independently, but agreed to pool certain common services: railways, posts and telegraphs, for example. They agreed upon a common customs tariff and, in a broad sense, taxation policy; they set up laboratories for veterinary, forestry and agricultural research near Nairobi, for virus research at Entebbe and for other inquiries elsewhere. Anti-locust campaigns were jointly mounted; a miniature East African Navy (two sloops and a fisheries research vessel) came into being at Mombasa; a bureau helped to supply the growing need for literature for schools and adult education; civil aviation codes were centralized; a common currency remained; higher education became a joint responsibility. Under a series of able administrators the system worked well, harmed none and became, in its limited field, a habit.

Although suspicion never wholly died, especially in

Uganda, fears that beneath the harmless clothing of this useful sheep lurked the old wolf of colonialism were at least allayed. And so when independence came, the territorial leaders were able without much difficulty to convince their followers that the High Commission should stay, renamed the East African Common Services Organization; the three Governors were replaced by three Prime Ministers; an able and experienced civil servant, Mr. A. L. Adu, was brought from Ghana to take over, as Secretary-General, from the British administrator. Expatriates yielded rapidly to Africans—"blackanization" is the latest term for this. (Another newly minted word, to stand for nepotism, is "brotherization.")

Among former colonialists the impetus to federate was economic and technical. A single campaign against locust hordes hatching in distant Arabian or Eritrean deserts is better than three campaigns; a common market for some five and twenty million more sensible than customs barriers in the middle of wilderness, lake or Masai Steppe; one railway system, one postal union, one policy on defence, one expensive centre of research into rinderpest, yellow fever or wilt in potatoes a great deal more economical than three such centres, and so on.

All this is undeniable, and Africans have never denied it. But matters of finance, efficiency, economy, organization— these have never touched their hearts. These do not appear to be human matters. In the long run, of course, they are; the users of railways and postal services, of libraries and bank notes, those whose crops will, or will not, be destroyed by locusts or potato wilt, whose cattle will, or will not, die of rinderpest and whose children are menaced by malaria, these are all human beings, for whose welfare a federal authority is

389

at work as surely as the teacher in the bush school or the dispenser in the clinic.

But it's all remote and seemingly impersonal. A statistician in the inland revenue, a pathologist in the laboratory, a radio engineer among his electronic tubes—they may be doing good to other people, but they can seldom be seen to be doing it. Arguments about customs duties on cameras lack the human warmth, the pulse-quickening excitement of attacks on rival party politicians for squandering public funds on bonanza trips to New York. Politics, that is what catches the imagination and stirs the African heart. Nkrumah's famous perversion of a Biblical text about seeking first the kingdom of politics, and then all things all be added, expresses a belief both widespread and popular.

Two Faces of Unity

From the ashes of colonialism is to arise the phoenix of unity. A noble aim: like most, with a positive and a negative side. The positive aspect is as President Nyerere, Mr. Kenyatta and others have defined it: to fight the dragons (so much more tenacious than colonialists) of poverty, ignorance and disease. With this goes the hope that Africa, so long a recipient of other peoples' ideas, will be able to give as well as to receive; that, for a change, men of other nations will look to an enlightened continent for inspiration and example. (In the case of West African art they have already done so—but only to the past.) This is the constructive side of the Pan-African dream.

It is the negative side that has hitherto been more in evidence, that aspect tinged with belligerence and bombast, chauvinism and sabre rattling—the side of anti rather than · pro. You can unite for something or against it; for betterment or for conquest, for the hoe or the spear. Heaven knows Africa needs the hoe, but the spear shines brighter—"burning spear." The hoe is the woman's weapon, the spear the man's.

Plain for all to see is the enemy, entrenched on a continent that Africans are coming to regard, with growing conviction, as exclusively theirs. (Surely a new, odd and unhistorical idea, that any particular continent is the property of any particular race or set of races? Should no migrations ever have taken place? At what point would you freeze all people in their positions? What would be the state of Europe, Asia and America if the frost had come down, say, ten thousand years ago?) There is the enemy—the Republic of South Africa, and Portugal, who has ruled her African territories for some four hundred years without any great objections being raised until the last ten.

In a sense—though no African would think so—this anticolonial *jihad* that is to be the next stage in Africa is a gigantic red herring. Fundamentally the issue is settled. Fundamentally the issue that must now be joined is that which the positive Pan-Africanists have defined, the fight to conquer backwardness and create a modern Africa. Of all the luxuries the newly independent states can least afford, the building up of armed forces is the greatest; yet most of them are affording it. Economically war against Portugal and South Africa would be a criminal waste of narrow, almost nonexistent resources—sheer lunacy. Have such basic economic facts ever yet averted war? Nations don't opt for peace because they are broke; on the contrary, they are more inclined to go to war in order to take the minds of their people off their poverty, fill them with vague but glorious hopes and condition them to accept a tighter discipline and more centralized control.

As always, the crystal ball is clouded and to look into it is profitless. All that can be said with certainty is that the setting up of the Organization for African Unity, embracing all the newly independent states, at Addis Ababa in the summer of 1963 appears to have been a turning point. Since then a new note of resolution and belligerence has resounded through the speeches of many African leaders, and the actions of their governments have become more bellicose. A committee sitting in Dar es Salaam has been planning military action and organizing sabotage. It has been said that one and a half million pounds ($4,200,000) a year is to be contributed, as a start, to a fund for training freedom fighters and supporting a central high command. A charter of African unity, drawn up at the Addis Ababa conference, has given firmer shape to the Pan-African dream.

There is a blueprint now to work to; from a haze of hope vision has emerged to be pinned down to a drawing board. There it is before the eyes, an outline only, but sketched in the form of a secretariat, officials, memoranda and committees.

Hope may turn at last to reality, and as for the forks . . . these must get busy in the bush, busier than ever turning the good earth; but they are, along with the poor crooked scythe and spade, dull and muddied objects, needed but prosaic symbols of servitude, fitted for use by women and for self-help schemes. The glory, the glitter, the prizes, the dream, the shining hope—these are elsewhere, in Addis and Conakry, Casablanca and Accra, in Paris and Peking and Moscow; and perhaps in the vision of a black commander leading his black armies and his black-flown aerial fleets victoriously into the last, beleaguered strongholds of colonialism.

What will the next word be? The road is at the fork. "Happiness, contentment and fulfilment, and a small bird singing on a mango tree"; or the command: "Go, bid the soldiers shoot."

392

INDEX

916.7 Huxley, Elspeth
H   With forks and hope. 7/64